THE BOOK OF CREATIVE
CRAFTS

THE BOOK OF CREATIVE
CRAFTS

EDITED BY
ELSIE BURCH DONALD

Art Editor: Elizabeth Palmer

Photographic Stylist: Maggi Heinz

Art Assistant: Anthony Lawrence

Editorial Assistant: Charlotte Edwards

 **Planned and designed by Tigerlily Limited
8 Berwick Street London W1**

First published 1978 by Octopus Books Limited
59 Grosvenor Street London W1

© 1978 Octopus Books Limited

ISBN 0 7064 0757 1

Produced by Mandarin Publishers Limited
22a Westlands Road Quarry Bay Hong Kong

Printed in Italy by New Interlitho SpA

CONTENTS

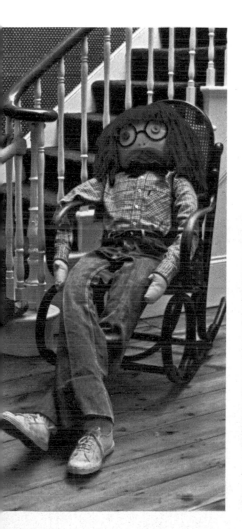

INTRODUCTION

The purpose of this book is twofold; it presents a comprehensive guide to the techniques of a dozen different crafts which can be learned by reading diagrams and instructions, and can be practised without expensive equipment. At the same time the book is a voluminous collection of patterns. It contains 150 things to make – all of them shown in colour and accompanied by step-by-step instructions and a list of necessary materials. The patterns range from simple beginners' projects to more intricate work. At all levels good design and clear instructions have been given prime consideration.

The book is arranged so as to be of use as a general work of reference as well as a textbook for learning the crafts and producing the projects in it. Each chapter has a general introduction followed by a colour section showing the projects. As a rule, the final part of the chapter contains the instructions for each project and, where applicable, a quick guide to the essentials of the craft. In this way, the reader can quickly find information pertaining either to a specific pattern or to a craft generally, and so the book can be used as a guide to projects outside its confines as well as those within. The colour sections provide an uninterrupted visual pleasure and a creative stimulus.

Throughout the book measurements are given both in metric and in feet and inches – the latter in parentheses.

There is also a section on how to transfer designs to different surfaces and a list of craft suppliers who provide mail order service.

NEEDLEPOINT

Needlepoint is any type of embroidery on open-weave canvas. It falls into two main categories, pictorial and counted. **Pictorial designs** tend to be painted on the canvas and worked by simply filling in each area with the appropriate colour yarn. The traditional stitch for pictorial designs is tent (basketweave) stitch, which is worked diagonally (fig. a).

Counted designs are worked on plain canvas and counted out stitch by stitch. The most popular counted needlepoint style is bargello, or Florentine. Bargello is normally worked over more than one canvas thread at a time (fig. b) and for this reason is relatively quick to do. The patterns are generally based on a zig-zag or 'flame' design associated historically with Hungary and northern Italy.

MATERIALS AND EQUIPMENT
For all needlepoint work you will need canvas, needles, yarn, scissors and masking tape. You may also wish to use a frame.

Canvas. There are two main kinds of needlepoint canvas, single thread (mono) and double thread (penelope). *Double thread*, or penelope canvas has pairs of threads and this allows you to work the background area over double threads but split them for the design area to give more detail (fig. c). *Single thread*, or mono canvas is woven with single threads – hence its name – and can be used for any stitch. It is easy to count the threads, so it is a good choice for beginners.

Canvas mesh and widths. Needlepoint canvas comes in several mesh sizes (a mesh is the open space between the threads). Canvas is sold by numbers of holes per 5 centimetres, 2.5cm, or per 1″. For example, 14 mesh canvas has 14 holes per 2.5cm (1″). The more threads there are per centimetre or inch, the finer the mesh. (In double thread canvas, holes per centimetre or inch refer to the holes between pairs of threads.) The size of the project and the wealth of detail you require dictate the mesh you should use. But different mesh also come in different widths so it is advisable to choose a mesh in a width which is suitable for your needs. For example, a metre of canvas 90cm wide (1yd. of 36″ wide) will give you four cushions 40cm

(16″) square. Finely meshed canvas tends to come in relatively narrow widths such as 58cm (23″) but 90cm (36″) is the average width. Some rug canvas, however, is available in 150cm (60″) widths. A chart in the instructional section of this chapter gives a guide to mesh sizes, recommended uses, and appropriate needles and yarn.

Canvas colour varies from white to ecru and pale yellow, but some sizes are available in one colour only. Colour is largely a matter of personal choice, but it is worth remembering that a white background is difficult to work on white canvas, likewise a beige one on ecru; however, it is easier to paint on white canvas.

Wool The following types of wool are the most suitable for canvas work:
Crewel wool is fine, stranded wool which is very versatile as you can use the exact number of strands a particular stitch and canvas need. Crewel wool lies flat and close on the canvas.
Tapestry wool is 4 ply and cannot be divided. It is most suitable for tent (basketweave) stitch, or when working one kind of stitch for a whole project.
Persian wool is a two ply wool sold primarily in America. Like crewel wool, it is stranded but the strands are thicker. It is sold in three strands which can be separated.
Rug wool is a heavy-textured wool specially designed for rug-making.

Needles. Special blunt-ended tapestry

needles are needed. These vary in size and it is necessary to select the right size for the thickness of wool you are using because the friction of an eye that is too small wears the wool thin. Packets of needles are available both all in one size and in a range.

Masking tape. Tape the cut edges of the canvas with masking tape before working. This prevents the canvas fraying and the cut edges snagging the wool.

Scissors. A large pair for cutting canvas and wool, and a small curved pair for snipping mistakes, are needed. Eyebrow tweezers for pulling out mistakes are also useful.

Frames are recommended though not essential. For projects with a variety of stitches, however, a frame should be used to avoid distortion. Another advantage of a frame is that it enables you to use both hands. If you are right-handed, work with your left hand above, and your right hand below the frame. Pass the needle back and forth through the canvas like a shuttle.

A *slate frame* can be balanced easily against a table edge or used on a floor stand. The canvas is lashed to the frame, and in some models the work can be rolled up, leaving only working areas exposed.

Round embroidery frames, either handheld or on a floor-stand, are portable and useful for working central motifs, but do not leave canvas on this frame when you are not working.

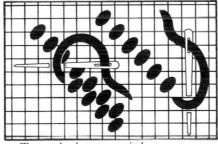
a. Tent or basketweave stitch

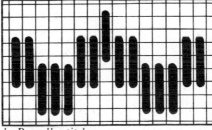
b. Bargello stitches

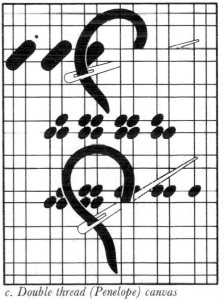
c. Double thread (Penelope) canvas

SAMPLERS

Sampler cushions incorporate numerous imaginative patterns by combining a variety of needlepoint stitches. They are also splendid demonstrations of the textural potential of needlepoint, and make good starting projects for anyone who wants to learn the true scope of the craft.

The square cushion combines 21 different stitches to form geometric patterns, plus a flower, central heart motif and pleasing border. It is worked in three shades of green and two of pink.

The tortoise has contours that adapt remarkably well into a cushion and its shell makes a cleverly segmented sampler. The form serves an additional purpose here in reiterating the moral of Aesop's fable that slow, steady, careful work wins in the end. It is a lesson for all needlepointers to bear in mind.

The instructions for the cushions are given on pages 32 and 33 respectively.

BARGELLO CUSHIONS

One of the fascinations of bargello is the use of gradations of colour to build up the well-known zigzag patterns that characterize it. Sometimes as many as seven shades are used to this effect and these are often coupled with contrasting colours which may be shaded also.

Details of the cushions on the previous page, along with charts showing how to work each of the patterns, are given here, but the colours can be changed according to taste and choosing them is one of the pleasures of bargello work.

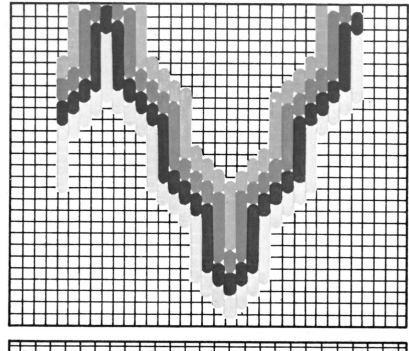

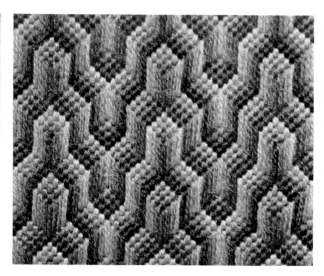

MOSQUE. One of the oldest bargello patterns, mosque is worked here in four shades of two different colours. The design is made by stitches made over 6 and 2 canvas threads. Easy.

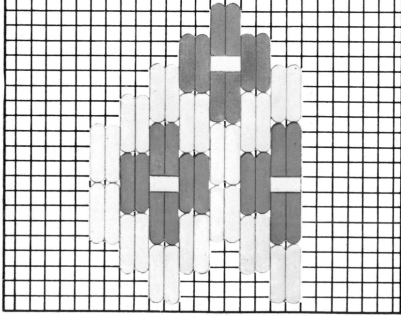

BLOSSOM. Worked in paired stitches. Begin by stitching the single colour 'blossoms', then fill in the background. Work over 4 threads, except centres which are over 2 threads. Easy.

Coral Mula

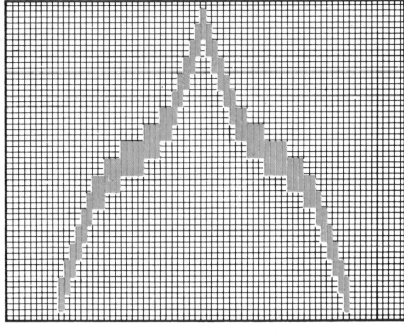

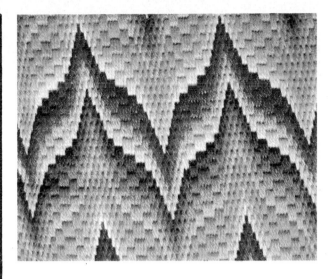

FLORENTINE FLAME. This classic bargello pattern is worked over six threads using four shades of three different colours. It is an excellent design for exploring colour. Easy.

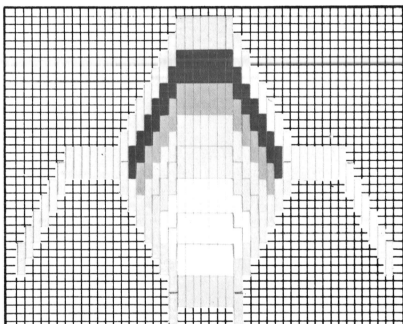

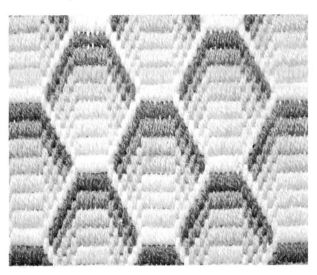

HONEYCOMB. Stitch the framework first, shown here in white, then work the honeycomb centres using four shades from one colour. Sew all stitches over 4 canvas threads. Medium.

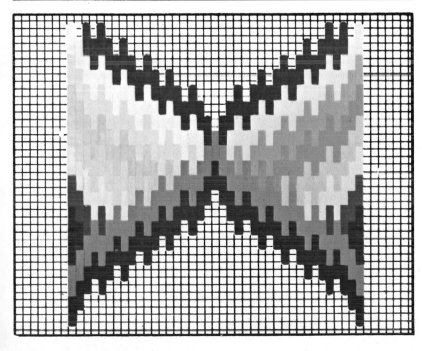

ISLAMIC. Seven shades of blue and four of yellow compose this interlocking pattern. Work dark outline, then fill ovals with random shading to give an antique effect. Medium.

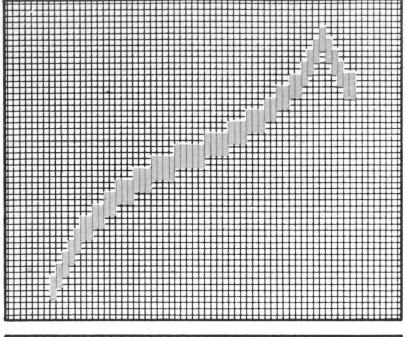

FLAME VARIATION. The broad, zigzag pattern is worked here in five shades of one colour and a band of two contrasting colours for emphasis. Note similarity to Florentine Flame on previous page. Easy.

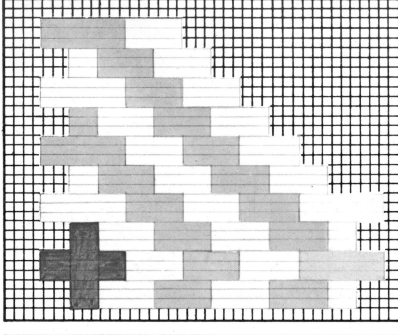

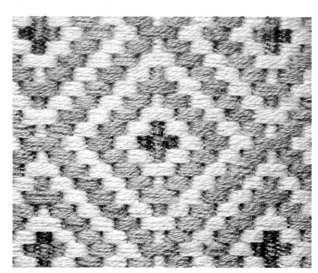

STONES OF VENICE. This inspired design is based on the brickwork of the Doge's Palace. It is worked in two random shades of pink and grey, plus white; and stitches are over 3, 6 and 9 threads. Advanced.

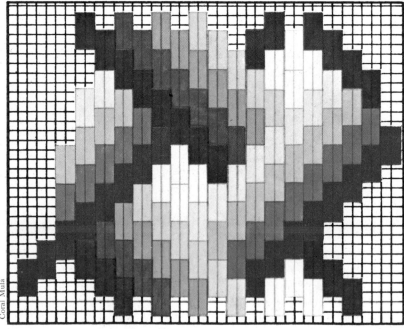

Coral Mula

BASKETWEAVE. By emphasizing different aspects of the pattern, different optical effects result. The pattern is worked in pairs of threads over four holes. Each 'band' is eight pairs of stitches long. Medium.

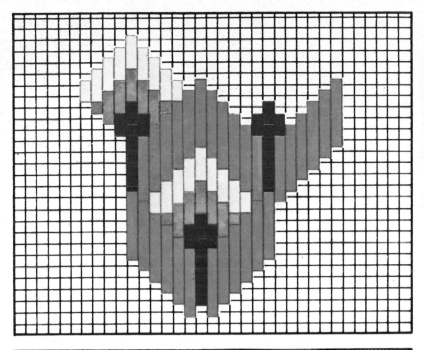

TREE. This repeat pattern is very useful for spectacle cases and other small items. The pattern is worked here in three shades of brown, plus background. Stitches are over 1, 2, 3 and 6 canvas threads. Easy.

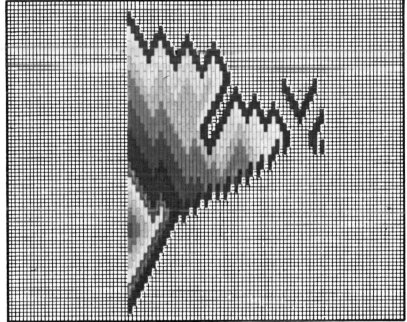

CARNATION. Five shades of pink and two of olive, plus drab background. Work centre flower on the canvas first and plan others round it. All stitches are over 4 threads. Advanced.

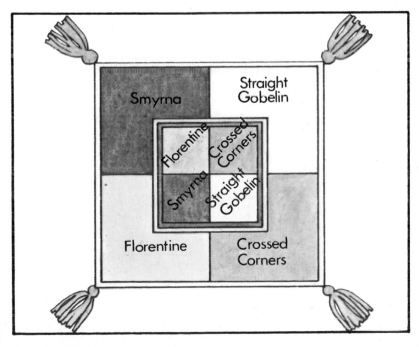

GEOMETRIC. This cushion combines bargello with textural needlepoint stitches: florentine, straight gobelin, crossed corners and smyrna. All are diagrammed in the Stitch Library on pages 29–31. Medium.

17

Dice, by nature, hold infinite potential and these needlepoint imitations are no exception for they can be made into pincushions as shown or, if you are feeling ambitious and are prepared to aim for bigger stakes, footstools or hassocks.
Instructions on page 33

Patchwork enters another exciting dimension when translated into needlepoint. This log cabin pattern shows the vivid gradation of colour associated both with log cabin patchwork and with bargello designs, and variations on this theme are possible by exploring the different 'shading' patterns which are characteristic of log cabin patchwork.
Instructions on page 34

This little piggie stayed home . . .
Working this bargello design before the fire on winter evenings will be as relaxing as the rest you will get when you put your feet up at the end of your labours. The hearts are a simple, charted motif and the background is worked in brick stitch.
Instructions on page 35

18

The elegant geometric pattern on the director's chair above is made more subtly interesting by the use of different needlepoint stitches to work the design. A stylized gardenia emphasizes yet softens the crisp, chequerboard squares, which are worked in a combination of cushion, moorish and tie stitches.   *Instructions on page 37*

Needlepoint can be used to 'paint' pictures, as the landscape design opposite illustrates. The simply drawn scene is given an evocative realism by the different textures of the stitches used to work the fields, hedges, trees and river. It is also a fertile source of inspiration for other painterly excursions in needlepoint.   *Instructions on page 38*

PURITY
AND SIMPLICITY IN
A NEEDLEPOINT
RUG

Milky white rug wool is used to work the six different patterns that make up this design and, because rug canvas has a very large mesh, it can be worked relatively quickly. You can adjust the overall size by adding or subtracting from the number of squares, or by changing the size of the squares. Small rugs such as this one can be worked on a single piece of canvas but in larger versions the needlepointed squares must be sewn together.

Diamonds are a
girl's best friend...

Dandy Waistcoat

This splendid waistcoat draws its inspiration
from the finely embroidered, flowered waistcoats
popular in the eighteenth century. A commercial pattern
is used for the shape, while the motifs which
make up the design are given below.

GENERAL GUIDE

ESTIMATING WOOL

It is important to buy sufficient wool for a project as dye lots can change slightly. But the amount of wool needed will vary according to the stitches used and the canvas mesh size.

For large projects it is advisable to work 2 sq. centimetres (1 sq. inch) and count the amount of wool used, then multiply this times the overall size of the design.

If, after all your careful calculations you do not have enough wool, take a hank to the shop to match (once it is sewn into the canvas this is more difficult).

Do *not* use all the original batch and then switch to the new but change it gradually.

WORKING

Starting the wool. Never knot the wool, except temporarily, to start; then, knot the wool on the right side of the canvas, about 2cm (1″) from where you begin and in the direction in which you will be working. When you get to the knot, snip it off, and the wool will now be secured by stitches you have made over it on the back of your work.

Finishing. Run the needle through the work on the underside of the canvas for about 2cm (1″) and cut it off close to the surface. This method is also used for beginning new wool once you have worked some of the canvas.

Sewing. Come up in an empty hole wherever possible and go down in a hole with wool in it. If a diagram shows a special order of working, follow it.

Mistakes. Pick out mistakes by cutting stitches on the front of the work with curved scissors and pulling wool out from behind with eyebrow tweezers.

STRETCHING FINISHED CANVAS

Always leave 5cm (2″) round the worked area for stretching. All needlepoint is freshened by stretching, even if there is minimal distortion. Pin the canvas to a board in its original shape and dampen work thoroughly with a sponge, but do not rub. Leave it to dry thoroughly in a horizontal position.

WORKING TIPS

Selvedge is the side of the canvas, so work with it at one side of your work. Mark one of the cut edges (not the selvedge) 'TOP' – this will ensure that stitches are not done sideways by mistake.

Wool. Cut yarn into lengths about 75cm (30″). Wool that is too long is difficult to handle and wears thin with friction before all is used.

Threading the needle. Hold the eye end of the needle in your right hand and loop the wool tightly over the needle; pull the thread off the pointed end and, keeping the loop tight, push it through the eye.

NEEDLEPOINT REFERENCE CHART

SINGLE THREAD (MONO) CANVAS

MESH SIZE Holes per 2·5cm or one inch	RECOMMENDED NEEDLE SIZES	RECOMMENDED WOOL		NUMBER OF STRANDS	RECOMMENDED USES
24	24	CREWEL		1	
		PERSIAN			
22	22	CREWEL		2	Small projects with very fine detail such as an evening bag or spectacles case
		PERSIAN		1	
20		CREWEL		2	
		PERSIAN			
18		CREWEL		3	Large areas of fine detail
		PERSIAN		1 or 2	
16		CREWEL		4	Bargello
		PERSIAN		3	
14	20	CREWEL		3	General stitching
		PERSIAN		2	
		TAPESTRY		1	
10	18 or 20	CREWEL		5	Quick projects without much detail. Projects for children
		PERSIAN		3	

DOUBLE THREAD (PENELOPE) CANVAS

11	20	PERSIAN		2	Projects with fine detail which can be worked over single canvas threads and background filled in more quickly over two canvas threads
		CREWEL		3	
		TAPESTRY		1	
10	18	PERSIAN		2 or 3	
		CREWEL		3	
		TAPESTRY		1	
5	13 or 14	RUGWOOL		1	
		TAPESTRY		2	
		CREWEL		5 or 6	
		PERSIAN		3 to 5	
3	12	RUGWOOL		1	Rugs and carpet squares
		TAPESTRY		3	
		CREWEL		6 to 8	
		PERSIAN		3 to 6	

STITCH LIBRARY

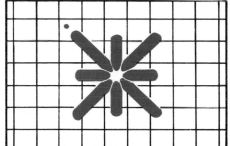

ALGERIAN EYE OR STAR
Always take needle *down* tightly through the centre hole. If the canvas is not covered sufficiently, a back stitch over two threads may be worked round star.

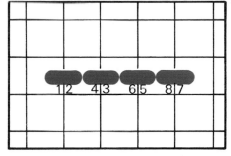

BACK STITCH
The numbers indicate the path of the needle.

BASKETWEAVE – see Tent

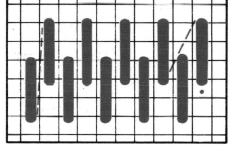

BRICK STITCH
Work over 4 threads of canvas with a space of 2 threads in between. The next row begins two threads lower and the stitches interlock neatly.

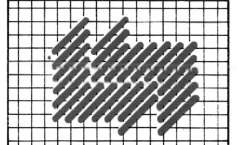

BYZANTINE
Work in steps of 6 stitches each. The dot marks the starting point.

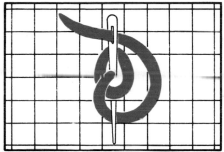

CHAIN STITCH
Work downwards over 2 threads of canvas, then, either start at the top and work down again, or use a vertical row of tent stitches to get you back to the top.

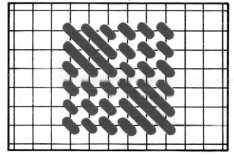

CHEQUER
5 stitches are worked diagonally to form a square and the spaces in between filled with 9 tent stitches.

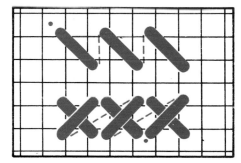

CROSS STITCH
Work first stich over whole area with straight stitch behind canvas: work second half of cross with long stitch behind canvas.

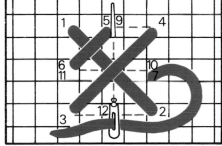

CROSSED CORNERS
Work large diagonal cross stitch first, then a stitch over 2 threads of canvas diagonally over each point.

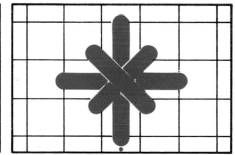

CROSS, DOUBLE
A straight cross worked over 4 canvas threads with a diagonal cross worked over 2 threads over it. Work in horizontal rows.

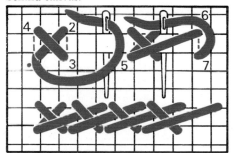

CROSS, LONG LEGGED
Work from left to right in alternate rows with tent stitch from right to left in between. The diagram shows the stitch in three stages of development.

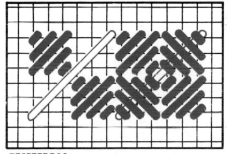

CUSHION
Work 'boxes' diagonally from right to left. Work 2 boxes in the same direction then work a long intersecting stitch and work stitches across it.

CUSHION VARIATIONS

DOUBLE CROSS – see under Cross
ENCROACHING GOBELIN – see under Gobelin

29

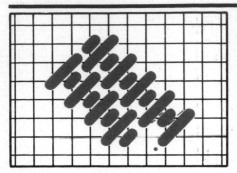

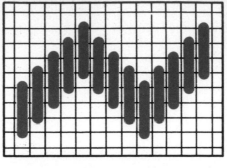

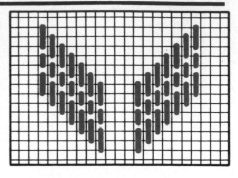

FLORENCE or DIAGONAL FLORENTINE
Work over 2 and then 1 threads. Bring needle up at dot.

FLORENTINE
This classic zig-zag stitch forms the basis of many bargello patterns.

FLORENTINE VARIATIONS

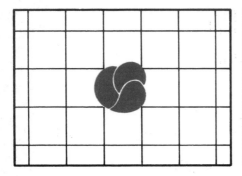

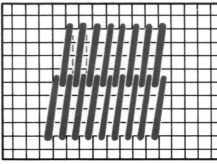

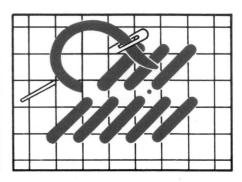

FRENCH KNOT
Bring needle to right side of work, wrap wool round needle once and gently take needle back through same hole.

GOBELIN, ENCROACHING
Work in horizontal rows with the second row overlapping the first row of stitches by one thread.

GOBELIN, SLOPING
Start at the right as the dot indicates and work stitches over 2 canvas threads.

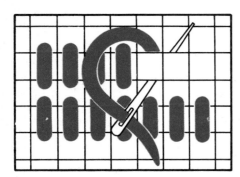

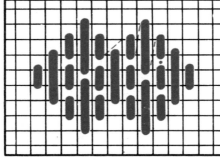

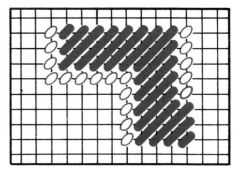

GOBELIN, STRAIGHT
This is a straight vertical stitch worked over 2 canvas threads.

HUNGARIAN

JACQUARD
Jacquard is a combination of Byzantine and a contrasting short stitch worked in between the steps.

HORIZONTAL TENT – see Tent

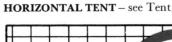

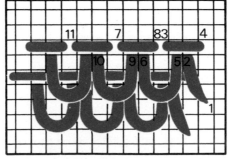

KNITTING STITCH
Work in vertical rows up and down the canvas so that the diagonal directions alternate. The result is a herringbone effect. The dot marks the start.

KNOTTED STITCH
Work right to left. Start with wool on right side. Work first row at the bottom of the area to be filled. At end of row, cut yarn. Start next row as shown.

LONG AND SHORT STITCH
The needle pierces previous short stitches, splitting the wool. Treat canvas as fabric. Do not count. Work on frame or hoop.
LONG LEGGED CROSS – see Cross

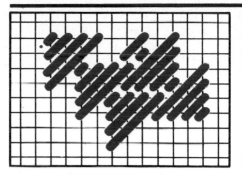

MILANESE
Work a row of triangles pointing up and a row of triangles pointing down. Stitch over 1, 2, 3 and 4 canvas threads respectively.

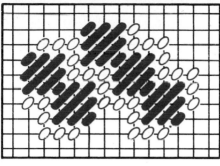

MOORISH
The short stitch of one row is in line with the long stitch of the next row. Use tent stitch between rows in contrast colour.

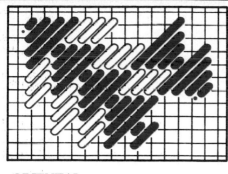

ORIENTAL
The long stitch over 4 threads meets the long stitch of the next row. The 3 fill-in stitches over 2 threads of canvas can be worked in a contrasting colour.

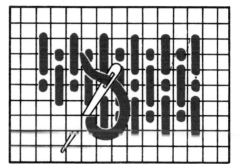

PARISIAN
Work from right to left, then back. Next row interlocks with the first.

RAY
Diagram shows ray used with blocks of 9 tent stitches to build up a chequerboard pattern.

RICE – see Crossed Corners

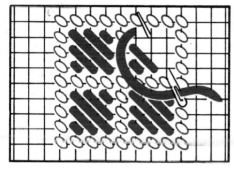

SCOTTISH
Groups of stitches, leaving 1 canvas thread between each square. A contrasting colour may be used to work the single threads between in tent stitch.

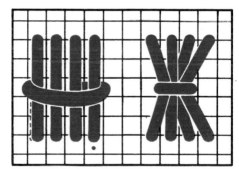

SHELL
Groups of 4 straight stitches worked over 6 threads of canvas and tied over 2 threads of canvas across the middle. The finished stitch is on the right.

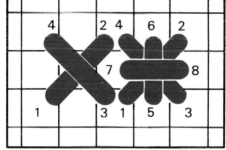

SMYRNA CROSS STITCH
This can be worked over 2 or 4 threads. The number on diagram shows needle's path. The stitch is shown in two stages.

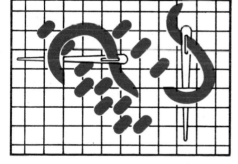

TENT (BASKETWEAVE)
Work first row on the diagonal then turn canvas upside down and work second row. Continue to alternate position every other row.

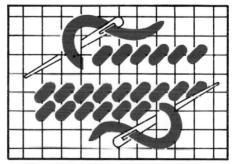

TENT, HORIZONTAL
Work first row then turn canvas upside down and work second row. Continue to alternate position every other row. Always work over 1 canvas thread.

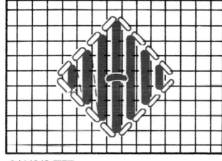

2/4/6/8 TIE
Work upright stitches to form a diamond. Then work back stitch between the diamonds. Tie central stitch. A variation has no tie or back stitches.

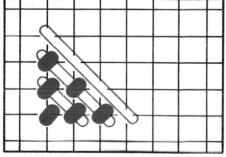

WEB
It is easier, with two needles, to work first the long diagonal stitch over area to be filled and then tie it down with the contrast.

Coral Mula

Cushions

Cushions form the most popular use of needlepoint. They can be a variety of sizes or, indeed, shapes – rectangular, round or following the contours of the needlepoint design. All of the designs in this chapter can be made up as cushions (and many of the designs on cushions can be made up as other items). Cushions should be made in the following manner, with or without piping. Piping is not essential but it gives a smoother look and helps disguise any mistakes made while sewing the sides together.

Note: if you are not using piping then follow the instructions, simply omitting directions about piping.

MATERIALS

Fabric backing the size of needlepoint plus turnings
Piping cord (optional), the length of the cushion edges
Note: extra fabric will be needed for piping.
Stuffing: terylene, kapok or pad
Needle and thread

ASSEMBLY

Trim turnings round the stretched needlepoint to 1.5cm (½″).
☐ Cut out fabric backing to same dimensions as canvas.
☐ Cut lengths of piping fabric on the bias and wide enough to cover piping cord plus 1.5cm (½″) turnings.
☐ Join lengths to make a

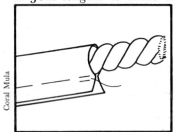

1. Piping for cushions.

strip long enough to go round cushion perimeter.

☐ Tack the bias strip round the piping cord, fig. 1.
☐ Tack the piping cord to the front of the cushion so that the raw edges of the canvas and cord covering are together, fig. 2.
☐ Tuck in piping ends and sew together by hand.

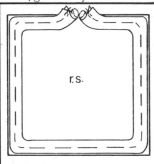

r.s.

2. Tack piping to cushion.

☐ Tack the fabric backing over the piping to make a 'sandwich'.
☐ Using a piping foot in the machine, stitch the 'sandwich' on three sides and stitch the piping to the canvas on the fourth side, leaving the backing free for turning through.
☐ Turn the cover right side out, press and insert the cushion stuffing.
☐ Hand sew the remaining side as the others.

Sampler Cushions

The chart below gives stiches and indicates the number of threads (not holes) to count in order to map the design on canvas. The finished cushion measured 33cm (13″) square. Use three strands of crewel wool unless chart says otherwise

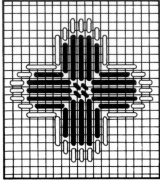

1. Sampler floral motif.

MATERIALS

Wool: 25gm (1oz) each of crewel in three shades of green and two of pink.
Canvas: 43cm (17″) square of 14 mesh single thread (mono) canvas
Sharp pencil
Fabric of canvas's dimensions
Piping and stuffing

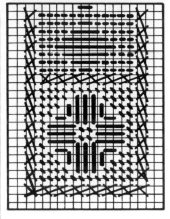

2. Sampler cushion border.

THE DESIGN

☐ Starting at centre, count 24 threads in all directions and draw a long line in the groove between the 24th and 25th thread (A in chart).
☐ Count one thread and draw lines in the next groove (B in chart), parallel with the first lines.
☐ Count 24 threads in corner sections and divide up as before (CD in chart).
☐ Pencil in diamonds.
Allow 16 threads for border design.
Fig. 1 diagrams floral motif, fig. 2 shows border pattern and fig. 3 gives central heart motif.
All stitches are diagrammed in the stitch library.

1. Hungarian; 2. Cushion;
3. Jacquard; 4. Cross;
5. Chain;
6. Tent (basketweave);
7. Algerian eye;
8. Brick;
9. Knitting; 10. Ray (2 strands);
11. Florentine (4 strands);
12. Crossed corners;
13. Long legged cross;
14. Sloping gobelin;
15. Chequer; 16. Scottish;
17. Double cross; 18. Web;
19. Tie (4 strands);
20. Diagonal florence;
21. Milanese.
All stitches are diagrammed in the Stitch Library on pages 29–31. The colours used in the cushion shown are three shades of green and two of pink. Use three strands of crewel wool unless otherwise indicated.

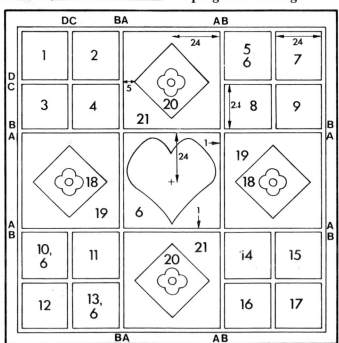

Coral Mula

3. Central motif on sampler cushion is worked over four threads.

WORKING
Work green corner squares first.
☐ Work diamond squares.
☐ Work centre motif (fig. 3).

☐ Stitch border last (fig ?)

ASSEMBLY
Make up following cushion instructions opposite.

Tortoise Cushion

This unusual sampler is worked in five shades of green on 14 mesh single thread (mono) canvas. It is made up like an ordinary cushion, described previously in the chapter.

The chart below shows the types of stitches used and general configuration of the tortoise.

You can either trace and enlarge the design following instructions at the end of the book, or, much easier, draw your own version freehand and divide the 'shell' into sections. Use a dinner plate to make the curve of the back.

The tortoise is 30cm (12″) high and 38cm (15″) wide at the base.

Diagrams of all the stitches appear in the stitch library.

Cording for eye. Use short length of piping cord: start at the centre of the eye and coil the cord. Secure it with a tieing down stitch to the needlepoint canvas.

Finish off by taking the cord through the canvas and securing it on the wrong side.

Dice Pin Cushions

These pincushions measure 7cm×7cm (2¾″×2¾″) but the design could be enlarged proportionately to make footstools or hassocks. In such a case, however, a different mesh canvas is recommended and the reference chart in the General Guide should be consulted. In the version shown, double thread canvas is used and the 'spots' are worked over one thread while the background is stitched over two threads for contrast. If you prefer, the pincushions could be worked on single thread canvas.

MATERIALS
For one pair of dice 7cm×7cm (2¾″×2¾″)
Wool: 4 skeins of 13.7m (15yd) white tapestry wool, 2 skeins of 13.7m (15yd) black tapestry wool.
Canvas: 30cm×24cm (12″× 10″) 10 mesh double thread.
No. 18 tapestry needle
Terylene or kapok stuffing
Pencil or indelible marker

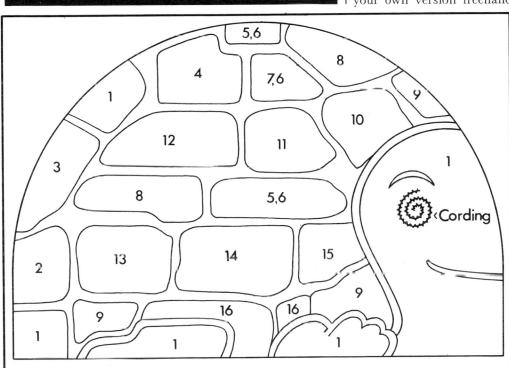

The stitches used to work the tortoise cushion are as follows:

1 Brick	2 Parisian	3 Florentine
4 Florentine variation	5 Long legged cross	6 Tent (basketweave)
7 Crossed corners	8 Byzantine	9 Diagonal florentine
10 Oriental	11 Straight gobelin	12 Scottish
13 Chequer	14 Milanese	15 Cross stitch
16 Encroaching gobelin		

All the stitches are diagrammed in the Stitch Library. The tortoise is 30cm (12″) high and 38cm (15″) wide. Draw the shape freehand using a dinner plate to make the curve, or trace and enlarge the pattern given here, following instructions at back of book.

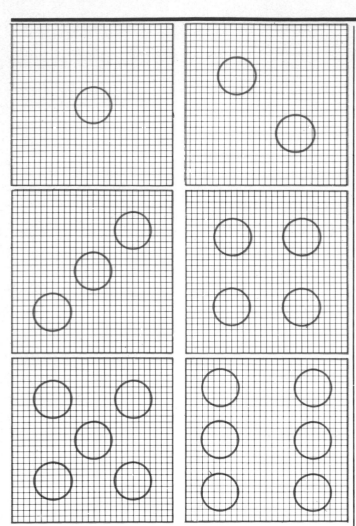

1. The dice chart.

4. Pincushion assembly.

THE DESIGN

Fig. 1 shows the six sides of the dice. Every background square of the diagram represents the double threads of the canvas. There are 28 double threads and 28 holes per side.

WORKING

Tape raw canvas edges.

□ Mark the outline of each dice side on the canvas, then add 1.5cm (½″) all round for seams.

□ Following fig. 1 count the correct number of threads from the edge of the design and work the first spot, as shown in fig. 2. Work over single threads of canvas.

□ Work the other spots by counting the number of threads and following the diagram in the same way.

□ Next, work background using horizontal tent stitch over pairs of threads, as shown in fig. 3.

□ Stretch canvas to correct shape. See General Guide.

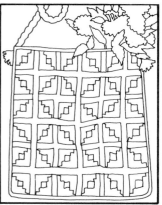

3. Working over two threads.

ASSEMBLY

Ladder stitch sides of each needlepointed cube as shown in fig. 4 to form an open box. Take one row of needlepoint stitch into the seam on each piece.

□ Trim corners.

□ Turn the dice right side out and insert stuffing.

□ Sew the remaining side on each cube, right sides facing.

Log Cabin Tote Bag

Bags such as this one present a happy alternative to cushions for needlepoint enthusiasts. One or both sides of the bag can be worked in needlepoint but a fabric back is advisable since wool worked over more than one thread tends to rub fairly easily. The instructions given here, therefore, are for needlepoint on the front only.

The design is worked in three shades of blue, three of yellow and in red. It measures 30cm (11¾″) square. By looking at other examples of log cabin patchwork you can find more ideas for colour and shading characteristic of the log cabin pattern.

MATERIALS

Canvas: one piece 36cm ×36cm (14″×14″), 16 mesh single thread canvas.

Wool: 4 skeins of 13.7m (15yd) tapestry wool in dark blue and dark yellow.

3 skeins of 13.7m (15yd) tapestry wool in each of the five other shades in the design.

4 skeins of 13.7m (15yd) tapestry wool in dark blue for the shoulder strap.

No. 22 tapestry needle
50cm (½yd) of 90cm (36″) fabric for the back
Lining fabric twice the amount and same colour as backing.
90cm (36″) piping cord
Indelible marker

THE DESIGN

Fig. 1, shown opposite, charts one square of 'log cabin'. There are 36 squares in the completed bag. All stitches are worked over four threads.

Because the design is worked in vertical and horizontal rows you may occasionally find that taking an extra stitch will fill small gaps where two colours join.

WORKING

Cut and tape the canvas. Start to work at the upper left-hand corner of the can-

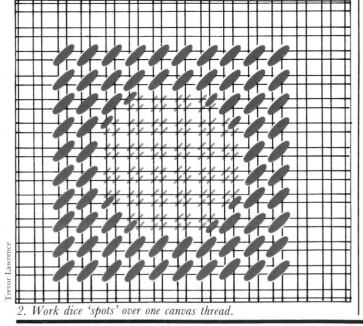

2. Work dice 'spots' over one canvas thread.

Trevor Lawrence

vas, leaving plenty of room for turnings later on.

☐ Mark a right angled guide line along a groove between two canvas threads. This represents the upper left corner of the design.

☐ Begin stitching a vertical row (stitching horizontally) over four threads using darkest yellow wool. Work downward.

☐ Work the horizontal dark yellow band next (stitching vertically).

☐ Work the other yellow bands, then a double row of red for the centre.

☐ Work the two lighter shades of blue.

☐ Work a horizontal band of dark blue across the entire canvas – 192 holes.

☐ Work a dark blue vertical band to complete first square.

☐ Begin the next square to the right of the first one. Both it and the blue stripe across the canvas give the outline. *Note* that in every other row of squares the colour scheme is reversed.

ASSEMBLY

Because of the rectangular design, the canvas may not need stretching.

☐ Trim the canvas, allowing turnings of 1.5cm (½") all round.

☐ Cut the backing to the

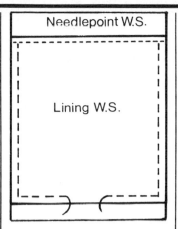

2. Stitching bag lining.

same size as the canvas.

☐ Cut the two lining pieces to the canvas size but increase the top turnings to 2.5cm (1").

☐ From the remaining fabric cut out several 4cm (1½") wide bias strips for the piping.

☐ Join strips to form a piece at least 90cm (36") long.

☐ Tack the bias strip round the piping cord.

☐ Tack the piping to the front of the bag on the edge of the tapestry – so that raw edges of canvas and cord covering are together (see fig. 2 under Cushions).

☐ Tack the bag back over the piping cord and stitch the bag on these three sides.

☐ With right sides together, stitch the lining pieces to the bag on top edge.

☐ Press the seam towards the front of the bag.

☐ Stitch the side and bottom edges of the lining taking 1.5cm (½") seams and leaving an opening for turning through, fig. 2.

☐ Turn through and press so that a 0.5cm (¼") wide turning on the top edge forms a 'piping'.

☐ Stitch on the seam line to secure, fig. 3.

☐ Cut the tapestry wool for the strap to 30 lengths 140cm (55") long each.

☐ Divide into three and plait firmly.

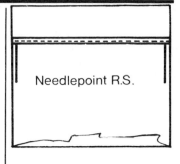

3. 'Piping' for top edge.

☐ Knot the ends tightly, leaving a small tassel of yarn ends, and stitch the strap to the bag at the top sides.
The bag is now complete.

Bargello Pig

The pig measures 38cm (15") high and 66cm (26") long. It can be used as a footstool, headrest or as a child's soft toy. The needlepoint design can be used to decorate any number of surfaces.

MATERIALS

Canvas: 2m (2½yd) 90cm (36") wide, 14 mesh single thread.

Wool: choose five shades of pink crewel wool ranging from pale pink to bright rose pink.

18 skeins of 25gm (1oz) very pale pink, 1 skein of 25gm (1oz) pale pink, 2 skeins of 25gm (1oz) for each of the three brightest shades.

No. 20 tapestry needle
2 pipe cleaners for tail
1kg terylene or kapok stuffing
10cm (4") of 90cm (36") wide pink felt
Carbon paper
Tracing paper
Indelible marker

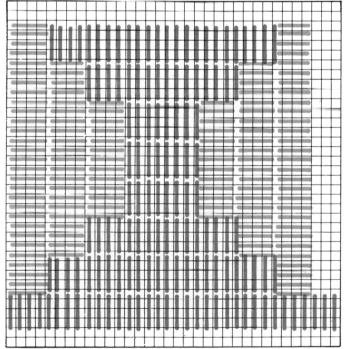

1. Log cabin patchwork design is worked over four canvas threads.

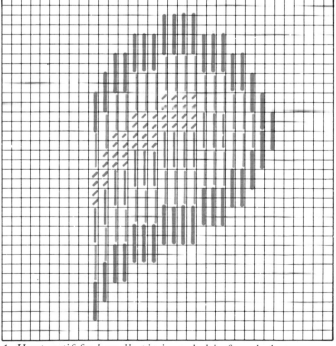

1. Heart motif for bargello pig is worked in four shades.

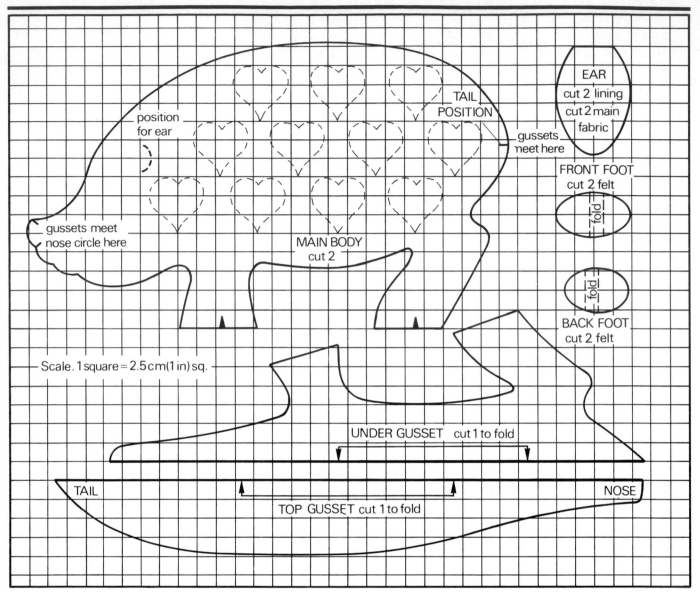

position for ear

gussets meet nose circle here

MAIN BODY
cut 2

TAIL POSITION

gussets meet here

EAR
cut 2 lining
cut 2 main
fabric

FRONT FOOT
cut 2 felt

fold

BACK FOOT
cut 2 felt

fold

Scale. 1 square = 2.5 cm (1 in) sq.

UNDER GUSSET   cut 1 to fold

TAIL

TOP GUSSET cut 1 to fold

NOSE

THE PATTERN

Trace and enlarge the graph pattern and transfer it to the canvas. Reverse pig side pattern when marking second side. A special section at the end of book gives method. Add 2cm (¾″) all round for seams.

THE DESIGN

Sides. Position the bargello hearts as you wish on the two side pieces, or use the repeat pattern given in graph.

□ Using four strands of crewel wool, stitch the hearts in four shades, according to fig. 1 on previous page.

□ Fill in the background with brick stitch using the palest wool.

Back gusset. Match the position of hearts on the back to those on the sides as closely as possible, but run the hearts along the back with the points toward the head.

□ Work as for the sides.

Tummy gusset. This is left plain and worked entirely in brick stitch in palest pink.

Ears. Work one heart on each ear and stitch background in brick stitch.

ASSEMBLY

Stretch the canvas to fit the original pattern pieces as described on page 28.

Body. First press canvas lightly on wrong side then cut out each piece allowing 2cm (¾″) for seams all round.

□ Cut out the feet and ear pieces from pink felt allowing 1.5cm (½″) turnings all round.

□ Snip small circles for nostrils and semi-circles for eyelids from remaining felt.

□ Matching the end of the under gusset to the point marked on the pig's back, tack and stitch firmly, just inside the edge of the tapestry, to both main body pieces. Leave the base of each foot and one entire leg seam open for stuffing.

□ Matching the top gusset to the point marked, tack and stitch to the two main pieces in the same way. It may be necessary to slightly stretch the tapestry around the nose.

□ Turn in the allowances on the nose ends of each gusset and slip stitch together.

□ Turn in the canvas of the base of each stitched leg and tack. Stitch the fold on each foot piece in place (fig. 2) and then turn in the seam allowance all round.

□ Oversew the feet to the legs.

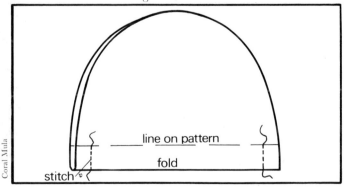

line on pattern

fold

stitch

2. Stitch the fold on the pig's foot, as shown. This gives a realistic, rounded effect.

Coral Mula

□ Stuff the pig from the nose backwards, making sure the stuffing is very firmly packed in the legs. When stuffing is half done, ladder-stitch the back leg to the band and attach foot.

□ Stuff the rest of the pig and ladder stitch final opening.

Tail. Bind two pipe cleaners together with cotton firmly.

□ Take a thick strand of each of the three tapestry wools used and bind them securely to one end of the pipe cleaner so that it is completely covered.

□ Poke the wrong end of the tail made in this way into the back seam point. Stitch very securely in place and bend into required shape.

Ears. With right sides together stitch the tapestry and felt ear pieces together, leaving an opening for turning through. Turn through and stitch up the opening.

□ Fold the ear and stitch to the pig very firmly using double thread.

□ Repeat with other ear.

Features. Stitch the eyelids over the eyes and embroider in long lashes using the darkest embroidery wool.

□ Stitch in a mouth with stem stitch using the medium shade of wool. If necessary, work chain stitch around the foot and nose seams to cover stitches. Attach the nostrils to the end of the nose by stitching them on. The footstool is now complete.

Director Chair

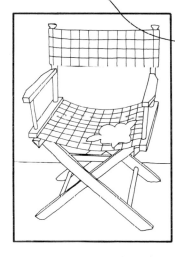

The advantages of designs for directors' chairs are that their dimensions tend to be standard, their fabric covers can be removed easily and the chairs themselves are readily obtainable and inexpensive.

In the design shown here, the back is 18cm×110cm (7″×43″) and the seat is 41cm×46cm (16″×18″). Use chair's original seat canvas to reinforce needlepointed seat and facilitate attachment to chair.

Unlike the ordinary director's chair back, this one wraps completely round the back so that the design can be seen on both sides.

It is advisable to measure the fabric already on your chair before beginning, in case some alteration is needed. Alteration can be made to the design shown by changing the number of squares or by adding a small border, or by enlarging or reducing the size of the squares.

MATERIALS

Canvas: 1.20m (1½ yd) 14 mesh single thread canvas 90cm (36″) wide.

Wool: 6 skeins of 25gm (1oz) crewel wool in camel and in chocolate.

3 skeins of black 25gm (1oz) crewel wool.

1 skein of cream 25gm (1oz) crewel wool.

No. 20 tapestry needle
Tracing paper for gardenia
Sharp pencil or indelible marker
Fabric glue
Chair's original seat canvas
Crewel needle

THE DESIGN

The stitches are as follows:
Camel squares – cushion stitch.
Chocolate squares – moorish stitch.
Black diamonds – tie stitch (without back stitch).
Outline of squares – vertical and horizontal tent stitch.

Gardenia: black outline of petals and leaves, back stitch. White petals and brown leaves, long and short stitches.

The diagrams for each of these stitches is given in the Stitch Library.

Three strands of crewel wool are used throughout.

□ Before you begin to mark out the design, cut two pieces of canvas to the finished dimensions plus at least 5cm (2″) for stretching and turnings, and tape the raw edges.

The back. Starting at the right-hand side of the canvas and leaving at least a 5cm (2″) margin at the top and the side of the canvas, draw a horizontal line, following the thread of the canvas, approximately 109cms (43″) long and a vertical line 18cms (7″) long.

□ From the top right hand corner count 26 holes and draw another vertical line.

□ Repeat until there are five lines (four squares) vertically and 25 lines (24 squares) horizontally.

□ Form a diamond in the centre of each square by counting six holes from the cross and drawing four diagonal lines (fig. A).

□ Repeat over back but mark half diamonds on short ends so design will be complete when joined.

The seat. Before the diamonds are drawn in, trace the gardenia on the canvas in the bottom right hand corner leaving about a 2cm (1″) margin from the edge of the design. To do this, trace the motif given here and place the tracing in position beneath the canvas. Then draw it on the canvas,

following the design which shows through from below. Like the back, the seat is begun by covering the oblong with 10 squares (11 lines) horizontally and 9 squares (10 lines) vertically.

WORKING

Thread needle with three strands of crewel wool.

□ Outline the squares in tent stitch worked horizontally and vertically.

□ Outline the gardenia in back stitch.

□ Fill in the diamonds.

□ Fill in the camel and chocolate squares in cushion stitch and moorish stitch respectively.

□ Fill in the leaves and petals of the gardenia in long and short stitch using a crewel needle.

When the two canvases are complete they must be stretched as described in the General Guide.

ASSEMBLY

Back. Glue top and bottom turnings of the back to the wrong side with fabric glue.

□ Stitch the two short ends together, right sides facing, to make a circular strip.

□ Glue seam turnings to underside of work and turn right side out.

□ Position the back strip so that it is double and flat with the seam at the centre of the back.

□ Machine stitch through both layers about 10cm (4″) from either end, being sure to stitch along black dividing line. This makes the slots for the back struts of the chair. Stitch the top and bottom edges together between the two slot seam lines.

Seat. Glue canvas turnings of the seat front and back to the underside of work with fabric glue.

□ Lay needlepoint centrally on original seat canvas, baste round the edges and machine stitch or stitch by hand round the edge to attach the needlepoint to the chair canvas.

□ Attach seat to chair in the usual way.

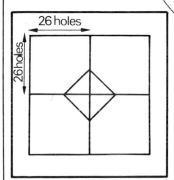

1. Making diamond motif.

26 holes

26 holes

Landscape Chair

Needlepoint can be used effectively for 'painting' pictures. The landscape design employs different stitches to impart shape and texture to the hayfields, hedges, river and mountains. The overall design is so simple that it can be drawn freehand on the canvas. If you prefer, however, the outline below can be enlarged and traced on the canvas. (Instructions for enlarging and transferring designs are given in a special section at the back of the book.) But trying to draw your own undulations and to shade the canvas as you work is part of the pleasure and the challenge of this particular project.

The landscape could be worked on one piece of canvas for a wall hanging, or made up as two cushions or a chair cover like that in the picture.

As a chair cover, the work must be backed with another fabric on the chair back, to give a finished appearance from behind. As a wall hanging, the aerial position of the trees on the seat should be changed to match the point of view shown on the back piece.

The dimensions of the chair cover shown are 51cm× 43cm (20″×17″) for the back and 42cm×50cm (16½″× 20″) for the seat. But the sketch is a fluid one and can be easily adapted to any size. By adding and subtracting elements, the worker can put as much creativity and imagination into the design as he or she wants.

MATERIALS

Canvas: 1m (1¼ yd) 14 mesh single thread canvas 90cm (36″) wide.

Wool: Skeins of 13.7m (15yd) tapestry wool are used throughout in the following amounts:

River and blue hill – 5 skeins each of blue and darker blue. Hedges and green mountain – 10 skeins of forest green and 2 skeins bottle green. Sky – 2 skeins each of turquoise in two shades. Ploughed field – 3 skeins each of orange and brown. Trees – 3 skeins kelly green, 2 skeins bottle green, 2 skeins forest green, 1 skein brown. Cornfields – 14 skeins bright yellow, 6 skeins pale green, 6 skeins chartreuse, 2 skeins khaki. Meadows – 6 skeins mint green, 5 skeins olive green. Mountains – 2 skeins pale grey, 1 skein dark grey.

No. 20 tapestry needle
Indelible marker or lamp black artist's oil
Paper for sketching
Fabric glue
Masking tape, scissors
Oil paints in shades given.
1 m (¼ yd) heavy cotton fabric for backing – or use fabric from chair
Stapler (optional)

THE DESIGN

Mark off the dimensions of the work, allowing at least 5cm (2″) for stretching and turnings.

☐ Apply the design freehand using the indelible marker, or make a preliminary sketch on paper. Place the paper beneath the canvas and trace the sketch on to the canvas by following the outline, which can be seen through the holes in the canvas.

The colours can be painted on the canvas in oils or you can stitch on the plain canvas, simply following the charted colour guide. Note the simple shading in the picture but add your own to achieve a more subtle, painterly effect.

The names of the stitches used to work the design are given in the chart caption and their positions indicated on the chart. Diagrams for each stitch are given in the Stitch Library.

WORKING

Cut the two rectangles out and tape the raw edges. Complete one rectangle before beginning the next.

☐ Begin by working the hedges in knotted stitch. This will outline the other areas of the work. Since knotted stitch is a looped stitch, the hedges must be literally trimmed with scissors to about 1cm (¼″).

☐ Stitch the river next if you are working the seat, or the mountains and river if you are stitching the back.

☐ Fill in the trees.

☐ Finally, work the fields.

☐ Stretch the canvas using the method described in the General Guide.

ASSEMBLY

If the canvas is for a chair such as the one shown in the photograph, you can use the chair's original fabric for backing.

☐ Trim the raw edges of the worked canvas to 2cm (⅝″) and glue raw edges to the under side of the work.

☐ Lay the needlepoint on the original fabric backing, baste round each rectangle and machine stitch a seam 1cm (⅛″) from the edges or hand stitch along the edges.

☐ Attach the seat and back to the wooden frame in the same way as the original fabric was fixed.

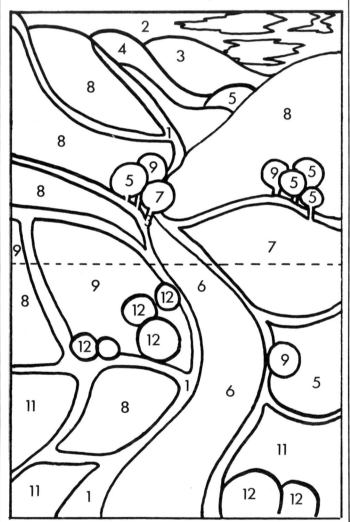

The following stitches are used to work the landscape: 1. Knotted stitch; 2. Alternating rows of horizontal tent and straight gobelin; 3. Brick; 4. Tent (basketweave); 5. Florentine variation; 6. Horizontal brick stitch; 7. Diagonal florentine; 8. Tent (basketweave) interspersed with shell stitch to make the 'haystacks'; 9. Straight gobelin; 10. Parisian; 11. Sloping gobelin; 12. Cushion.

White Rug

The finished rug measures 135cm×188cm (53″×74″). Each square is 32 holes long and 32 holes wide.

Because the canvas holes are large, the design can be worked comparatively quickly. If you have any great difficulty finding rug wool, two strands of tapestry wool, five strands of crewel or three strands of Persian wool can be substituted.

MATERIALS
Canvas: 2m (6′6″) of 3 mesh double thread rug canvas, 150cm (60″) wide.
Wool: 36 balls of 50gm (2oz) white or cream rug wool.
Rug needle
Sewing needle and thread
Indelible marker
Metre (yard) stick

THE DESIGN
Mark the outline of the rug on the canvas, being sure to keep a straight line along a horizontal and vertical thread. (The rug will be 158 stitches (holes) wide and 222 stitches (holes) long.)
Leave enough canvas at the edges for turning under later.
The diagrams indicate positions of the squares and also show the six different patterns that fill the squares.

WORKING
Work the first square 15 stitches from the outline.
☐ Work all the squares, following the diagrams.
☐ Stretch the canvas to remove distortion, as des-

cribed in the General Guide; then work the border.
The border
Work one line of cross stitch round the finished squares, then work a band of oblique stitch five holes in length.
☐ Work another row of cross stitch followed by another band of oblique stitch slanting in the opposite direction from the first.
☐ Fold over the edges and finish by straight gobelin worked over the edge three stitches in length.
☐ Trim excess canvas. This completes the rug.

The numbers indicate the correct placement of each pattern.

1	2	3	4
2	3	4	5
3	4	5	6
4	5	6	1
5	6	1	2
6	1	2	3

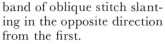

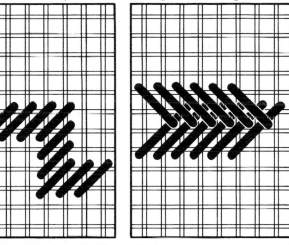

1

2

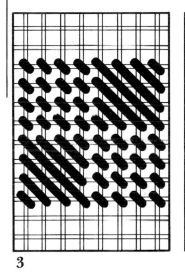

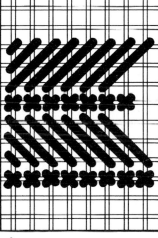

3

4

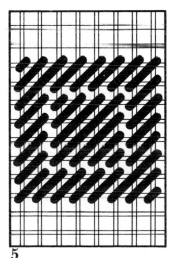

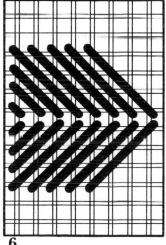

5

6

The patterns above are worked over double mesh rug canvas.

Coral Mula

Desk Set

The diamond pattern on the blotter, notebook cover and pencil bin shows how a simple design can be enriched by varying its position.

The pencil bin is made from a tin can and the blotter is constructed from hardboard. (Needlepoint could also be glued to an old blotter with fabric glue.)

The dimensions of the desk set shown are as follows:
The blotter needlepoint – 30.5cm×5cm (2″×12″).
The total width of the blotter is 46cm (18″).
The folder measures 16cm×25.5cm (6½″×10″) and the pencil bin is 12.5cm×27cm (5″×10⅝″).

MATERIALS
Canvas: 0.5m (¾yd) of 68cm (27″) 16 mesh single thread canvas.
Wool: skeins of 25gm (1oz.) crewel wool are used throughout.
4 skeins of white.
2 skeins each of three shades of blue.
1 skein each of three shades of yellow.
No. 20 tapestry needle
1 piece of thin hardboard 30cm×46cm (12″×18″)
1 piece of fine plain cotton fabric 50cm×36cm (20″×14″)
1 piece of thick matching cardboard 30cm×46cm (12″×18″)
Sharp pencil
Fabric glue
Tin can with lid removed
20cm (¼yd) of fabric for folder lining
Stiff interfacing for folder to needlepoint dimensions
Masking tape and scissors

THE DESIGN
The design and background are worked over four canvas threads using four strands of wool throughout.
The border is worked in cross stitch over two threads and the background is in brick stitch (see Stitch Library). Fig. 1 charts the design motifs.
Each diamond measures 7cm (2¾″) or 48 holes long and 3.5cm (1½″) or 23 holes wide.
□ Using a sharp pencil and following the groove between two threads, mark on canvas the outer dimensions of cross stitch borders (of the piece). Leave at least 5cm (2″), for turnings and stretching, between each piece.

WORKING
Cut out the pieces, plus turnings but keep the two blotter pieces together as it will make balancing the counted design easier.
□ Tape all raw edges.
The blotter – start in the middle of one panel and work the motif to the required length in one direction.
□ Work the remaining end from the centre.
□ Work a single row of cross stitches over two threads round the four sides (see Stitch Library).
□ Fill in the background with brick stitch (see Stitch Library).
□ Work the other blotter panel in the same way.
The folder – Mark with pencil the centre of the area which will be the spine of the pad.
□ Work the interlocking design, counting carefully, so that it is placed centrally on the front of the folder.
□ Work the same motif on the back of the pad if you wish.
□ Work a single row of cross stitch over two threads round the edges.
□ Fill in the background with brick stitch.
The pencil bin – The diagram gives the pattern repeat

1. Bargello diamond patterns are worked over four threads. Three shades of blue and yellow are used to make the interlocking designs.

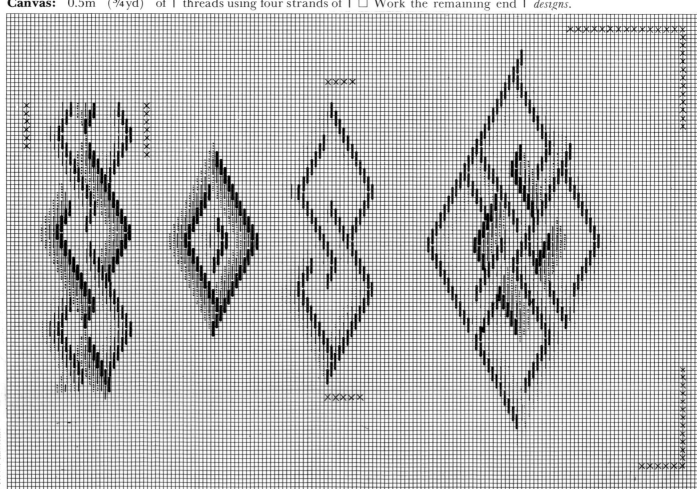

for a pencil bin with the dimensions mentioned above. If your tin can is larger or smaller, position each motif so that the pattern will join at the seam, e.g. if there is a double diamond at the left-hand end, finish with a single diamond at the right-hand end. Remember, it is easier to join background areas than through the pattern.

☐ Work the motifs, border and background, in that order. Stretch the canvas as described earlier.

ASSEMBLY

Pencil bin – Trim the turnings to 1cm (½″) and glue them to the underside of the work.

☐ Glue the needlepoint to the tin can.

1. Hardboard on fabric.

Blotter – Place the hardboard centrally on fabric, making sure the fabric is stretched evenly (fig. 1), and glue edges down. This side is the front of the blotter.

☐ Glue one long raw edge of each needlepoint panel under the worked area.

☐ Place panels on each end of hardboard, turn raw edges under and stick canvas edges to top edges of hardboard. Be sure to mitre the corners and cut away surplus. You should now have a rectangle of card with two shallow pockets.

☐ Carefully glue thin card on top of hardboard.

The folder – Press finished work on back lightly.

☐ Trim seams to 1.5cm (½″).

☐ Cut lining to same size as folder.

☐ From lining fabric cut two rectangles 28.5cm×19.5cm (11¼″×7¾″) for pockets.

☐ From buckram cut out a rectangle to exactly fit finished size of folder.

☐ Tack buckram stiffening

to the needlepoint on wrong side.

☐ Press rectangles for pockets in half with wrong sides together.

☐ Position pockets on right side of needlepoint, matching raw edges, and tack.

☐ Lay lining rectangle over pockets and stitch on the very edge of work nearly all round, but leaving an opening for turning through.

☐ Turn through, turn in raw edges and stitch opening.

Dandy Waistcoat

Needlepoint lends itself to a number of garments, jackets as well as coats, hats and waistcoats. You simply mark the canvas, using an ordinary paper pattern, and work the areas that will show e.g. the darts and turnings are left bare. Then cut out, make up and line the garment.

MATERIALS

For a woman's waistcoat you will need:

Canvas: 60cm (¾yd) 14 mesh single thread canvas 90cm (36″) wide.

Wool: 13.7m (15yd) skeins of tapestry wool are used throughout.

1 skein brown
2 skeins yellow
2 skeins pale pink
4 skeins deep pink
3 skeins pale blue
3 skeins dark blue
5 skeins pale green
5 skeins dark green
16 skeins white

No. 20 tapestry needle
Indelible marker
Sharp pencil
Oil paints, white spirit and paint brushes

Metre (yard) stick
Masking tape and scissors
Waistcoat pattern
Tracing paper the length of the waistcoat
Coloured pencils and crayons
Backing and lining fabric in amounts specified by paper pattern
Piping cord (optional)

THE PATTERN

Using the pencil, mark the outline of the paper pattern on canvas. Be sure to mark the seam and dart lines. Note that the design shown requires a considerable overlap in front so that the panels remain regular. The panels are 8cm (3″) wide so add to the front edge of the paper pattern or space the flowers in the panel to accommodate the overlap on the pattern.

THE DESIGN

Outline the green stripes by marking two points on each canvas piece 8cm (3″) from the side and front seam lines.

☐ Run the pencil vertically between two threads to make a straight vertical line at the marked points.

☐ Make two more lines on each piece, four holes inside the first lines. This marks the green stripes.

☐ Trace the motifs shown opposite the waistcoat photograph, repeating the motifs according to their arrangement in the photograph and so that there are six columns of motifs for the six waistcoat panels. Note that the roses and blue flowers are reversed in each column to make the design more interesting. The design for one side of the waistcoat must also be reversed.

☐ Colour and shade the tracings as in the design using crayons or coloured pencils.

☐ Place the tracings beneath the canvas, centring them between the stripes.

☐ Pin tracing papers securely in position.

☐ Using oil paints and brushes, commence to transfer the design to the canvas

by following the tracing beneath the canvas. Where the darts fall leave the space bare, but remember that on a man's waistcoat there are no darts and so the area must be painted in all the columns.

☐ Mark the buttonhole areas on the canvas.

☐ Paint in all the motifs.

WORKING

Separate canvas into two pieces and tape raw edges. Work one side at a time.

☐ Stitch the green stripes first, working horizontally over four stitches.

☐ Work one straight vertical row of tent stitch in white on either side of the green stripe, followed by a vertical row of blue. This completes the stripes.

☐ Work the floral motifs next. You will find that it is better to work in horizontal tent stitch than diagonal (basketweave) because of the smallness of the areas.

☐ Fill in the background in tent (basketweave) stitch.

☐ Work the other side of the waistcoat in the same way.

☐ Following method described in General Guide; stretch both sides to fit original paper pattern pieces.

ASSEMBLY

Assemble according to directions for making a waistcoat in the paper pattern.

The buttonholes should be cut and machine stitched last, after the garment has been lined. Centre them in the middle of the panel so that the design completely overlaps its counterpart.

Consultant:
Anna Pearson
Designers:
Sampler cushions and bargello desk set are by Anna Pearson; log cabin patchwork adapted by Phyllis Kliger; pig footstool, Eleanor Harvey; director's chair and waistcoat by Glorafilia; landscape chair by Frances Duncan and Stones of Venice cushion, Susan Gaskell.

The principle of the candle is fuel plus a conductor and the earliest candles were probably pine branches dipped in fat. Not until the Middle Ages did candles as we know them come into widespread use, but these, too, were usually made of fat (tallow) – an inferior material since it burns rapidly, splutters and smells. The few who could afford it burned beeswax and although this excellent but expensive material is still used in candlemaking today, it has been largely replaced by paraffin wax, an efficient and a comparatively inexpensive material.

Basically, there are two types of candle, dipped candles and moulded candles; and, while both provide fascinating possibilities for the candlemaker, moulded candles have by far the greater scope.

Dipped candles are made by repeatedly dipping a wick in hot wax and building up layers.

Moulded candles are generally cast and occasionally manipulated. Three kinds of moulds can be used for casting candles: commercial moulds specially made for candlemaking, improvised moulds, made from household containers such as milk cartons or tin cans, and home-made moulds.

In moulded candles, the wick is either inserted with a special needle, or it is suspended in the mould and wax poured in round it.

Detailed information on casting, wicking and dipping methods appears in the General Guide on page 52.

CANDLEMAKING EQUIPMENT

Paraffin wax. Grades of paraffin wax vary greatly and, in general, it is advisable to use a fully refined wax with a melting point of 57–60°C (135–140°F). Paraffin wax is available in solid blocks and in powdered form. The powder is the easier to use.

Paraffin wax also has different degrees of translucency. Translucency is a desirable quality if, for instance, you wish to embed something beneath the wax such as pressed flowers. The most opaque paraffin wax is usually called overdipping wax because it is designed for putting the final coloured layer of wax on dipped candles.

Beeswax is available in blocks or in honeycombed sheets. It is very expensive, but has the advantage of burning for longer and having a glossier finish than paraffin wax. It is a good idea to add a little to the paraffin wax.

Re-cycled wax. It is also possible to melt down old candles for re-use but, if doing this, do not mix several colours together or you will end up with a brown mess.

Stearin. This is a white, flaky material which makes candles opaque and helps dye dissolve. It also causes the wax mixture to shrink a little, making it easier to remove the candle from the mould.

Stearin is generally used in the proportions of 10% stearin to 90% wax.

Wax dyes. It is essential to use special candle dyes. These are available in powder or solid disc form and can be mixed to produce different shades. Never exceed the recommended amounts of dye as an over-dyed candle will not glow; start with a little dye and build up to the desired strength. The final effect can be tested by dropping a spoonful of the coloured wax into cold water.

A pinch of powdered dye will colour 0.5kg (1lb) of wax. The solid disc dyes will each colour about 2kg (4½lb) of wax. Add less for a pale colour, more for a dark shade. Overdipping wax takes about four times as much dye as other waxes (and no stearin).

Powdered dye is cheaper than the solid discs, but it is more difficult to control its depth of colour.

Wicks. Candle wicks are made of bleached linen thread, plaited together. The wick is soaked in a solution of various salts which helps it to burn.

Wicks are sold by the diameter of the candles they are intended to burn. A 2.5cm (1″) wick will burn a candle 2.5cm (1″) in diameter. It will also burn a 2.5cm (1″) hole in a larger candle. Therefore it is essential to choose the correct size of wick.

Thermometer. A sugar or confectionery thermometer with temperature readings of up to 205°C (400°F) is essential for candlemaking. As different types of candle require the wax to be at certain temperatures, accuracy is very important.

Saucepans. You need a saucepan in which to melt stearin and dye and a double boiler in which to melt the wax. For complicated projects, you will obviously need more pans.

Kitchen scales are necessary in order to weigh out wax and stearin in the correct proportions.

Miscellaneous supplies. Other candlemaking supplies which are sometimes needed for wicking candles are a *wicking needle*, a special gum called *mould seal* which seals the gaps round the wick hole, and a metal disc, or *wick sustainer* which weights the wick in the mould. Occasionally, special *wax glue*, *wax whitener* and *wax varnish* are needed as well. All of these materials are available from candlemaking suppliers and some craft shops.

MOULDS

The three types of moulds used in candlemaking are commercial moulds, improvised moulds and home-made moulds.

COMMERCIAL MOULDS

Commercial moulds are available in a number of different materials, but they can be classed in two basic categories – flexible and rigid.

Flexible moulds are made of rubber or plastic. They are the most commonly used type of mould since they are flexible enough for the candle to be removed easily.

They are always embossed or engraved, and thus make highly decorative candles. However, they do not allow much variation in method. A maximum of one per cent of stearin to wax should be used in rubber moulds as stearin attacks the rubber.

Rigid moulds are obtainable in a number of shapes, sizes and materials. They can be bought in metal, glass and plastic.

Since *plastic* moulds are both strong and cheap, they are the best moulds for the inexperienced candlemaker. All the candles shown opposite were made in rigid plastic moulds and it is possible, using any rigid mould, to make a variety of multi-coloured candles with one mould.

Metal moulds are the strongest and have smooth interiors which produce equally smooth candles. They also have the advantage that metal conducts heat quickly, and thus cools the wax mixture rapidly. This means that air bubbles are less likely to occur. *Glass* moulds have the disadvantage of being breakable, but they also give an exceptionally smooth finish, and, being clear, enable you to see any pattern that is being built up inside.

IMPROVISED MOULDS

Improvised moulds include such basic household items as glasses, bottles and baking trays. In fact, any object, which will not leak, burst or distort in shape when hot wax is poured into it, is suitable.

But bear in mind that, in order to remove the finished candles, improvised moulds must be larger at the top than at the bottom; unless, they are made of plastic or glass which can be cut away or broken off — providing you do not mind ruining the container in question.

HOME-MADE MOULDS

Home-made moulds are made by casting cold rubber round an object – thus making a flexible, rubber copy of the object chosen. This method is described in detail later on.

Rigid plastic moulds (see below) are both strong and cheap, and a variety of candles can be made in any one of them. The candles opposite are a good example of how mould shapes can be shown off to great advantage by casting plain, white candles and emphasizing their outlines with delicate, pressed flowers. Multi-coloured candles cast in the same moulds as the flower candles are shown overleaf and serve to illustrate the versatility of moulded candles.

Instructions on pages 54 and 56.

FRUIT CANDLES

Whether you use flexible moulds or mould fruit candles by hand, the secret of success is in the final touches and you do not need a chef's skill to produce them. Brown wax on the wick makes a 'stem', for example, while tapping a pear candle with a wire brush and rubbing in brown paint, makes a natural speckle.
Recipes on page 56 and 57.

Theo Bergström

Kim Sayer

48

Joke Candles

Amuse yourself and your friends with the lighter side of candlemaking. An ice-cream cone, some sticks of dynamite and a champagne bottle – all are in fact real candles and should illuminate the surprised faces of the recipients.

The ice-cream cone is concocted very easily from whipped wax and a sheet of beeswax, while the dynamite is basically a dipped candle. Most eye-deceiving of all is the champagne bottle, moulded entirely of wax with the champagne label pasted on later.

Instructions on page 57.

51

Wicking up

Containers such as plastic cartons and commercial, flexible moulds need to have a hole pierced centrally in the bottom with a wicking needle so that the wick can be threaded through. Commercial rigid moulds already have holes pierced in the bottom.

Fig. 1. shows the correct procedure for both types.

☐ Wax a piece of wick of the correct size and length for the chosen mould, by dipping it into molten wax. Then, thread the wicking needle with the pre-waxed wick and insert it down into the bottom of the mould.

☐ Make a hole in the centre if there isn't one already and draw the wick through.

☐ Seal round the hole on the underside of the mould with a dab of mould seal. This end will be the top of the candle.

☐ Tie other end of the wick around a short stick or pencil, and lay the pencil across the top of the mould so that the wick is taut and is positioned centrally.

In improvised moulds which cannot be pierced, such as glass ones, the wicking method shown in fig. 2.

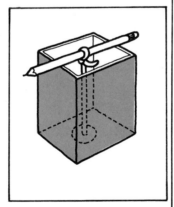

2. Another wicking method.

should be used. The wick must be weighted to the bottom of the mould with a wick sustainer – a metal disc – or glued with wax glue.

It is also possible to wick a candle after it has set. This is done by drilling a hole in the candle with a hot needle or twisting in a very fine screwdriver. Dip the wick in wax to stiffen it, and then thread through the hole.

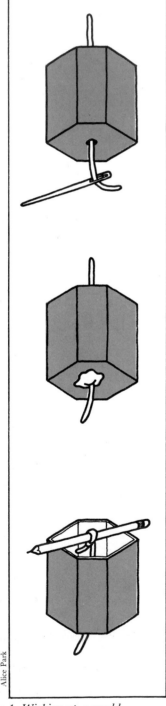

Alice Park

1. Wicking up a mould.

Casting a Candle

Melt stearin in a saucepan and sprinkle a little solid disc dye into it. Heat on a gentle heat and stir until all the dye is dissolved.

☐ In another pan, melt paraffin wax, (90% to 10% stearin). Twelve tablespoons of paraffin wax are sufficient to make a square candle 5cm×5cm×6cm (2″×2″× 2½″).

☐ Add molten wax to the stearin and dye, and heat gently to 82°C (180°F).

☐ Pour heated wax mixture into the mould and, after a few minutes, give the mould a tap to displace any air bubbles that may have formed. After about an hour, a well will form around the wick as the cooling wax contracts.

☐ Prod surface skin to break it, and top up with more wax mixture, reheated to 82°C (180°F).

☐ When the candle is completely cold and hard, remove it from the mould, either by slipping it out if it is rigid and the top larger than the bottom, or by cutting or breaking an improvised rigid mould. A flexible mould is removed by peeling it back on itself. To make this easier, moisten the outside of the mould with washing-up liquid to give it more slip.

Finishing off

All candles should be finished off in the following way. Level the base by lowering the candle, holding it by the wick, into an empty saucepan over a low heat. It is also possible to carve off lumps with a knife, but this will not give such a smooth finish.

Blemishes can be removed from the rest of the candle by wiping with a soft cloth moistened with white spirit or turpentine.

Buff with a wet tissue for a really shiny finish. Finally, trim the wick to 6mm (½″).

Warning. Whenever heating wax, a double boiler is the safest container. Do not put wax in too small a pan and do not heat it on too high a heat. Also, take care not to splash yourself with hot wax. It is rare to overheat wax to the point at which it bursts into flames but, should you do this, turn off the heat immediately, and cover the saucepan. Do not attempt to extinguish the flames with water, and do not pick up the saucepan.

Home-made Moulds

Silicone rubber-moulds can be made at home using household objects such as bottles, tins, light bulbs or eggs for 'masters'. You simply mix the silicone rubber and its catalyst, following manufacturer's instructions, and paint it on the surface of the shape you wish to reproduce.

The materials are available from candle supply and DIY shops. Always buy a long-curing catalyst or you may get bubbles in your mould. It is wise to test the mould mixture on a small part of the object before casting.

To test: stir both the silicone rubber and the catalyst well, before mixing the two.

☐ Paint a dab of the mixture on the bottom of the object. If the rubber remains sticky and will not set (this will take from one to five hours, depending on the catalyst used), then it is necessary to coat the master with a sealer such as shellac before casting the mould.

Casting. If the test presents no problem, proceed to coat the 'master' with a release agent such as wax furniture polish which will enable the mould to be removed more easily.

☐ Make a plinth (base) in clay or plasticine.

☐ Mix the rubber and catalyst, then paint a very thin coat of the mixture over the bottle and plinth.

After about five minutes, air bubbles will appear on the surface. Blow on them to burst them, or prick with a needle.

Filling a home-made mould.

☐ When there are no more bubbles, spoon the rest of the rubber and catalyst mixture over the 'master'.

☐ Leave the rubber to set for a day or two – the longer the better.

☐ Lubricate the mould with washing-up liquid and peel it back on itself to remove. You now have a flexible, rubber mould which should be wicked up and used in exactly the same way as any bought, flexible mould.

Estimating Wax

To estimate the amount of wax you need for a moulded candle, fill mould with water, then pour the water into a measuring cup. This will give you the liquid measurement.

0.6 litre (1pt) of liquid wax is the equivalent of 454gm (1lb) solid wax. The chart opposite gives conversion.

As a guide for the moulds shown, the cylinder needs 227gm (8oz), the polygon 454gm (16oz) and the star 114gm (4oz).

Dipping Candles

Dipped candles can be made in a variety of lengths and widths, depending on the size and length of wick used and the number of dips made into the wax.

Choose a wick of the correct size for the intended diameter. The most convenient diameter of dipped candle is 2.5cm (1″), as this is the standard size of most candlesticks.

The core of a dipped candle is usually made in undyed paraffin wax, and the final dips are made into dyed overdipping wax, which gives the candle a strongly coloured, opaque finish.

MATERIALS.

In addition to the equipment mentioned in the introduction you will need two tall jugs, a little deeper than the height of candle you intend to make. One is for dipping the wicks into the wax, and the other is for dipping the candles into cold water to harden them. You will also need a pencil or small stick.

DIPPING

Cut off a length of wick equal to the desired height of candle, plus about 10cm (4″). Alternatively, cut the wick more than double the length of the candle. This enables you, with a little practice, to dip two candles at once.

☐ Heat plain paraffin wax to 82°C (180°F).

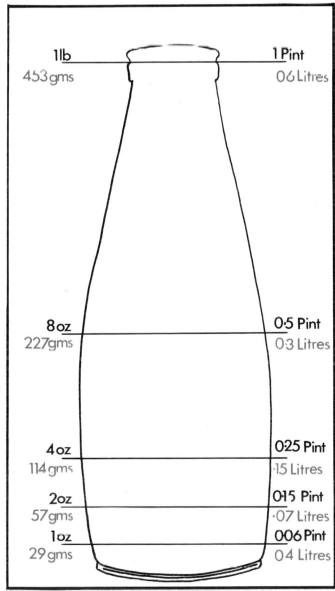

Conversion chart shows equivalent amounts of liquid wax (right) to solid wax measures (left).

☐ Fill jug with hot wax.

☐ Tie one end of the wick to a pencil or small stick and, holding the pencil, dip the wick into the hot wax. To dip two candles at once, hold the double length of wick in the centre, as shown in fig. 1, and dip ends into one large container or two narrow ones. Pull the wick straight

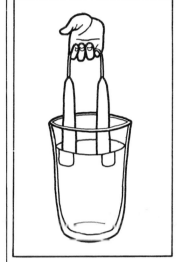

1. Dipping two candles.

up and out of the wax, and hold it in the air for about half a minute, until the wax hardens.

☐ Continue dipping until the candle is almost the correct diameter.

Note: If the wax in the jug begins to cool down before you have finished dipping – bubbles on the surface of the wax mixture or on the candle itself will indicate this – reheat the wax to 82°C (180°F) again before you continue dipping.

☐ Melt overdipping wax and add dye, stirring until dissolved. Do *not* add stearin.

☐ Stir and heat gently to 82°C (180°F).

☐ Dip the white candle into the coloured wax in the same way as before, until you build up the colour you want.

☐ Dip the finished candle in a jug full of cold water to harden it completely. Alternatively, you can hang the candle up to dry naturally, but this will obviously take longer.

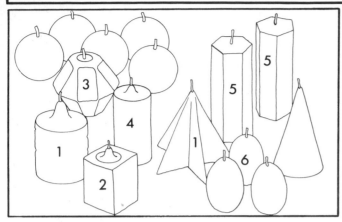

Multi-coloured candles on pages 46–47: 1. Pour-in pour-out; 2. Layered; 3. Cut-back dipped polygon; 4. Bull's eye; 5. Spread dye disc candle; 6. Powdered dye.

Pour-in Pour-out Candle

This method can be used in any rigid mould but the star mould is particularly suitable since the wax in the 'blades' cools more rapidly than the rest. (For this reason, the wax must be heated to a higher temperature).

MATERIALS
Mould and wick, mould seal and pencil
Saucepans, thermometer
Paraffin wax
Stearin
Wax dye
Pair of dividers (compass) and small craft knife (optional)
Soft cloths, white spirit and tissues.

MAKING THE CANDLE
Wick up candle mould as shown in the General Guide.
□ Heat undyed paraffin wax (with stearin) to 93°C (200°F) for a star mould, or 88°C (190°F) for a square or cylindrical mould.
□ At the same time, make dyed wax mixture with four times as much dye as usual, and heat to 93°C (200°F) for star or 88°C (190°F) for other moulds.
□ Fill the mould with the undyed wax mixture.
□ Tap the mould to release air bubbles, and, after two minutes, place the mould in a cooling bath. Leave for two minutes for a star mould, six minutes for a square or cylindrical mould.
□ Then pour the liquid wax back into the saucepan.
□ Pour strongly dyed wax mixture into the mould.
□ Tap, wait two minutes, and place in cooling bath as before.
□ Tip out liquid wax again and refill with hot, undyed wax.
□ Tap and wait a minute before replacing in water.
□ When candle is hard, remove from mould.
If you have used a star mould, (see chart) the finished effect will be attractive enough in itself. If you have used a square or cylin-drical mould, you will need to carve into the white layer to reveal the coloured wax. The cylindrical pour-in pour-out candle shown in this chapter has had a circular repeat pattern drawn on it with a pair of dividers (compass), and the pattern was then carved out with a small craft knife. The finished effect is one of gradual shading of colour.
□ Finish off the candle as described in the General Guide.

Layered Candle

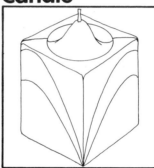

The layered candle is the simplest of the multi-coloured candles and is made by pouring layers of differently coloured wax, heated to 82°C (180°F), into the mould.

MATERIALS
Mould and wick
Mould seal
Pencil
Saucepans, thermometer
Paraffin wax
Stearin
Wax dyes
Soft cloth, white spirit or turpentine, and tissues

MAKING THE CANDLE
Wick up candle mould, following fig. 1 in the General Guide, and heat the wax.
□ Pour the first layer and tap the mould once to release any air bubbles.
□ Place the mould in a saucepan of cold water until a skin forms which, if prodded gently, will give but not

1. Making angled layers.

break. Diagonal layers may be produced by tilting the mould at an angle in the cooling bath (fig. 1).
If a layer sets hard before the next one is poured in, the two layers will not fuse. If, on the other hand, it is soft and not partially set, the colours will blend.
□ Pour in the next layer.
□ Top up, and finish as described in the General Guide.

Cut-back Dipped Polygon

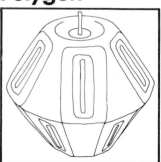

This unusual candle combines the two methods of casting and dipping.

MATERIALS
Polygon mould
Wick, mould seal, pencil
Saucepans, thermometer
Paraffin wax
Stearin
Wax whitener
Overdipping wax
Wax dyes
Broad-bladed knife
Soft cloth, white spirit or turpentine and tissues

MAKING THE CANDLE

Wick up the mould (see the General Guide), leaving about 5cm (2") at each end.

☐ Cast a white polygon in the mould, using paraffin wax (85%), stearin (10%) and wax whitener (5%) at a pouring temperature of 93°C (200°F).

☐ Remove hardened candle, but do not trim wick.

☐ Then dip into different colours, using overdipping wax and four times as much dye as usual (no stearin). Hold alternate ends of the wick each time, so that the wax runs down the candle in opposite directions with each dip.

☐ To reveal the underlying layers of colour, 'iron' off the corners of the polygon with a broad-bladed knife, heated in a flame. Place the candle on top of the knife, to prevent hot wax dripping on your hand.

Bull's-eye Candle

This type of candle combines dipping and casting.

MATERIALS

Saucepans, jugs
Thermometer
Paraffin wax
Overdipping wax
Wax dyes
Clear plastic or glass mould
Wick, mould seal, pencil
Sharp knife
Wax glue
Wax whitener
Spoon or fork
Soft cloths, white spirit, and tissues

MAKING THE CANDLE

First make a white, dipped taper, about 12mm (½") in diameter, using plain, undyed paraffin wax.

☐ Continue dipping the candle, but dip into a variety of different colours, using overdipping wax and four times as much dye as usual. Dip five times into each colour but allow candle to cool for about ten minutes before dipping into the next colour. This will ensure that the colour changes remain well defined.

☐ Cut off bottom end every now and then to see how pattern is progressing.

☐ Build up the candle to a diameter of about 4.5cm (1¾").

☐ While the candle is still warm, pull the wick sharply out of the candle with one hand, while pressing gently but firmly against the top centre of the candle with the other, so that the central core of the candle does not come out with the wick.

☐ Working quickly, so that the candle does not cool and harden completely, cut off a slice of candle between 6mm (¼") and 12mm (½") thick. If the mould is rounded, press slice against the inner wall of the mould, so that the slice of wax takes on the contour of the mould. The wax can be squashed to give a slightly elongated shape.

You do not need to arrange the discs at this point, merely to shape them. Ten discs are shaped in this way for the bull's-eye candle illustrated.

☐ Leave the discs to set for about 30 minutes. Cut two of the discs in half with a sharp knife for the design shown here.

Each of the wax shapes is glued in position (fig. 1) in the mould with wax glue as follows:

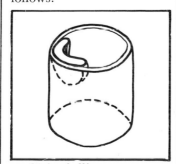

1. Gluing bull's eye.

☐ Take a little ball of wax glue and push it into the side of the mould, in the position where the centre of a disc is to be. Then press the disc on and move it very slightly from side to side and up and down until the glue ball becomes flat, so that there is no space between disc and mould.

☐ Glue in all wax discs in this way.

☐ Wick up the mould as described in the General Guide and cast the candle. For a white candle, use 85% paraffin wax, 10% stearin and 5% wax whitener, which, heated to 93°C (200°F), will, to some extent, prevent the last outer circles of colour in the discs from spreading into the white. (You may prefer to cast a coloured candle, in which case, simply use dyed paraffin wax as usual.)

Note. A little wax is bound to have seeped between the discs and the mould and will be found on top of the bulls' eyes. Rub this off with the edge of a heated spoon, and wipe the loose bits off with a rag.

☐ Finish the candle as described in the General Guide.

Spread Dye Disc Candle

This technique involves melting solid dye directly on the candle with a blow torch. It takes some practice to control the flow of colour and it is better to use a square-faced candle, as the colour will run uncontrollably on a rounded surface.

MATERIALS

Square-faced core candle
Dye disc
Scalpel or craft knife
Blowtorch
Soft cloth, white spirit or turpentine, and tissues

MAKING THE CANDLE

Shave off little bits of the dye disc with a scalpel or craft knife, and place on the core candle.

☐ Direct the blowtorch flame on the dye shavings, and melt them on the surface of the candle. Remove the flame as soon as the colour begins to run. Tilt the candle to direct the flow of the dye.

☐ Allow the candle to cool and the dye to dry. Finish off as usual.

Powdered Dye Candle

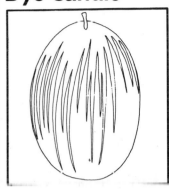

This is a simple method of producing an unusual effect with powdered dye.

MATERIALS

White, dipped candle
Stearin
Saucepans, thermometer
Powdered dye
Paintbrush
Paraffin wax
Soft cloth, white spirit or turpentine, tissues

MAKING THE CANDLE

Melt the stearin and heat to 82°C (180°F).

☐ Dip the paintbrush into the stearin and then into the powdered dye, and lightly touch the top of the candle round the wick with the loaded brush.

☐ Dip the candle in 90% wax, 10% stearin mixture, heated to 82°C (180°F) and, when you see the colour begin to spread down the candle, pull it straight up, out of the hot wax.

☐ Allow to cool and finish off as usual.

Note. If you do not like the finished effect, dip again in 88°C (190°F) and hold there for about a minute until all the dye has run off. Allow to cool and start again.

Pressed Flower Candles

These candles are made in rigid plastic moulds, then pressed flowers, leaves or grasses are applied to the surface, and a final dip into hot wax holds them firmly in place. Obtain paraffin wax with a translucent quality.

MATERIALS
White candles with untrimmed wicks
Pressed plants
Saucepan, thermometer
Paraffin wax
Metal dessertspoons and jam jar
Tissues and soft cloths
Wicking needle, black poster paint, paintbrush (optional)
White spirit or turpentine

MAKING THE CANDLE
Heat some metal spoons in hot water.

□ Place a pressed flower in position on the candle and press on with the back of the hot spoon, which has been dried quickly on a tissue or cloth. Blow on the flower to cool it as you work.

□ Continue working in this way, using a hot spoon each time, until all plants are in place.

□ Hold the candle by the wick and dip it in plain, undyed paraffin wax at 99°C (210°F) for about six seconds. Do not worry if the surface goes cloudy – it will become clear again as it gets cold.

□ Write the names of the pressed plants on the candles by carving them with the wicking needle, wiping off the loose pieces of wax as you work.

□ Then paint on black poster paint over the carved name, using a paintbrush. Wipe with a soft cloth to remove excess paint, so that only the name stays black.

□ Finish off as usual.

Fruit Candles

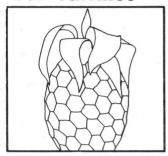

Flexible moulds for fruit are available from some candle supply shops. The candles are wicked up and cast as for any flexible mould (page 52) and coloured in the manner described here.

Two alternatives to bought moulds are to make your own flexible moulds using the method described in the General Guide or to mould the wax by hand. Hand-moulded results are not so eye-deceiving as cast versions but there is great pleasure in the tactile process and more individual results in the end.

MATERIALS
Flexible moulds (optional)
Saucepans, thermometer
Paraffin wax
Stearin, wax dyes
Wick and wicking needle – a 2.5cm (1″) wick for average size fruit
Paintbrush, wire brush
Poster paint
Soft cloth, white spirit
Metal baking tray, Scissors, palette knife wax glue (optional)

MAKING THE CANDLE
The chart below shows how to colour candles and produce a realistic effect.

Flexible moulds. If you are using a flexible mould, cast the candle as described in the General Guide, but remember to use only one per cent stearin for rubber.

Hand-moulded. Mix the dye, stearin and paraffin wax in the normal way.

□ Stir and allow to cool until the wax has congealed. You should be able to remove the wax in one piece.

□ Mould shapes by hand.

□ Then push the wicking needle through the centre and thread wick through the hole, tying a knot in the bottom to secure it.

Leaves. Add a little green dye to molten paraffin wax. (Do not use stearin as it makes wax less malleable.)

□ Heat to 82°C (180°F), and pour into a clean, rust-free, metal baking tray to form a layer 3mm (⅛″) thick.

□ Allow wax to congeal, lift it off the tray with a palette knife and cut into shapes using scissors.

□ Allow leaves to set and dip into plain, undyed paraffin wax at 88°C (190°F).

□ Mould the leaves, while still warm, into a realistic curve, and stick on candle with wax glue or 'weld' on with hot wicking needle.

Type of fruit	Colour of core candle	Colour of dip	Finishing off
APPLES	Yellow	Green with no stearin 82°C (180°F)	The wick can be made to look like a stalk by coating it with brown wax. For a red apple, paint on a little strongly dyed, hot, red wax. Then a hot dip in yellow or green wax at 105°C (220°F)
GRAPES	Green, dark grey for purple	Green with stearin	Press the balls round a pre-waxed wick. For a final effect, dip the bunch into plain, undyed wax at 105°C (220°F).
LEMONS	Yellow	Yellow with stearin 82°C (180°F)	Stipple with a wicking needle.
ORANGES	Yellow	Orange with stearin 82°C (180°F)	
PEARS	Yellow	Green or yellow, no stearin 82°C (180°F)	Tap pear all over with a wire brush, and rub brown poster paint over it. This will sink into the little holes made by the brush. Polish off excess paint with a soft cloth dipped in white spirit. Dip again in hot yellow or green wax at 105°C (220°F). Coat the wick with brown wax.
PINEAPPLE	Orange		If you are hand-moulding the candle, carve the spikes with a wicking needle while wax is still malleable. In either case, rub the candle with brown poster paint, then remove excess

Fruit Flan Candles

These candles, like their prototypes, are made in ordinary pie tins.

MATERIALS
Paraffin wax
Stearin
Wax dyes
Moulds for fruit, sharp knife
Wicks, 2.5cm (1″) size
Mould seal, pencil
Saucepans, thermometer
Wax whitener
Metal flan tray
Fork or metal whisk (optional)
Wicking needle or very fine screwdriver (optional)
Candle varnish (optional)

MAKING THE CANDLE
Before you make the flan case, make the fruit filling. *Apricot and peach halves* can be cast by filling a round, wicked-up, rigid mould one third full. *Cherries* and *grapes* can be rolled by hand or cast in round ice-cube trays if these are available. Make *fruit slices* by hand, moulding an apple or apricot as described earlier, and then cutting it into slices with a sharp knife while the wax is still malleable.

Use your imagination and improvise moulds from everyday items you will find around the house.
☐ When you have prepared the fruit 'filling', cast the flan case using a metal flan tray. Use paraffin wax (85%), stearin (10%), wax whitener (5%) and a little dye, heated to 93°C (200°F).
☐ Allow to congeal and, as a very fine skin begins to form on the top, after about ten minutes, pour the liquid wax out. This will leave you with a hollow flan case.
☐ Arrange fruit shapes as desired.
☐ Paint candle varnish on the tart to give a glazed finish.

Note: if you are dealing with fruit slices which do not have wicks, you will need to drill holes in the finished candle, either with a hot wicking needle, or by twisting in a very fine screwdriver, but do not push too hard or you will break the wax. Thread pre-waxed wicks into the tart.

Champagne Candle

The champagne candle was made from a mould which has been cast round an unopened bottle. An alternative is to use an empty bottle, slice the bulbous end off the champagne cork and glue it to the bottle top to simulate an unopened bottle. Then cast the mould.

A quicker method is to fill an empty bottle with wax and, when cool, wrap it in a cloth and break the 'mould'. Then, add a wick with the wicking needle. The results are less perfect, however, since bubbles are more likely to form in wax which has been poured into the bottle. The former method is given here.

MATERIALS
Champagne bottle
Wick, 4cm (1½″) size
Green dye, stearin
Paraffin wax
Spirit-based glue
Wax furniture polish
Silicone rubber such as Silastic, and a suitable catalyst
Clay or plasticine
Gold paint
Spoon, muslin
Washing-up liquid
Mould frame

MAKING THE CANDLE
Float all the labels off the champagne bottle in warm water and keep them.
☐ Wipe the bottle clean and dry it with a cloth.
☐ Cast the mould following the method described on page 52 but put a little piece of muslin over the cork end of the bottle, and cover it with the remainder of the rubber mixture so that it is not exposed. This will strengthen the area where the wicking hole is to be made, so that the mould will last for more than one casting.
☐ Wick up the mould following fig. 1 on page 52.
☐ Mix bottle green dye and stearin.
☐ Heat wax and dye mixture at 82°C (180°F).
☐ Fill the mould and cool wax as quickly as possible.
☐ Break surface skin and top up the mould.
☐ Level off the base of the bottle candle as described in the introduction.
☐ Paint gold label on the top of the candle with gold paint such as Goldfinger, which you simply smooth on with a finger and allow to dry. Buff with a soft cloth.
☐ Finally, buff the rest of the candle with a wet tissue, and stick the bottle labels in position with adhesive.

Dynamite Candles

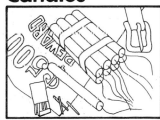

Here is an amusing idea to give your guests a gentle fright.

MATERIALS
Saucepans, jugs and thermometer
Paraffin wax
Overdipping wax
Yellow and red dye
Craft knife
Paintbrush

MAKING THE CANDLE
Make a plain, white, dipped core candle, following the dipping method (page 53).
☐ Dip the core candle repeatedly into the red over-dipping wax heated to 82°C (180°F), dipping the candle from opposite ends each time to obtain a perfectly straight candle.
☐ Between each dip, cut out circle of wax at the centre of one end, so that you obtain a hollow.
☐ When you have built up the desired diameter, roll the candle on a table to make it evenly cylindrical.
☐ Paint hollow centre at top end of the candle with hot, yellow wax.

Ice-cream Cone Candle

MATERIALS
Sheet of beeswax
½ cup of cold whipping wax
Electric whisk or mixer
Icing bag with potato nozzle
Wick, 4cm (1½″) size

Roll beeswax sheet into a cone round a pre-stiffened wick.
☐ Whip the wax in the mixer until it is the texture of stiff cream.
☐ Put the whipped wax into the icing bag which has been fitted with a potato nozzle and squeeze the wax round the wick into the cone.
☐ Prop cone up and allow to set for two days.

Sub editor: Anne Johnson
Designers: pressed flower candles by Janet Wedgwood; tarts by Colburn Lys; all others by David Constable.

BEADS SEEDS SHELLS

The decorative use of shells, beads and seeds involves two very simple and straightforward techniques – stringing and sticking down. The most elementary threading or discreet use of the glue pot can produce excellent results very quickly and simply or, with more studied application, elaborate work with a wealth of fine detail.

The challenge of working with natural objects you have collected yourself, or with beads of different types, is the creation of designs that give full play to colour, texture and shape of the material. Snail or scallop, split pea or sunflower seed, tiny 'rocaille' bead or elongated 'bugle' – each has properties whose careful exploitation is going to add interest to the project and require a fusing of your own ideas with the dictates of the substance.

Before embarking on the actual work, time must be spent in adequate preparation. It is important to work out a design so that you can ascertain how much material you need or, alternatively, how far your material will stretch. Jewellery can usually be strung and re-strung to get different results, but with collages it is advisable to work out the design on paper first. Once you have begun gluing the pieces it is difficult to alter them and you do not want to have a race against the drying tackiness of the glue.

MATERIALS AND EQUIPMENT
Suitable glue and string or wire are the main things needed to work beads, seeds or shells. Jewellery fastenings, called findings, are often also needed, and, occasionally, a small drill is necessary to make holes for threading natural objects. Collage work necessitates a background surface such as card or board, or a three-dimensional object.

Glue. In nearly all cases polyvinyl acetate (PVA) can be used. This is a reasonably strong adhesive, particularly suitable for wood and cloth.

A much stronger glue, and one suitable for metal, is epoxy resin. It is initially fast-setting but needs several hours to dry completely. A mixture of one part plaster of Paris to two parts epoxy resin makes a good base for laying slightly embedded shells.

Plastic is a more inconvenient material for collage work since no particular glue can be relied upon to hold different materials to it. It is necessary therefore to investigate which glue will work with the substance you wish to stick down by reading the recommendation on the label.

But whatever the glue or material used, sticking down should be done in a horizontal position.

Backing. Collages must be worked on a rigid backing such as hardboard or plywood. When decorating a three-dimensional object such as a box, flower pot or mirror frame, choose wood, plaster, metal or unglazed ceramics.

In all instances, whether pictures or objects, small sections of the background may show through, so select a surface that is as near the colours you will be working with as possible.

In the case of seeds, the colour and density of translucent ones like rice can be radically altered by background colour, so that certain sections of the background may need to be painted. This is easily done once the design has been outlined.

Shell and seed pictures often have some background left uncovered and, in such cases, interesting background colours can be obtained with coloured card or a cloth such as hessian. Card must be stuck down fast to the rigid backing and cloth pulled taut. Cut cloth slightly larger than the backing board so that it can be stretched across the backing and glued, then mitred at corners and glued again so that the entire cloth surface is stuck to the backing and the raw edges are glued to the back of the board.

Thread. It is of the utmost importance to choose a thread tough enough to carry the weight of the finished article and withstand friction. It is not much use threading a carefully designed necklace and having the whole lot break and roll away. Only you will know how much you expect a string to withstand, so either test it yourself or ask any reputable craft shop for advice.

Terylene and polyester. Necklaces of tiny shells, beads or seeds are best strung on a terylene or polyester thread, both of which are more hard-wearing than traditional sewing cotton. This includes bead weaving.

Plastic-covered wire. Heavier shells usually require something substantial and fine steel wire covered in plastic can be bought from craft shops. This wire, sometimes called Tigertail, has the added advantage of its own very simple clasp mechanism that needs neither sewing nor gluing.

Chain. A small chain can be used to great effect with large beads. Leave a short length of fine stringing chain on either side of the fastening so that the back of the neck will be free of bumpy beads. The necklace of course should not be too heavy or the chain will not rest comfortably.

Thread and leather. Large wooden beads are usually strung on a thick linen or cotton thread but narrow leather thongs, which come in several colours, and traditional leather bootlaces make excellent alternatives. They provide a robust threading for wooden, china or metal beads and the ends can simply be tied into a secure knot, rendering a bought clasp unnecessary.

Beading needles are available for stringing beads and a packet normally includes several sizes but, as long as the thread will go through the eye and the needle through the beads, any needle will do.

Some threads do not need a needle as they are already stiff enough to thread. Another alternative is to stiffen the end of thread with a little beeswax.

DRILLS AND DRILLING
Seeds and most shells have to be drilled in order to be threaded. Tiny trochus shells and soft seeds such as melon pips may need only a needle or a slim skewer and light hammer to pierce them. Cushion the shells on a soft pad so that they do not crack on impact.

All large shells and tough-skinned seeds will need drilling. Use a jeweller's bow drill, which can be operated with one hand and is not expensive, or an ordinary twist drill with a fine steel bit. This is normally part of any well-equipped tool kit.

You will need to secure the shell or seed you are drilling, so it can be properly pierced and this can be done either by sticking the object to a work surface with beeswax or with lapidary cement (dop wax), which can be bought at jewellers' and rock shops.

A mottled cowrie shell on a strand of heishi mosaic makes an unusual shell necklace. First, fix a bridge of epoxy resin across the mouth of the shell and allow to dry. Then, thread the mosaic and pass both ends of the thread underneath bridge. Tie and secure with bead. Add back fastener.

Swathing plastic beads in silk is an excellent way of making a glossy and stylish decoration. Take skeins of silk embroidery thread and carefully enclose the beads, securing each by wrapping more thread on either side, as illustrated. Fasten ends with a hook and eye.

A bright, flower chain necklace made entirely of felt and buttons. Use two colours for the flowers and another for the stem-like neckband. Cut out the petals and sew the stamen buttons through all three thicknesses. Finally fasten the band with a button and buttonhole.

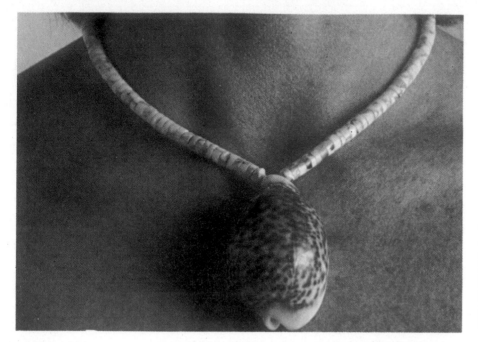

STRINGING and THREADING

While the number of beads available in the traditional materials of glass, wood, metal, 'pearl' and ceramic provides a vast treasury of colour and texture for beadwork, there are many other small objects that can be threaded as well. It is by thinking of beads in their broadest sense – as any thing that can be strung – that some of the most inspired and exciting creations are made.

Seeds and shells are two such materials and are given special emphasis here, but do not neglect those opportunities offered by using improvised beads such as metal nuts and washers, sequins, fabric, bone and buttons. Each gives a totally different effect on a string and working out the most satisfying arrangement is an exciting design challenge, no matter what degree of experience is involved.

Stringing methods can be enlarged upon by looping and re-threading to produce remarkable effects – small flower shapes or a daisy chain, for instance, or a mesh fabric such as the rings illustrated.

Alternatively, beads can be stitched on other materials as the leather bracelet shown, or worked into a firm, beaded fabric in colourful patterns using a bead loom (this technique is explained further on in the chapter).

But while the examples on this page show some of the ways in which simple threading methods can be used to obtain very diverse effects, the designs opposite illustrate how different interpretations of 'stringing' or 'threading' produce striking results.

Types of beads. As well as being of different materials, some conventional beads have special designations. The very small, round, glass beads in the jewellery shown here are called rocaille, while the slightly larger, flattened beads used at intervals in the necklaces are rotelles. Small cylindrical beads are known as bugles. These form the most common types used in beadwork and they are all sold by the gramme or ounce in millimetre sizes. Three and four millimetre rocaille and six millimetre rotelles are the most popular.

Rocaille beaded ropes, rings and a bracelet worked on leather. Instructions on page 78.

Sandra Lousada

Beaded collar. This striking necklace, worked in brilliantly coloured rocaille beads, evokes the sun-drenched and carefree life of the South Seas. The meshed pattern is worked in an easy, looped manner with tiny daisies at the end of each section. The small beads enable the collar to sit comfortably on the shoulders. By experimenting with different colour combinations, the whole appearance of the collar can change. Black, glossy beads, for example, would produce a definite element of drama.

The beaded petal flower is a versatile decoration that might be used on a belt or a necklace. As a hair ornament the impression is distinctly Polynesian. The method of making the petals is not as difficult as might appear. The beads are threaded on beading wire and they can then be bent and shaped into position. The pattern of colouring can be altered by the order of threading.

Instructions for the collar and the flower are on pages 78 and 79.

Wood beads. The splendidly painted beads are decorated by hand and serve to illustrate how individual creations can be made by carefully painting wooden beads to suit your fancy, and using the simplest possible threading. The pattern shown can be copied and transferred, but a free-hand interpretation is recommended.

The large beads are painted with acrylic colour in the following manner: first, the bead is stuck on the end of an artist's brush, so that it can be steadily held in one hand while it is being painted with the other. Start with a layer of base colour and build up to the application of the design, but allow each coat to dry before applying the next. To obtain a brilliant luminosity, undercoats of white should be used between layers. Finally, each bead should be given a coat of polyurethane varnish. The small intermediate macramé beads are available already coloured, and once the main beads have been painted, the necklace can be threaded on a leather thong.

Rex Bamber

63

Iridescent abalone shells make natural soap dishes
and small holes in the back let water drain out.
Opposite: a rope of pyrene shells, a cockle-encrusted
choker and translucent wedge shell necklace.
Instructions for necklaces are on page 80.

Stringing beads is carried a step further when used in conjunction with crochet to make three-dimensional jewellery or eye-deceiving decorations.

Rope of beads. Worked in slip stitch, the design automatically spirals into a twisted rope. In the photograph on the left, the finished rope has been twisted double to make a heavy choker.

Blackberries make mouth-watering decorations lodged temptingly in their faery-like basket, or used in jewellery. Such trifles were popular in Victorian times and have lasted to enchant and trick us still.

Instructions, page 80.

Shells must be among the most wonderfully varied and versatile of natural objects. There are over a hundred thousand known molluscs and, with mussels, whelks, winkles and cockles waiting to be collected from almost every temperate shore, there are immense resources for the designer.

Although shells have been used as currency, insignia and decorative motifs down the ages, few examples of shell art survive, largely due to their extreme fragility. Nineteenth century shell flowers, usually bouquets preserved under glass domes and the so-called sailors' Valentines – intricate shell patterns with a few flowers or words of greeting, encased in hinged octagonal frames – can still be found. On a grander scale there are instances of Rococo plasterwork inlaid with shells and fanciful, encrusted grottoes made to enliven garden architecture.

Modern shell designs often employ the texture as well as colour of shells to characterize the work: concave mussel shells for the ruffled plumage of a chicken; tiny pearly trochus shells on a feminine mirror; pointed and whorled turritellas marking out a brown linear ground; brilliantly shiny convex cowries displaying a sea of pale lipped mouths – a single scallop cemented in a magisterial position. The contrasts are evident and the opportunities become apparent. Juggle with the shells, lie them flat or overlap them; look at the shallow concave bowls of a pair of bivalves, or the pale teeth of an aperture, the glossy surfaces and spiralling shapes; in fact, know all you can before you begin.

THE FRAME

The encircling frame is a choice of small shells laid and overlaid, built in from the edges, to give a densely encrusted border; the shells taking over the art of both carver and painter. Row upon row of tiny white and mottled shells, glossy, greenish money cowries half hidden by orange pyrere, and finally the splendid projecting row of trochus shells – pearly whorls crowning the design.

COLLECTING SHELLS

Sometimes shells can be bought in shops, but collecting them yourself has an inherent pleasure which should not be missed. Take only those that are as near perfect as possible because the gentle washing which is necessary cannot take out stains or tar.

Preparing shells. Most live animals float out by being brought to the boil, but small gastropods (single shell animals) may need easing out with a pin, or soaking in spirit for a week or two.

Wash the empty shells in warm soapy water and rinse. You can get rid of some seaweed stains using household bleach.

Next, grade the shells for size and colour and sort out the bivalves. These are the hinged shells and those such as mussels separate out into lefts and rights.

The plumage of barnyard fowls is brilliantly suggested by the shapes, textures and colouring of the cowries, conch, neritas and mussel shells that cover these terracotta shapes.

Instructions on page 81.

SEED COLLAGES

Multitudes of different seeds are used in picture-making and for ornamentation, and the vast majority of them can be bought from health food and from pet shops.

Boxes. Radish and canary seed are used for the round box. The pattern is based on a North American design. By contrast, the cat on the cigarette box is inspired by a modern primitive. Striped sunflower seeds suggest the cat's fur while canary and radish seeds convey background vegetation.

The fish mosaic is made from several varieties of seed: the upper part of the body is Cyprus tares, gunga and yellow peas make up the middle, and dari, the belly.

Bird. Fantasy ruled in the creation of the serene, crested bird standing sentinel against a jungly background and overhung with a veil of small flowers. Care and precision were used to give a casual, impressionistic background to this imaginative creation.

Instructions on pages 82 and 83.

Theo Bergström

Rex Bamber

72

BEAD WEAVING

Theo Bergström

Bead weaving on a loom produces narrow strips of closely-woven mesh which can be used for trimming or for jewellery, such as the bracelet shown here. Alternatively, lengths of mesh can be sewn together to make fabric for clothes. The bolero opposite is a good example: lengths worked in a diagonal pattern are joined to make a chevron, while the bracelet design forms a contrasting border. The bead weaving technique is described overleaf and diagrams of the designs charted. Detailed instructions, page 83.

Bead weaving is a simple method of making strips of bead fabric using a wood or metal loom. Bead looms are available from craft shops, but looms can also be improvised using a cardboard box (fig. 1). The advantage of a bought loom is that it enables you to wind the fabric up as you work. In either case, the strips of fabric which are produced are limited in width by the width of the loom, but strips can be sewn together to make wider or longer fabric, as illustrated in the beadwork bolero on the previous page.

HOW TO WEAVE

Pull threads tightly on the loom by winding it round the rollers as shown in fig. 2. Use about 30cm (12") more thread than the finished work needs. Make sure each thread is in a groove and double the outside threads for greater strength.

☐ Thread up a beading needle and fasten thread with a knot (fig. 3).

☐ Thread up the same number of beads as there are spaces between the threads.

☐ Pass beads under stretched threads and push one bead up into each space from below.

☐ Pass the needle back through the beads from above (fig. 4), this secures the beads in position. Continue to weave in this way, following bead pattern diagrams for appropriate colours of each row of beads you weave.

Joining new threads. To join new threads, overlap the new length of thread with the end of the old by at least 5cm (2"). To finish ends, weave them back into the beads for 2.5cm (1") and trim off excess.

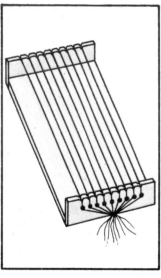

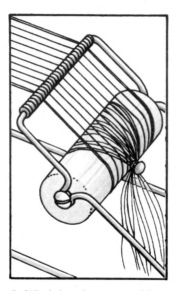

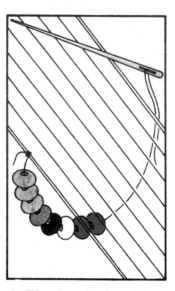

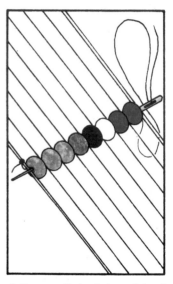

1. Cut down a cardboard box to make an improvised loom.

2. Wind threads taut round loom roller as shown here.

3. Thread up beads and fasten thread as shown, before weaving.

4. Pass needle back through beads to secure them in position.

Wooden bead loom with work in position. The warp threads can be seen wound around the removable bar, or roller, on the left. For a longer piece of work they would also be wound round righthand roller, ready to be pulled forward as worked areas are rolled up.

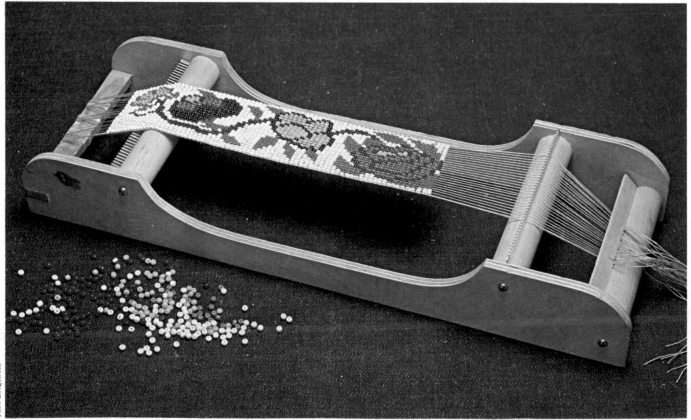

In bead weaving patterns, one square represents one bead. Use beads of the same size or the results will be uneven. The patterns shown below are for the bolero and bracelet (full instructions on page 83). The patterns on the left can be used for belts, bracelets or trim. Using graph paper, it is easy to chart your own designs.

Graph pattern shows size of weaving strips and assembly.

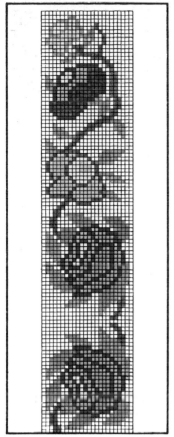

Flowers in a traditional border pattern.

Geometric design worked in five colours.

Chart showing repeat pattern for bead woven bolero.

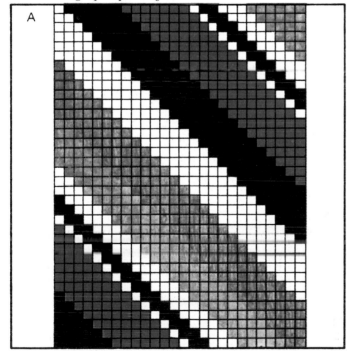

One square=6mm(¼")

cut neck higher
for back of bolero

A   A   A   B

B

BOLERO PATTERN one front(reverse for opposite side)

A Chevron B Border of flowers ▬ strip of plain beadweaving

Below: stylized floral design for the bracelet, including repeat pattern for the border of the bolero shown on page 74.

B   repeat of design for border

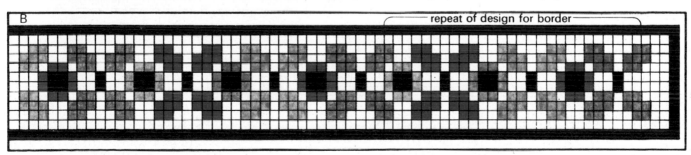

Bead Rings

Following the basic instructions and diagrams given below, you can make any of the rings shown on page 87, or invent a pattern of your own.

MATERIALS

Beading wire: one reel of very fine beading wire or 5amp fuse wire.
Beads: small amounts of blue, red, yellow, green and orange.

WORKING

Using 1m (1yd) of wire, thread the number of beads required for the centre width (fig. 1) of the ring you are making. Position beads in centre of wire.

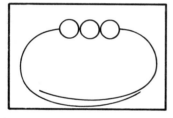

1. Place beads in centre.

☐ Thread second row and pass other end of wire through beads in the opposite direction (fig. 2).

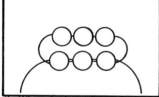

2. Thread up second row.

☐ Tighten wire and continue design in this way.
☐ Finish ring by working wire back through beginning (fig. 3) for three rows.

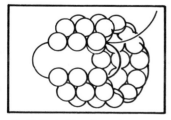

3. Rethread to close up.

Bead and Leather Bracelet

MATERIALS

Beads: 28gm (1oz) of 2mm blue beads; 14gm (½oz) each of 2mm beads in white, red, yellow and green.
Leather: one strip of leather 4cm×23cm (1½″×9″) and another strip of leather 2.5cm×23cm (1″×9″).
Bead and sewing needles
Terylene thread
Polyvinyl acetate glue
Craft knife; paper clip

WORKING

Turn 6mm (¼″) down either side on the wider strip and glue (fig. 1).

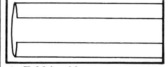

1. Fold in sides.

☐ Fold other strip in three (fig. 2) and glue down. Then glue roll to first strip.

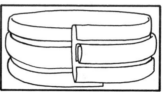

2. Attach glued roll.

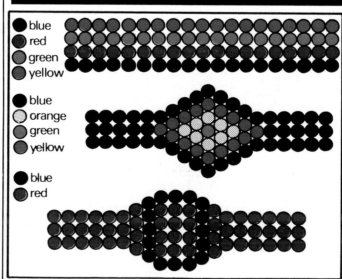

Ring patterns: a plain band, two with centre decoration.

☐ Form the bracelet into a circle with padding facing outwards (fig. 3). Keep it in shape by clipping with a paper clip.
Begin the pattern shown on the chart 2.5cm (1″) in from the end of the bracelet and just inside the edge.

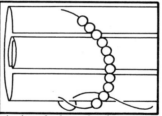

3. Reshape into bracelet.

☐ Make a stitch, then thread 11 white beads (fig. 4) and make another stitch at the opposite edge of the band.

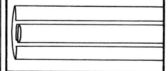

4. Attach eleven beads.

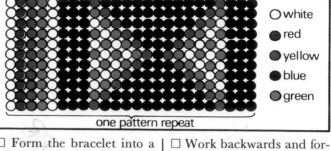

○ white
● red
● yellow
● blue
● green

one pattern repeat

☐ Work backwards and forwards, including a row of beads between each stitch (fig. 5). Thread up the beads according to the pattern on the chart.

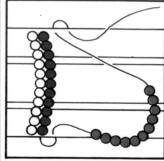

5. Stitch between rows.

☐ Work two repeats of the pattern but measure one repeat and, using this measurement, overlap the ends of the bracelet to the correct finished size.
☐ Trim away excess padding and leather.
☐ Work the final repeat of the pattern through the overlapped section, thus disguising the join.

Beaded Collar

MATERIALS
Beading needles
Terylene thread
Beads: 50gm (2oz) each of 3mm beads in blue, red, green and yellow.
Fastening

WORKING

Thread up 204 red beads on double thread. Leave 15cm (6″) of thread free at either end, and knot thread close to last bead at each end to prevent unthreading. This string of beads forms the basic circle of the necklace and the design is worked in long loops off this circle.

Use long thread and work, following chart opposite:

Row one. Pass needle through first two beads on collar circle and anchor thread by knotting. Thread up seven red beads, nine blue, 15 green and 20 yellow.

☐ Continue on the same thread, make a daisy in blue with a red centre (fig. 1) by threading eight blue beads.

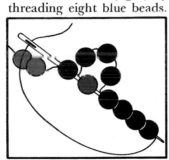

1. To make daisy.

☐ Then pass needle back through first blue bead, add one red bead and pass needle back through blue beads five, six, seven and eight. Tighten up thread and a daisy will result.

Row two. Thread 19 yellow beads and, following the pattern diagram, slip needle through first yellow bead threaded on row one.

☐ Thread up 15 green and slip needle through last blue bead threaded on previous row.

☐ Thread up eight blue beads and slip needle through last blue bead on previous row.

☐ Thread up six red beads and pass needle through first red bead on previous row, then pass needle through five beads on actual necklace.

Row three. Thread up three red beads and pass needle through fourth red bead on previous row.

☐ Thread three red and four blue beads, then pass through fifth blue bead on

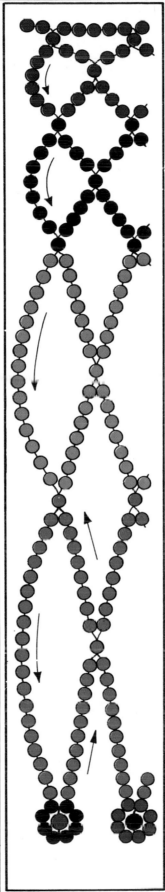

⬤	red
⬤	blue
⬤	green
⬤	yellow

Diagram for making meshed necklaces with daisies.

previous row.

☐ Thread five blue and seven green beads and slip needle through eighth green bead on previous row.

☐ Thread seven green and eight yellow beads and slip needle through ninth yellow bead on previous row.

☐ Thread 10 yellow beads and make a daisy in red with a blue centre, following fig. 1.

☐ Repeat rows two and three, making alternate red and blue daisies, and finish with a knot in the same way as the beginning.

☐ Knot the necklace ends onto a fastener and thread loose ends back into beads for 5cm (2″).

Beaded Petal Flower

MATERIALS

Beading wire: one reel of beading wire or 15amp fuse wire; 1m (1yd) very fine beading wire or 5amp fuse wire.

Beads: 25gm (1oz) each of 3mm beads in red and yellow.

Florist's tape: 1m (1yd) to bind stem.

WORKING

A description of the technique (fig. 1) is followed by the precise amounts of beads needed for each petal.

☐ Thread up the total amount of beads on the wire needed for each petal (a).

☐ Bend hook at end of wire to prevent unthreading (b).

☐ Count out required number of beads for centre length (c).

☐ Allow a spare 2.5cm (1″) of wire below hook, then gather a loop of wire below the beads and twist (d).

☐ Take up correct number of beads for first side length (e).

☐ Encircle straight length (f).

☐ Push up correct number of beads for second side (g).

☐ Continue working bead leaf/petal until all the beads are used up (h).

☐ Cut wire free of reel and wind around petal base (i).

☐ Trim off straight length to 6mm (¼″) and bend round to back of petal (j).

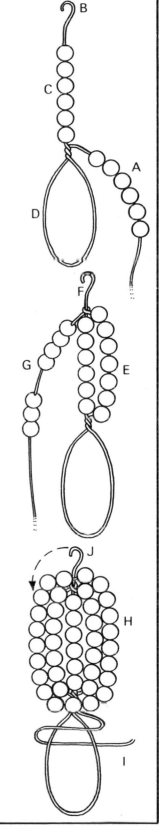

1. Technique for petal.

Flower pattern

Three small petals. Thread up five yellow, eight red, seven yellow, five red. When these have been bent according to the technique described, the result will be a centre length with five red and two yellow, two outer lengths of four red and five yellow each.

Five middle petals. Thread up six yellow, 16 red, 10 yellow, eight red, seven yellow and five red.

Centre length is five red and two yellow, two middle lengths, four red and five yellow, two outer lengths eight red and five yellow.

Six outer petals. Thread up 51 red, 10 yellow, six red, 14 yellow, 19 red and 10 yellow.

Centre length is 10 yellow. Adjacent sides 12 beads. Next sides 17 beads long. Outer length 21 beads.

Finishing. Using the very fine beading wire, bind the three small petals into a triangular shape right sides down.

☐ Next, bind the five middle petals, right sides up, around the smaller ones.

☐ Finally, bind on the six outer petals, right sides uppermost. Wind self-adhesive floral tape around the stem to fasten.

☐ Bend the three small petals up into a bud shape and curve up the others appropriately.

Crocheted Bead Rope

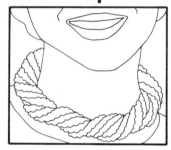

MATERIALS
Beads: 80gm (3oz) black 4mm beads and 80gm (3oz) white 4mm beads (approximately 740 beads). The necklace is 85cm (33½″) long.
Crochet cotton: 1 ball black cotton no. 20.
Crochet hook size 3 (3D)
Beading needle
Fastening

WORKING
Thread up the complete 168gm (6oz) of beads on the crochet cotton, two black and two white repeating. Leave this string attached to the ball of cotton.

☐ Make a chain of eight stitches and form into a circle (see Crochet chapter).

☐ Work three rows round in slip stitch.

☐ Begin to stitch in beads as shown in figs. 1 and 2, eight beads per row. The spiral effect will happen automatically.

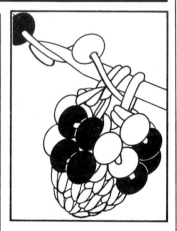

1. Slide each bead along thread and stitch into the work.

2. Complete by pulling thread through loop.

☐ Continue working until all the beads are used.

☐ To finish, work three rows of slip stitch as at the beginning.

☐ Oversew a necklace fastening at each end of the crocheted rope.

Blackberries

The blackberries are made by simple crochet in slip stitch. For basic crochet instructions see Chapter 10.

MATERIALS
To make 12 blackberries:
Beads: 25gm (1oz) of 3mm black glass beads; and 12×12mm black wood beads.
Beading needle
Crochet hook size 2 (1B)
Black embroidery cotton

WORKING
Thread 30 beads and make an eight chain circle.
1st row. Slip stitch around chain once.
2nd row. Slide a bead up and slip stitch into first slip stitch of previous row.
3rd row. As second row, put crochet hook through the loop to the right side of the bead on the previous row.

☐ Work three rows of eight beads and slide the wood bead into the centre of the crochet beads. Continue crocheting beads close over the wood bead by working into every other slip stitch. Cast off.

Shell Necklaces

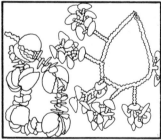

MATERIALS
Beading needle
Terylene thread
Epoxy resin glue
Small hand drill
Purchased clasps
Shells and beads in quantities given below

SHELL ROPE
This simple rope of pyrene shells needs a small hole bored in one end of each shell. (Information on drilling is given in the chapter introduction.)
Thread beads and knot securely. There are 210 shells in the rope shown.

WEDGE SHELL NECKLACE
Beads: 14gm (½oz) off-cut white glass beads.
14gm (½oz) white rocaille beads.
48 wedge shells

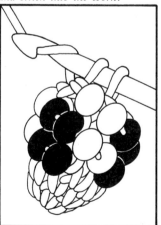

1. Detail of necklace pendant.

Working. Take a thread long enough to complete the entire necklace. Thread up 30 off-cut beads, 10 rocaille, one wedge shell, six rocaille, one wedge shell and re-thread the last three beads.

☐ Thread another six rocaille, a shell, rethread three and continue as in fig 1, down to the bottom of the pendant. Then work up the string again so that there are eight shell drops, each with three beads.

☐ Re-thread the last 13 rocaille beads and shell.

☐ Thread 10 cut beads and continue to work a further five shell pendants.

☐ Finish with the 30 cut beads and a purchased fastening secured by thread and glue.

COCKLE NECKLACE
Beads: 10 pairs of cockle-shells, approximately 15gm (½oz) shell sequins and 15gm (½oz) off-cut translucent beads.
Working. Using double terylene thread, thread up 10

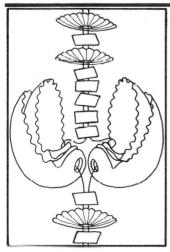

1. Threading of cockles.

beads; then alternate one sequin and one bead for 10 sequins; then add five beads.

☐ Divide the threads and thread each through two shells so that they cup around the beads (fig 1)

☐ Combine thread and continue alternating 10 sequins and 10 beads; five beads and then cockles. Do this four times.

☐ Thread up 10 more beads and finish with a purchased clasp. This is attached to the threads which are then glued into place for extra safety.

Mirror Frame

MATERIALS
Frame: use either an old wooden frame or have one made up to specific measurements.
Glue: one part plaster of Paris to two parts epoxy resin.
Shells: tiny trochus for border and a selection for the bouquet – scallop, tellins, white nerita and turritellas are shown here.

WORKING
Old frames must first be cleaned of any varnish with paint and varnish remover. The frame illustrated here has a slightly convex surface so that the design is gently rounded.

☐ To build up a rounded surface, spread a thick layer of the glue mixture on the frame, moulding it to make a gentle curve, then let dry.

☐ Fix shells with another batch of glue mixture, working a small area, and one row at a time.

☐ Leave space for the 'bouquet' and affix this last.

Câche Pot

MATERIALS
Unglazed earthenware pot
Glue: one part plaster of Paris/two parts epoxy resin.
Polyurethane varnish (optional)
Shells: money cowries and moon snails.

WORKING
Apply the cementing mixture to part of the pot at a time and fix shells, being careful not to show too much of the adhesive.

☐ Work a row of money cowries around the bottom edge, then two more rows of cowries (convex side out) followed by a row of money cowries showing the apertures.

☐ Then, work two rows of horizontal cowries, convex side up and another of cowries with apertures exposed.

☐ Next, glue down two rows of mottled neritas and top with a row of small money cowries. If you are going to put a plant pot inside, varnish the base to prevent moisture escaping.

Shell Birds

Several bases can be used for shell birds. Papier mâché worked on a chicken wire frame will enable you to make chickens and ducks of any size or type. Bought shapes include unglazed terracotta chicken bricks and decoys from a sporting supply shop; or you can carve specimens as described in the Wood chapter.

MATERIALS
Base and appropriate glue: one part plaster of Paris to two parts epoxy resin is recommended for the unglazed terracotta birds shown on pages 70 and 71.
Antique wax polish and thinning spirit
Shells

WHITE CHICKEN
Concave mussel shells for the wings and cowries over the back and breast. Shell beak and purchased eye.

☐ Spread on a bit of glue mixture at a time and work that area, then proceed to the next. Work from the bottom up.

SHELL DUCK
Small brown conch shells overlaid with white nerita are used here.

☐ Work as for the chicken but do not put white shells in place. Leave spaces instead.

☐ After applying the brown shells, coat the bird liberally with a solution of antique wax polish thinned down with spirit and use a dry cloth to rub over the shells, leaving the glue and base of some shells brown.

☐ Then add white shells.

BROWN CHICKEN
Small conch shells showing apertures and circular patterns of conelike turritella are used. The bird's comb is a larger conch.

☐ Work as for white chicken, then coat with wax as for duck.

Round Box

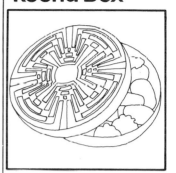

MATERIALS
Wood box measuring 15cm (6") diameter.
Glue: large tube of a clear general purpose glue.
Seeds: 75gm (3oz) radish or similar small dark coloured seed; 100gm (4oz) pale canary seed or other small, light coloured seed.
Applicator stick for glue
Polyuretherne varnish
Black felt tip pen
Carbon and tracing paper

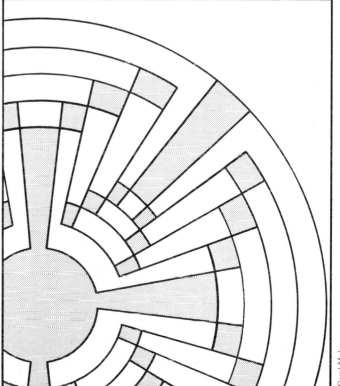

Full size detail of geometric design for the box lid. Use quarter section and repeat it four times, for circular design.

Coral Mula

WORKING

Transfer design on to box lid using the method described at the back of this book and colour dark areas with a pen.

☐ Beginning with the dark patches, apply small areas of glue, spreading the glue smoothly with a flat stick or piece of cardboard.

☐ Sprinkle a thick layer of seeds on the glue.

☐ Continue until all dark areas are covered.

☐ Shake off excess seeds when the glue dries.

☐ Then work the light areas in the same fashion.

☐ To work sides of box, fill in dark areas, as shown in photograph, down sides of box.

☐ Mark with a line the point where the edge of the lid finishes on the side of the box base and work a fine line of dark seeds at this place.

☐ Complete all other areas in light seeds.

☐ When glue is completely dry, shake off excess seeds and apply a thin coat of varnish over all seeds.

Oblong Box

MATERIALS

Wooden box measuring approximately 17×10×5cm (7″×4″×2″).

Large tube of clear, general purpose glue such as Uhu.

Seeds: 25gm (1oz) large corn seed; 25gm (1oz) sunflower seeds; 100gm (4oz) mixed canary seed or 50gm (2oz) radish seed or similar dark seed and the same amount of a light seed, such as grass seed.

Carbon and tracing paper

Polyurethane varnish and brush

Black felt tip pen

Tweezers and applicator stick

Sharp knife

WORKING

If you are using canary seed, you will have to separate the light and dark shades before beginning to work the design.

☐ Transfer design to box lid, following instructions for transferring designs at the back of this book.

☐ Colour all dark areas with the black felt tip pen.

☐ Slice the sunflower seeds in half and, applying only a small area of glue at a time, begin to lay the sliced seeds on the body of the cat with the tweezers. Press each seed firmly down in the glue.

☐ Work the features of the cat's face in dark seed before applying light areas. Sprinkle seeds on the glue and shake off excess when dry.

☐ Sides of lid are worked in mixed radish and canary seed.

☐ When the work is completely dry and excess seeds have all been removed, apply a light coat of varnish to add a gloss and fix seeds.

Fish Mosaic

The fish opposite is 48cm (19″) long and 24cm (9½″) at the widest point. The seeds used to make the design are obtainable from health shops, supermarkets and pet shops.

MATERIALS

Cardboard for backing
All-purpose clear glue
Polyurethane varnish
Tracing paper (optional)
Seeds: Cyprus tares, millet, lentils, long grain rice, paddy rice, golden pleasure, blue maw, gunga peas, yellow peas, dari and milo.

WORKING

Draw a simple outline of a fish to the dimensions given here or enlarge and trace the shape on the chart.

☐ Transfer the image to the cardboard.

☐ Lay the seeds as previously described, working a small area at a time.

☐ Varnish upon completion.

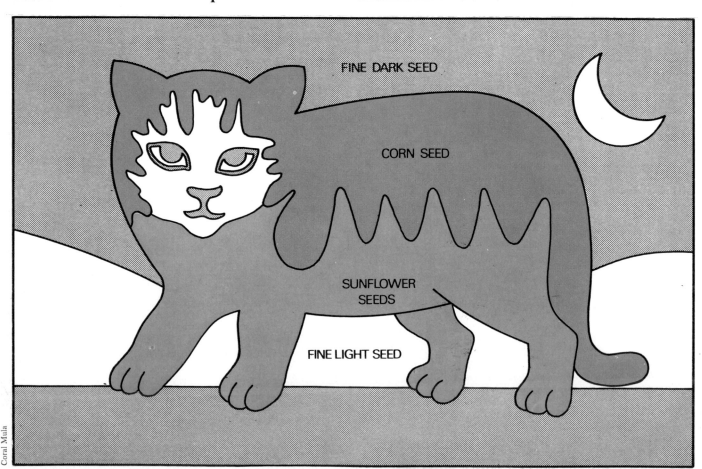

FINE DARK SEED

CORN SEED

SUNFLOWER SEEDS

FINE LIGHT SEED

Coral Mula

The prowling cat is worked in four types of seed. The design is for the lid of a rectangular box.

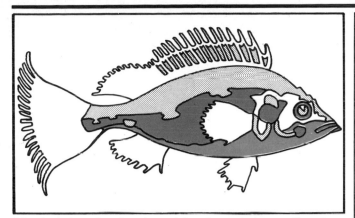

Mosaic design of an imaginary fish to be worked on cardboard.

Design for the crested bird against jungle foliage.

Crested Bird

The seeds which make up the bird motif are laid closely and evenly, while the background is worked much more loosely and spontaneously in order to create the impression of wild, exotic foliage.

If you have difficulty in obtaining some of the seeds listed, then replace them with others of a similar shape and texture from health shops and delicatessens.

The finished picture measures 61cm×46cm (24″× 18″). This includes a 1cm (¼″) border which is left bare to facilitate framing.

MATERIALS

Hardboard or heavy cardboard for backing
All-purpose clear glue and applicator
Tweezers
Polyurethane varnish
Tracing paper and pencil
Seeds: lentils, tares, wheat, dari, rice, melon seeds, oats, split peas, mung beans, milo, hemp, paddy rice, marrow seeds, sweet chestnut, rhubarb, date pips, dried berries, white sunflower seeds, mung.

WORKING

Enlarge and transfer the design on to hardboard. (See the section at the back of the book on enlarging and transferring designs.)

☐ Work the bird motif first.

☐ Then work the background, gluing a small area at a time. Aim for an uneven texture.

☐ Finally, overlay the seeds to build up a relief surface on the background.

Bead-woven Bolero

MATERIALS

Beadweaving loom
Beading needles
Terylene thread: approximately 3 reels
Beads: 200gm (8oz) each of 3mm beads in black, white, orange, dark red and brown.
Black needlecord: 0.5m (½yd) for jacket back
Lining fabric: 0.5m (½yd)
Hooks and eyes

THE DESIGN

The stripes in the jacket use 26 beads across. You will need 29 lengths of thread (doubled at the edges) measuring the length of the strip, plus an allowance of 15cm (6″) at each end for tying on to the loom.

☐ Following method described on page 76, use charted pattern to weave strips of the diagonal design of the exact length shown.

☐ Oversew these strips together, reversing alternate panels to create a chevron.

☐ Weave four short lengths of red beads 6mm (¼″) wide (see pattern) and oversew in positions shown on diagram, page 77.

☐ Weave border lengths by following chart for bracelet design, beginning and ending each border length as shown in the design.

☐ Oversew borders into position.

ASSEMBLY

Cut out exact size pattern for jacket back plus 2cm (⅝″) for a seam allowance, except at shoulder joins. On the chart the dotted line shows where the neck should be cut higher for the back, also two darts are marked in for the jacket back.

☐ To cut out the lining place four pattern pieces as shown in fig. 4, page 97, leaving seam allowance all round.

☐ Sew up darts on jacket back and lining.

☐ Back stitch bead fronts to jacket back at sides and shoulder. Turn in seams on jacket back and lining and slip stitch lining on to complete jacket.

☐ Fasten front with hooks.

Bracelet

The design given is for a bracelet approximately 18cm (7″) in circumference and 3cm (1½″) wide.

MATERIALS

Beads: small amounts of white, black, red, orange and light brown 3mm beads.
Bead loom
Bead needle
Terylene thread
Two small hooks and eyes

WORKING

Thread loom with 15 threads (outer edges have two threads).

☐ Thread up 12 black beads and, following the pattern chart and the instructions already given for working on a loom, proceed to weave.

Section editor:
Rosemary Lamont

Designers:
Beadwork designs by Jackie Short; painted beads by Elizabeth Pleydell-Pearce; shell necklaces, Paula Rieu; shell chickens, Anthony Redmile; seedwork, Roger and Glenda Marsh.

PRINTING

Printing is universally practised both as a means of conveying information and creating works of art and decoration.

In its less mechanical forms it is wonderfully simple, yet remarkably flexible and effective; and for these reasons it is enthusiastically practised by beginners and experienced designers and artists alike.

The recent development of modern dyes and inks makes it possible to print on most materials and this has contributed greatly to the revival of interest in some of the earlier and more straightforward forms of this ancient craft. (Information on appropriate inks and dyes is contained in the General Guide at the end of this chapter.)

DIRECT PRINTING

Direct printing is the simplest of all printing methods since there is no block to be cut and no image to be incised. Instead you use as your printing block the object whose image you wish to print.

Choosing natural blocks for printing is in itself a stimulating occupation. Leaves such as those shown here make quick, effective designs and are easily obtainable from trees, flowers or houseplants. Select perfect leaves with interesting outlines, which will lie flat. Avoid glossy, hard leaves like laurel or holly and remember that any flaw in a leaf will appear in your print.

Vegetables and fruits are also natural printing blocks. Simply slice cleanly in half any firm-fleshed vegetable or fruit with an instantly recognizable outline – an apple, green pepper, carrot or onion, for example. Dry the surface, apply dye and use as a printing block.

Note: before beginning to print, see instructions overleaf for preparing printing surfaces, working and fixing dyes to make them permanent.

Leaf table linen. The mat and napkin below are printed with freshly picked geranium leaves. The picnic cloth opposite, a leafy September song, is printed with leaves from several trees. In both cases, fabric paint is applied to one side of each leaf with a brush. In the autumnal version, however, several colours are merged to give a realistic effect. This can be difficult at first and it is worthwhile practising on a spare piece of fabric.

Lay a painted leaf carefully in place on the fabric, cover with scrap paper and press firmly down with your hand. After printing all leaves in your design, fix the colours by ironing.

RELIEF PRINTING

The general name given to printing with stamping blocks is relief printing, and some of the most rudimentary methods are among the most effective; matchsticks, washers and hairpins, for instance, are ready-made 'blocks' in that they have outlines which will print interesting geometric or abstract shapes. But more conventional blocks can be cut from malleable surfaces such as corks, erasers and potatoes.

HOW TO PRINT

Place the paper or fabric to be printed on a firm but yielding surface, such as an old, folded blanket or several newspapers. Cover this with plain paper to protect the printing surface from absorbing newsprint, or the blanket from absorbing dye.

Cover the surface of the block with colour, using a brush, sponge or stamping pad. Then press the block face down on the fabric or paper. Unless you wish to make gradations of colour in the design, re-ink the block between each printing.

Note: always test-print first, either on newsprint or, better still, on a spare piece of the actual fabric or paper you are using.

When printing on fabric, always wash fabric first (if it is washable) to remove any dressing and then fix the colour after printing by ironing on as hot a setting as the fabric permits.

Geometric design. The suede belt is a good example of how familiar forms can be used to build up abstract designs. The pattern is made by alternately printing the end of a cork and the end of a piece of square wooden beading. The belt is printed with suede dye and an ordinary ink stamping pad is used to hold the colour.

Tulips. This pretty little motif was cut out of an eraser with a sharp craft knife. Used here to decorate a salt box, it would be equally appealing on the border of a pinafore, kerchief, or the edge of a kitchen shelf.

Apply the design to untreated wood by brushing acrylic paint on the surface of the carved eraser and stamping at regular intervals. Use a ruler as a guideline to keep the design straight. A good waxing or two coats of polyurethane varnish will give a lustrous finish.

Theo Bergström

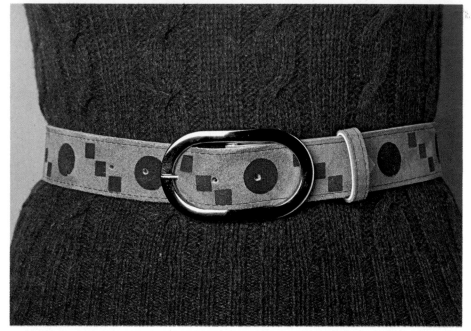

Rex Bamber

POTATO PRINTING

Potatoes make good printing blocks because they can be carved easily with a kitchen knife, and yet they are firm enough to be stamped again and again. They have relatively short lives, however, remaining firm for only about a day; consequently, they are recommended for small projects only.

Peel the potato first, then cut it in two crosswise. You can gouge out designs in the flat surface by making small V-shaped cuts so that the motif stands out in relief. Alternatively, you can slice the potato into geometric shapes – dots, triangles, squares – which can be used independently or combined to build up more complex designs. By slicing the geometric shape from the entire piece, as shown opposite, you will obtain a better-defined edge and a block which is immediately identifiable.

Note: never use oil-based paints or inks when printing with potatoes. Potatoes contain water and the old adage about oil and water not mixing may become painfully apparent.

If you are printing the same image in more than one colour, cut a different block for each. Otherwise, the potato may absorb some of the first colour and affect the second application.

Potato-printed shoes. Shoes are well-known keys to the wearer's personality, a fact beyond dispute in the potato-printed examples below. The triangle, large spots, flower and stripes are all cut out of potatoes. The end of a matchstick makes the small spots on the clogs and the flower centres on the dancing shoes. The colour on the plimsoll laces is painted on with a brush. The potato blocks and matchsticks are shown opposite, along with the improvised blocks used on the belt and salt box.

Stuff the shoes firmly with screwed up newspaper and apply the designs using shoe dye. You will probably have to apply a conditioner, so read the manufacturer's instructions first to find out.

Use a sponge for a stamping pad and dab the potato blocks first on the pad and then on the shoes. But test the colour first on a piece of rough fabric, to check the quantity of dye and amount of pressure required. Any mistakes made while printing can be removed quickly with a damp cloth.

Sandra Lousada

FELT BLOCKS

Felt printing blocks give considerable scope to the needs and imagination of amateur printers. Unlike more sophisticated techniques, they require no special training to use, and they have an advantage over most other improvised blocks in that they can be cut to virtually any size and shape. Furthermore, it is easier to cut out intricate shapes in felt than to gouge them out or incise them in other surfaces.

Choose the design and draw or trace it on paper. Cut the paper out and pin it to a piece of heavy felt, about 2mm (1/16″) thick, then cut out the felt and glue it with PVA to a square of thick cardboard, slightly larger and at least as thick as the felt. This automatically puts the motif in relief, ready for printing.

Felt blocks can be inked up on stamping pads if they are small enough, or colour can be applied with a brush.

To print, hold the block by the edge, lay it in place on the surface you wish to print, and press down. Remove the block carefully so as not to smudge.

The peasant-style skirt illustrates the charming use made of a naive folk motif which has been cut from felt and printed on plain white cloth. The round motif is the end of a cork. Remember to wash fabric before printing to remove any dressing that might prevent proper printing. If you are making a skirt with trimmings, like the one in the photograph, work out the arrangement of the ribbons before you print and mark the positions on the edge of the fabric. Make a fine straight line with a row of pins or tailor's chalk where you wish to print the design. By aligning the printing block with this base line you will be sure of printing the motifs in a straight row.

After printing, remember to 'fix' the colour by ironing with a hot iron. Finally, machine stitch the ribbons and trimmings in position, gather the fabric and make up as you would any ordinary gathered skirt.

Rex Bamber

STENCILLING

Stencilling involves blocking out the areas you do *not* want to print and this is done by cutting the design out of stencil paper and laying it on the surface to be printed. You then spread colour over the stencil, and those areas which are not blocked by the paper will print.

Stencils can be made cheaply from thin card coated with polyurethane varnish, or you can buy stencil paper from craft shops and art suppliers. Stencil paper has a glossy finish so that it resists paint absorption and can be used repeatedly.

Cutting. Cut out stencil designs with either a craft knife, such as a Stanley knife, or a scalpel (obtainable from art supply shops).

First trace the design on the stencil paper, then anchor the paper to a cutting board with masking tape. (If you are cutting round motifs, you will have to re-position the paper from time to time as you work.)

Grip the knife as you would either a table knife or a pencil and, if you are cutting a straight line, work with the blade alongside a metal rule. This gives a guideline and is a safety precaution as well. Keep fingers of the other hand on the ruler and well out of the path of the blade. Always work with the blade absolutely straight. Do not angle it to left or right. If the card or paper is too thick to slice through easily, cut a bit at a

90

time, going over it until you cut through.

To apply colour, use a blunt-ended stencil brush specially designed for the purpose, or a small piece of sponge, and choose a paint or dye which is suitable for the surface you are stencilling. (See the General Guide at the end of this chapter.)

Hat. Birds, or their feathers, have always been popular decorations for hats and here the idea is used effectively at its simplest. Choose a hat made of smooth felt or some other flat fabric.

The stencil is cut from ordinary greaseproof paper which bends more easily to the rounded contours of the hat than would normal stencil paper or card. Trace and transfer the design on to the greaseproof paper with a soft pencil. (See special section at the back of the book for information on how to transfer designs.) Make several stencils. You can cut out the motifs with a pair of scissors.

Place the hat on a hat block or stuff the crown with newspaper.

Pin the stencils into position, bending the paper to the curve of the crown and carefully paint the birds, making sure not to get paint behind the stencils, which is a hazard when working on a curve.

When dry, shade the birds by overpainting in a slightly darker hue. Finally, 'fix' the design by blow drying with a hair dryer for about two minutes on each bird.

The blue bird has long been a symbol of happiness, recognizable the world over. On the previous page the motif takes the form of swooping swallows cavorting on a hat brim, while here its associations are definitely of a more romantic nature – a cloud of bluebirds passionately chasing red hearts across a pair of jeans. The two motifs used are given in full size on page 98 and can be traced on to stencil paper and cut out. By varying the birds' positions as you print, a realistic sense of flying is achieved.

Like the blue birds, the heart is a universally recognizable symbol, and there is no mistaking the intentions of this 20th century Artemis who is plainly in the mood for love, and armed and dressed for the delights of the chase. The motif would also be appealing on white, ruffled, kitchen curtains, or combined with the folk motifs shown previously, to make a Pennsylvania Dutch design for a box or a chest. Originally, most stencils were cut from tin so that they could be stored away and used again. In America, professional stencillers travelled the countryside with ranges of stencil patterns for floors and walls. Today, however, commercially obtainable stencil paper like that shown below is perfectly adequate for most needs, as it too can be re-used.

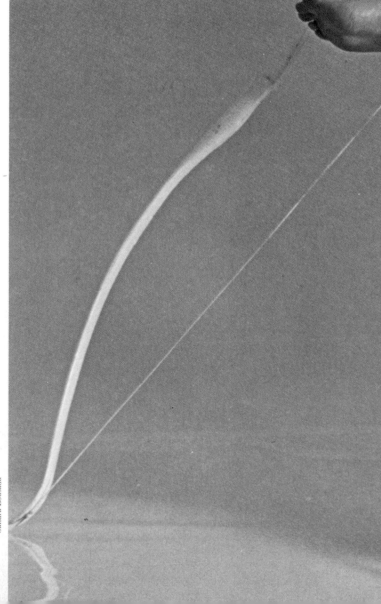

SCREEN PRINTING

Screen printing, an advanced form of stencilling, is done by scraping colour across a stencil placed on mesh fabric. The process is shown 'before and after' below. Trace patterns of motifs are on page 99.

Silk screen printing is a form of stencilling which requires the use of a simple rectangular wooden frame with cotton organdie or terylene screen fabric stretched across it. The areas which are *not* to be printed are blocked out, as in an ordinary stencil, and colour is scraped across the mesh fabric on to the surface below with a kind of rubber spatula called a squeegee. The screen stencil has the advantage over an ordinary stencil in that isolated areas do not need 'bridges' because the frame holds them in place. Screen printing also facilitates rapid repeat printing of a design on to different surfaces, such as posters and writing paper, or on to the same surface, such as the cup motif shown opposite.

A silk screen printing kit will contain everything you need for the process, but be sure to buy one with a large enough screen.

Stencils for screen printing can be cut out of ordinary newspaper or a paper specially made for them called Profilm. Or you can use a screen printing liquid to paint directly on the screen, blocking out the parts you do not want to print.

Colour. Use waterproof screen ink to screen print on paper and paste dye to screen print on fabrics.

Printing. Cut out the stencil and lay it on the screen, or paint it on. Then position the paper or fabric carefully under the screen. Place the squeegee at the far end of the screen.

If you are using paste dye, apply a line of it across the top of the screen (the area furthest from you), hold the squeegee in both hands and pull it firmly across the screen, dragging the dye across the screen towards you. The colour is pushed through the screen on to the printing surface below.

If you are using screen printing inks you must first thin them with a little white spirit until they are of a creamy consistency.

Raise the screen and, if you are printing on paper, remove your print and hang it up to dry. Screen-printed fabric must also be hung up to dry. After printing on fabric, remember also to fix the dye by ironing. After a little practice you will be able to print evenly.

Repeated motifs. To print a repeat design such as the coffee cups illustrated on the previous page, work out the spacing first. Draw a line on the printing surface with tailor's chalk to mark where the bottom of the screen will fall during printing. Calculate the number of times you can get the motif comfortably on the surface you are printing and mark the position of each motif on the line with tailor's chalk. (If the motif is small enough, you can facilitate repeat printing by using more

than one motif on the screen.) Always wait a minute after each printing and then cover the newly printed motif with a piece of paper so that the ink will not off-print on to the screen and spoil the next application.

Cleaning up. When you have finished printing, it is important to clean the screen. Place newspapers underneath it and scrape off any surplus ink or paste with a palette knife. Remove the stencil and discard it. Pour white spirit on the screen (or water if you are using dye) and clean the screen with a rag, renewing the newspapers when they get too messy.

Personalized notepaper is one of the most popular creations for home screen printing. Motif on page 98.

Theo Bergström

96

GENERAL GUIDE

Paint, Dyes and Inks

Water-solvent paints such as poster paints, powder colours and printing water-colours are designed for use on paper.

Poster paint can be used undiluted and applied to the printing block with a stiff, hog-hair brush or a sponge. But remember that it dries very quickly and this can present difficulties by clogging up the printing block. Generally, it is best to dilute the colour slightly. These colours are not washable and if waterproofing is required, the paper must be coated with paper varnish after printing.

Printing watercolours should also be diluted with a little water and, like poster paint, applied to the printing block surface with a stiff hog-hair brush or a lino roller.

Oil-based printing inks, while best-suited for paper, can also be used on cloth (check ink manufacturers' label).

You may find you have to dilute the ink with a very little white spirit. You will certainly need white spirit for cleaning up afterwards. These inks are applied to the printing block with a lino roller.

Spread colour on a piece of glass or mirror and roll the roller over the surface in different directions until the ink consistency is even. Then ink up your printing block with the roller.

To mix colours, blend them with a palette knife at the side of the glass first, then roll them out as described. Do not try to mix colours by rolling them out together.

Fabric dyes. These include a number of different brands, some of which are for special fabrics only – silk, for instance – but other brands, such as Dylon Color-fun can be used to decorate almost any cloth and many other surfaces too. When choosing fabric dyes, always read and follow the manufacturers' instructions. It is also wise to test the dye on the cloth first.

Fabric dyes are washable, provided the colour is fixed on the cloth after printing. To do this, cover printed fabric with a clean cloth and iron it on a setting suitable for the type of fabric. This fixes the dye.

Screen printing inks and dyes. Although some all-purpose colours can be used for screen printing, special screen printing inks and dyes are recommended. These are stocked by some craft shops and by screen printing supply shops. They are usually used in conjunction with special thickening agents, available from the same sources.

Surfaces

Cartridge paper is the best paper to use. It does not have to be white; in fact, using a coloured paper can give extra interest to a design. But the shade used must be considerably lighter than the one you are printing. Avoid glossy papers which are non-absorbent, especially if you are relief printing, because the printing block

will slide on the glossy surface and give a smudged effect.

Newsprint is excellent for trials only as it does not age well – it tends to yellow and tear easily.

Cloth. Until very recently, it was possible to print successfully only on fabrics made from natural fibres, but new fabric paints have made it possible to print on synthetics too. However, there are certain man-made fibres which are not colour-fast when printed. If you are in doubt, print a separate test piece and wash it.

All fabric which is washable should be thoroughly washed and ironed before printing to remove any finish which might impede the printed colour.

Leather and suede. Small projects can be printed using shoe colour and this can even be applied to previously dyed leather. For more important leather projects using undyed leather, you may wish to follow professional policy and use spirit-based aniline leather dyes. Use suede dyes on suede.

QUICK COLOUR GUIDE

	DIRECT AND RELIEF PRINTING	STENCILLING	SCREEN PRINTING
PAPER	Poster paints Printing watercolours Oil-based printing inks* *except potato blocks	As for direct and relief printing, also household paint	Oil-based screen ink
CLOTH	All-purpose dye such as Dylon Color-fun	As for direct and relief printing	Paste screen dyes
WOOD	Acrylic paint	Acrylic paint	Oil-based screen ink
LEATHER	Shoe colour	Shoe colour Aniline leather dyes	Special screen ink
SUEDE	Suede dye	Suede dye All-purpose dye such as Dylon color-fun	Special screen ink

Section editor:
Judy Allen

Designer:
Janet Allen

SEWING

Conventional paper patterns can be perplexing, yet they are not really necessary in order to make many types of very wearable clothes. The illustrations on these and the following pages show how several different designs can be made up from basic geometric shapes and cut out directly from the fabric. All movement and shape come from well-placed gathers, pleats and bands on wrists and waists. The designs depend on fullness for a comfortable fit.

MATERIALS

Fabric. It is very important to choose suitable fabric for this kind of dressmaking. Stiff or very firm material will not hang well when gathered but will tend to stick out and look awkward. Soft, fine fabrics – particularly crepe, silk, wool or cotton – hang beautifully and make the most of soft, billowy sleeves and skirts. If you are not sure whether a fabric will work, simply drape it over your shoulder and look at it in a full length mirror before you buy.

Measuring stick. Since the patterns are marked directly on the cloth, you will need a metre (yard) stick. A right angle marker is also very useful.

Tailor's chalk. This is the best marker for fabric and is available in colours, as well as in white, for marking white fabric. Simply brush chalk away when fabric has been cut.

SIZING

The pattern dimensions used to make the clothes in this chapter can all be

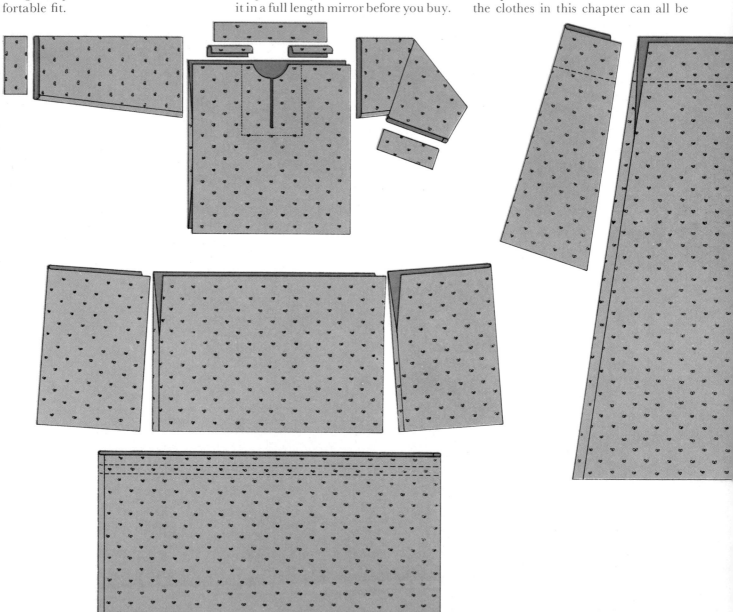

Barbara Firth

used for several sizes, though obviously the garments will be larger or fuller in smaller sizes. More precise measurements can be applied to the patterns simply by taking body measurements of sleeve length, waist, etc. and adjusting pattern dimensions accordingly.

SEWING TIPS

Before you cut the fabric, always find the straight grain, which runs parallel to the selvedges. Mark your centre back or front on the straight grain.

Mark out any cutting lines with tailor's chalk on the wrong side of the fabric and, if you are not using the whole width of the fabric, or if there is any slight shaping, make sure you fold the fabric in half before you cut, to get two absolutely equal halves.

To make the sewing process even simpler, you can avoid tacking fabric together by pinning so that the pins lie at right angles to the edge of the fabric and the machine will easily run over them without damaging the needle. Be

more wary with slippery fabric, and if you are quilting, tacking is almost essential.

Gathers should be drawn up with three rows of large stitches to make them even.

Attention to finishing touches avoids a home-made look, so take care to hem edges by hand neatly, to finish off button loops well and to neaten edges inside and, most importantly, to press seams as you sew them to give a professional finish.

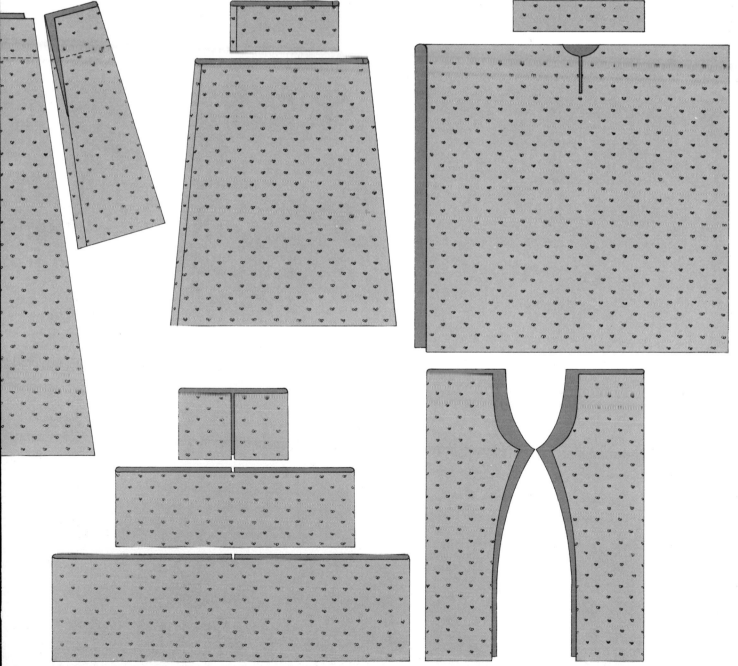

The principle of sewing rectangles
together to make clothes, instead
of using conventional dressmaking
patterns, is well-illustrated in
the shirts opposite. The same
design is used for each shirt; it
is based on a traditional, peasant
style which pre-dates the invention
of darts, curved armholes and other
subtleties of shaping. Instead the
pattern depends on fullness of cut
to make it fit comfortably.
Variations in style can be made by
altering the neck opening. On the
mother's shirt, for example, the
neck facing is put on the outside
as a decorative device, while on
the man's version, the neck has
been opened down the front and a
strip sewn on each half for
buttoning.
Complete instructions, pages 120 and 121.

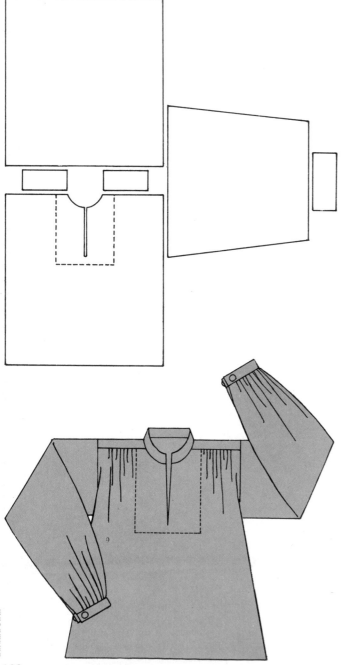

Barbara Firth

102

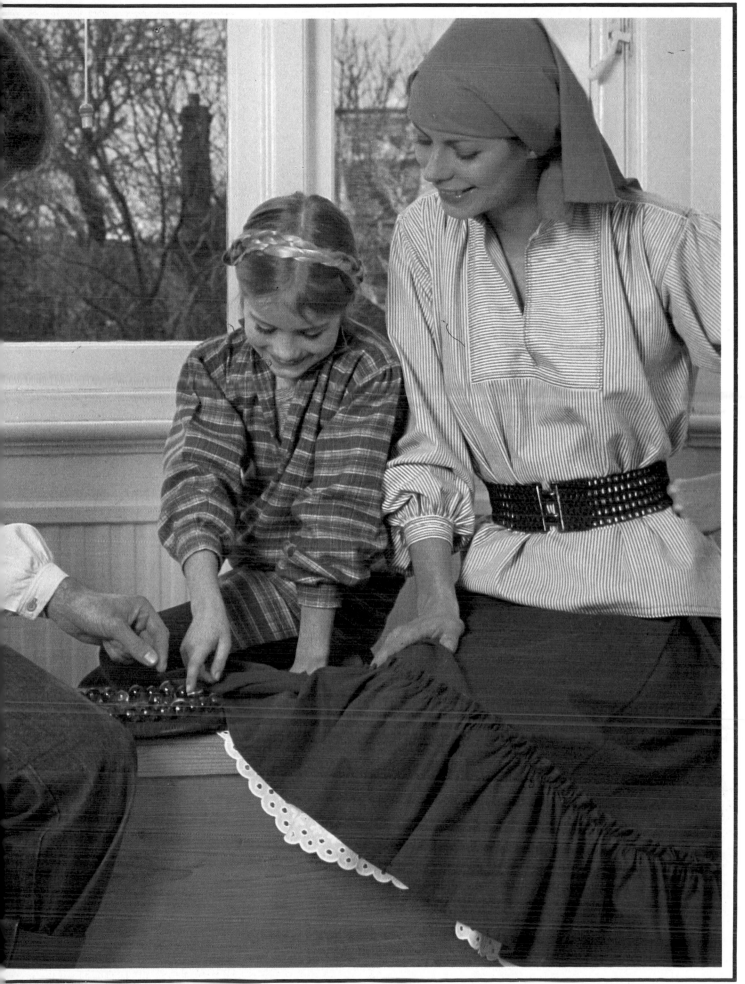

An enduring elegance reminiscent
of the great French fashion houses
characterizes the clothes in the
photograph opposite. It is easy to
imagine these fashionable ladies
going to and from their fittings in
imposing establishments along
the Faubourg St. Honoré. But modern
living – and clothing – styles make
such time-consuming occupations
unnecessary, even for those who can
afford them. The garments opposite
are of the simplest construction.
The drawstring skirt is made from
two rectangles sewn together, while the
silk blouse and woollen dress are
the same shape, except that the
blouse is fuller and the dress has
extra fabric above the gathering
line, to make the collar. All three
depend on gathers for their effect.
Instructions on pages 122 and 123.

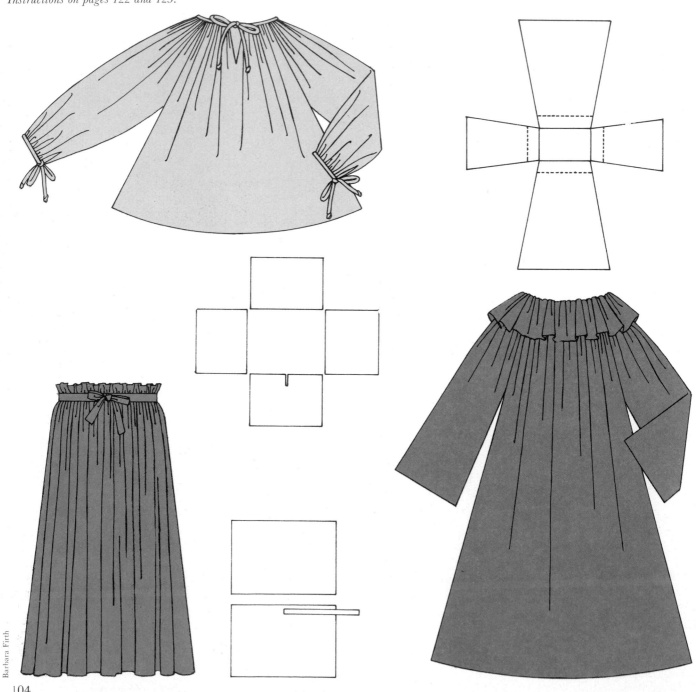

Barbara Firth

104

Play it again, Sam . . .

in Casablanca, Cornwall, or Connecticut; whether it is on a night out or a night in, this is a composition that will wear well. It is made of two pairs of rectangles, joined together; the top pair forms a yoke, on which the other pair is gathered. A drawstring creates the waistline. Left-over fabric is used to make the shawl-like collar, while the blouse is the same as shown on previous page.
Play it *again*, Sam.
Instructions, pages 124 and 125.

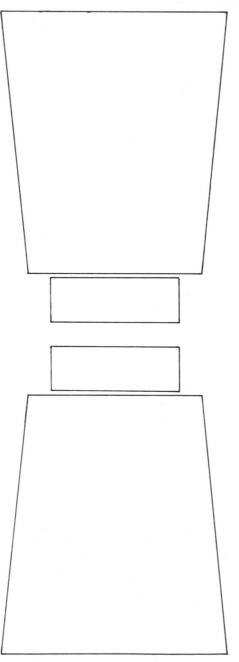

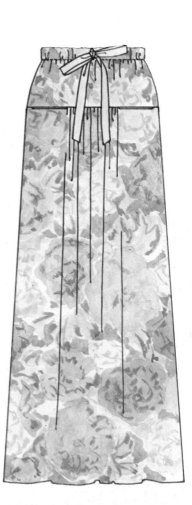

Barbara Firth

This 'waif-faring' couple proclaim a stylish insouciance. The clown-like bagginess of the tweed trousers is emphasized by large tucks at the waist and tapered, or 'peg', legs. The cut is simplified by the fact that there are no side seams and the waist is bound rather than belted.

The tiered skirt carries the idea of rectangles a step further. Three rectangular strips are gathered and joined together, then the waist is pulled in with a drawstring.

Instructions are on pages 125 and 126.

Barbara Firth

Brilliant colours in a painting by
Matisse suggested this quilted poncho.
Wadding is sandwiched between two
rectangles of curtain lining. The
top layer is decorated with abstract
shapes, drawn freehand, and applied
with zigzag machine stitch. The
appliqued scalloped border folds
over to bind the sides together.

Instructions are on page 126.

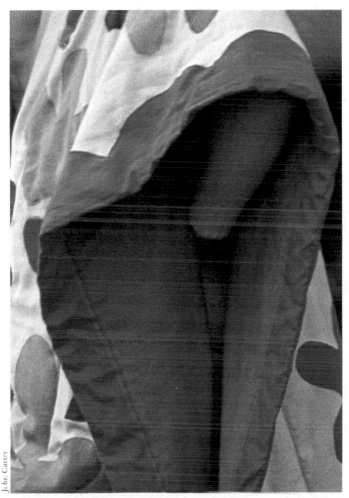

These little girls' dresses are
both made from the same pattern – a
basic 'T' shape with tucks at the
shoulders and top of sleeves. The
pinafore slips on over the head and
ties at the sides of the waist.
Instructions are on pages 127 and 128.

Barbara Firth

112

Sandra Lousada

PATCHWORK

Traditional patchwork hexagons are
used here on a gigantic
scale to make a colourful quilt
cover. The hexagonal pieces are worked as
in ordinary patchwork, then joined
to make a giant 'bag' with a zip.

Instructions on page 128.

APPLIQUÉ

Appliqué quilts are a traditional and much loved form of patchwork. Here, the technique is carried to an imaginative and modern dimension, using felt. And like so many good ideas, it is wonderfully simple.

The motifs are drawn from eighteenth and nineteenth century patchwork and stencil patterns but, because they are worked in felt, the laborious task of turning under raw edges is avoided.

The bedspread is made up of 56 squares – each 30cm (12″) square – and has a border 20cm (8″) deep.

To make a similar version, trace and enlarge the motifs given, or use designs from patchwork or stencil books. Craft shops and some haberdashers sell ready-cut felt squares which can be used for the background. Pin or tack, and sew motifs to felt squares and then attach squares to a cotton backing by stitching round the edge of each.

Note that each colour must be sewn in matching thread, and you may find it easier to attach felt of one colour in several of the squares and then sew other colours.

Felt appliqué can also be used to make quilts, wall hangings or cushions. The more ambitious may wish to draw inspiration from the headboard, in which felt appliqué is used in a three-dimensional way by stuffing motifs such as the clouds. The design is carried on to the wood frame with gloss paint.

The naive style of the figures, combined with meticulous sewing round the edges, makes it an example of how skill and imagination transform craft into art.

DOLL MAKING

Dollmaking is a delightful pastime at any age. Here the elements are reduced to the most basic conception and at the same time enlarged to the most tremendous size.
Larry the Layabout is as much a dummy as a doll, but he can be cut down to size simply by reducing the dimensions of the pattern pieces' proportionately. If a change of gender is preferred, just omit the moustache.

Detailed instructions are on page 129.

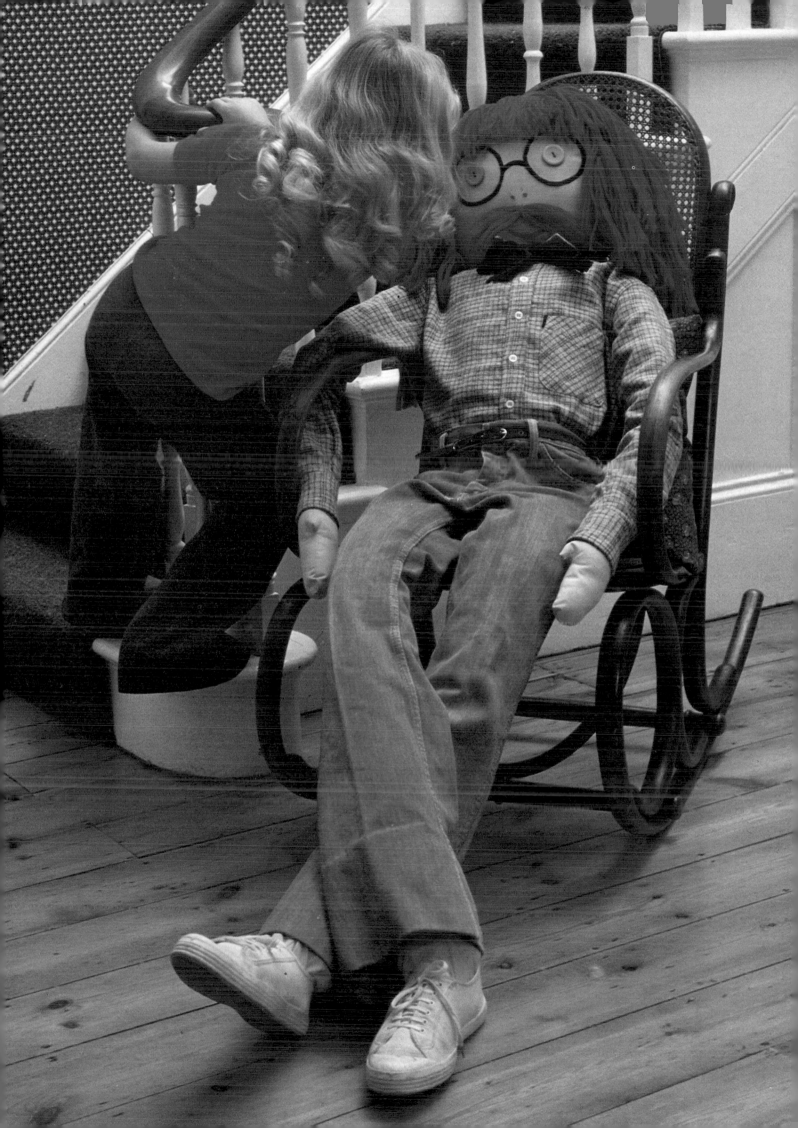

Sewing Abbreviations

The following abbreviations are used throughout the sewing chapter:

CF   centre front
CB   centre back
RS   right side of fabric
WS   wrong side of fabric
RST right sides together
WST wrong sides together
SS   side seam

Family Shirts

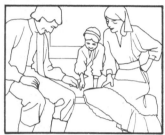

Instructions are the same for all three versions, except for neck openings and for a front opening on the man's shirt.

MAN'S SHIRT

Chest: 95–105cm (37½″–41½″)
Finished length: 71cm (28″)

MATERIALS
2.8m (3⅛yd) of 90cm (36″) wide fabric

20cm (8″) of 90cm (36″) wide iron-on interfacing
7 buttons

WOMAN'S SHIRT

Bust: 85–96cm (33½″–37½″)
Length: 66cm (26″)

MATERIALS
2.7m (3yd) of 90cm (36″) wide fabric
Iron-on interfacing for neckband and cuffs

CHILD'S SHIRT

Chest: up to 71cm (28″)

Length: 69cm (27″)

MATERIALS
1.4m (1⅝yd) of 90cm (36″) wide fabric
Iron-on interfacing for neckband and cuffs

Woman's shirt

60cm(23½″)

63cm (25″)

5cm (2″)

Sleeve

63cm (25″)

2.68m (3yds)

60cm(23½″)

slit

16cm (6½″)

65cm(25½″)

s. seam

Back

30cm (12″)

Yokes

71cm(28″)

armhole

25cm (10″)

5cm (2″) — 13cm (5½″)

armhole

28cm (11″)

20cm (8″) slit facing

25cm (10″)

Cuffs

71cm(28″)

s. seam

22cm(8½″)

Front

CF

30cm (12″)

Neckband

slit

16cm (6½″)

Front Facing

90cm(36″)

CUT
1 neckband 44 × 8cm(17½″ × 3½″)
1 front facing 28 × 22cm(11″ × 9″)
2 cuffs 22 × 8cm(9″ × 3½″)
4 yokes 17 × 7cm(7″ × 3″)

Man's shirt

78cm(31″)   78cm(31″)   60cm(23½″)   60cm(23½″)

slit   s. seam   armhole   armhole   s. seam   slit

90cm (36″)

Front

75cm (29½″)

4cm (1½″)   1cm (⅜″)

12cm(5″)

Back

Sleeves

60cm (23½″)

shoulder notch

70cm (27½″)

13cm (5½″)   35cm (14″)   30cm (12″)   30cm (12″)   35cm (14″)   13cm (5½″)

5cm(2″)

Neckband   Cuffs   Frontbands

Yokes

CUT
1 neck 50 × 8cm(19½″ × 3½″)
4 yokes 21 × 9cm(8½″ × 3½″)
2 cuffs 26 × 8cm(10½″ × 3½″)
2 front bands 10 × 73cm(4″ × 28½″)

Trevor Lawrence

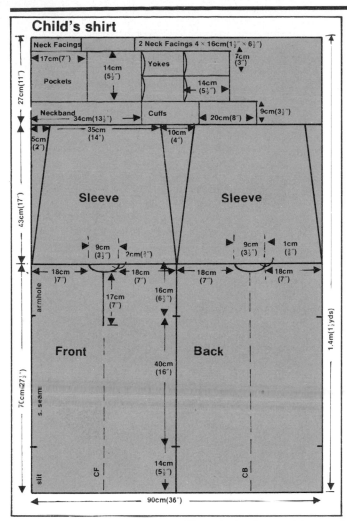

Child's shirt

Neck Facings

2 Neck Facings 4 × 16cm (1½" × 6½")

17cm(7")

27cm(11")

14cm (5½")

Yokes

Pockets

14cm (5½")

7cm (3")

Neckband 34cm(13½")

Cuffs

9cm(3½")

35cm (14")

10cm (4")

20cm(8")

5cm (2")

43cm(17")

Sleeve

Sleeve

9cm (3½")

2cm(¾")

9cm (3½")

1cm (⅜")

armhole

18cm)7")

18cm (7")

18cm (7")

18cm (7")

17cm (7")

16cm (6½")

1.4m(1½yds)

Front

Back

s. seam

40cm (16")

70cm(27½")

slit

CF

14cm (5½")

CB

90cm(36")

WORKING

Cut fabric from correct layout chart.

Child's neck opening. Lay RS of neck edging bands on WS of slit, overlapping lower end of slit by 9mm (⅜").

☐ Sew each edging band to front slit with a 6mm (¼") deep seam, and press ends up 9mm (⅜").

☐ Press bands towards CF, fold over raw edges of slit to RS of shirt. Press along centre front and also free edges under 6mm (¼").

☐ Stitch band to shirt close to edge and across lower edge.

Woman's neck opening. Place RS of facing on WS of shirt and sew round slit with 6mm (¼") seam, making point at base.

☐ Double stitch round point and clip into point.

☐ Place facing on RS of shirt and press seam.

☐ Press again, rolling seam onto WS slightly to hide it.

☐ Press free edges under 9mm (⅜"), and pin down.

Topstitch down sides and across lower edge, as shown in the photograph.

Man's neck opening. Cut two pieces iron-on interlining 5cm × 78cm (2" × 31").

☐ Press front in half along CF line and cut along fold.

☐ Press front bands in half lengthwise, WST, and iron interlining on WS of one half of each band.

☐ Lay RS of interlined side of band to RS of CF. Pin and sew with 9mm (⅜") seam.

☐ Press seam under band.

☐ Press free edge under 9mm (⅜") and pin down on WS over first seam.

☐ Topstitch on RS close to seam and to folded edge. Make second row of topstitching 3mm (⅛") from first.

Child's pocket. Fold and press under one short end and both sides 9mm (⅜"), press top down 2.5cm (1") and raw edge in 6mm (¼").

☐ Topstitch close to both edges, pin pocket in place and topstitch.

All three shirts. Gather shoulder seams on front and back between notches and gather wrist edges of sleeves.

☐ Lay RS's of one pair of yokes to RS's of front. Draw gathers up to fit, pin and sew yoke seams (fig.1).

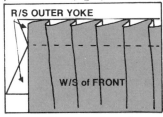

1. Attaching top yoke to front.

☐ Do same at back.

☐ Lay RS's of second pair of yokes to WS's of fronts, matching edges. Pin, (fig. 2) to first seam. Press.

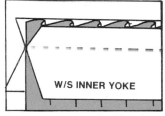

2. Sandwich front inside yokes.

☐ Press free edge of inside yokes at the shirt back under 9mm (⅜") and pin and tack down to original seam.

☐ Turn to RS and topstitch 6mm (¼") above first seam line on back and front yokes.

☐ Cut iron-on interlining to fit half width of cuffs and neckband.

☐ Press bands in half lengthwise and iron on interlining to one half – these are now outer sides.

☐ Mark CB on neckband and shirt and pin, RST, so band overlaps CF of shirt by 9mm (⅜") either side.

☐ Sew with 6mm (¼") seam and press seam up. Fold band back in half, RST, pin and sew across ends.

☐ Turn right side out, press ends. Press raw edge under 6mm (¼"). Pin along seam line on WS.

☐ Topstich on RS 6mm (¼") from edge along top and ends of band, and very close above seam on inner neck edge.

☐ Cut notch 5cm (2") above wrist on each side of sleeves. Neaten from wrist to notch

on each edge, fold back 9mm (⅜") and sew again. This will form sleeve opening.

☐ Lay interlined RS of cuffs on to RS of sleeve edge – draw gathers up to fit, so that cuffs are 15mm (⅝") longer each side than sleeves.

☐ Sew with 9mm (⅜") seam and press seam under cuff.

☐ Fold cuffs in half lengthwise RST, stitch across ends, turn out and press.

☐ Press free edges of inner cuffs under 9mm (⅜") and pin along seam line, stitch close to edge.

☐ On RS topstitch all round cuff 6mm (¼") from edge.

☐ Lay sleeves on shirt RST, matching centre top of sleeves to centre of yokes and sides of sleeves to armhole notches.

☐ Pin, making small tucks at top of sleeves until they fit.

☐ Sew with 2cm (¾") seams, starting and finishing 2cm (¾") in from edge of sleeve.

☐ Press seams up under yokes, neaten edges and top stitch 6mm (¼") from seams.

☐ Pin underarm seams and sew with 2cm (¾") seam from top to opening. Neaten edges.

☐ Pin SS's from armhole to required length above hem for side slits – see cutting layout for lengths.

☐ Sew with 2cm (¾") seam. Neaten edges by turning under 6mm (¼") and sewing close to edge, continue down sides and across hem.

☐ Press SS open all way down to hem.

☐ Turn up hem 9mm (⅞") and sew.

☐ Sew buttons and thread loops on edges of cuffs and front band if required.

☐ Topstitch facing, cuffs, neckband, yokes, hem and slits, and the armhole on woman's shirt, in zigzag stitch and contrasting thread.

☐ Make buttonholes on left band on man's shirt and each cuff. Sew on buttons to correspond. This completes the garment.

Drawstring Skirt

Waist: 60–70cm (23½″–27½″)

Hips: 90–100cm (35½″–39½″)

Length: approximately 88cm (34½″)

MATERIALS
1.8m (2yd) of 136cm (54″) wide fabric (or twice your length)
Matching thread
Ribbon for waist tie

MAKING
Cut fabric as shown in layout chart.

☐ Pin SS's of front and back RST along selvedges. Sew with a 2.5cm (1″) seam. Press open.

☐ Neaten bottom and top edges by rolling over narrow hem, about 3mm (⅛″), to WS. Zigzag stitch down with small stitches and use point of scissors to hold folded edge down in centre of machine foot as you sew – this helps to stretch fabric slightly. Stitch edging round top and bottom of skirt.

☐ Make three rows of gathering stitches 2.5cm, 4cm and 5cm (1″, 1½″, and 2″) below top edge of skirt, all round. Put pins in to mark CB and CF.

☐ Pull gathers up.

☐ Press long edges of waistband under 9mm (⅜″), and ends under 15mm (⅝″). Put pins in to mark CB, CF and two sides.

☐ Pin WS of waistband to RS of skirt 4cm (1½″) from top, with ends meeting at CF, see fig. 1.

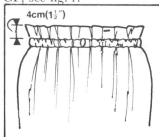

1. Detail of skirt waistband.

☐ Match CB and SS marks. Pin along each edge of band, adjusting gathers to fit.

☐ Topstitch with small zig-zag stitch along each edge of band.

☐ Thread drawstring in through opening at CF and pull up to fit.

Silk Blouse

Bust: 85–100cm (33½″–39½″)

Length: 64cm (25″)

MATERIALS
2.6m (2⅞yd) of 90cm (36″) wide fabric
Matching silk thread

MAKING
Cut fabric as shown in layout chart below.

☐ Mark CB of blouse back and centres of sleeves at top and bottom.

☐ Cut neck slit and make narrow rolled hem round slit.

☐ Join SS's RST. Join underarm seams RST but leave 5cm (2″) open at cuffs.

☐ Lay sleeves on blouse RST, pin and sew armhole seams. Neaten raw edges and press open.

☐ Make three rows of gathering stitches all round neck edge and pull up to 70cm (27½″).

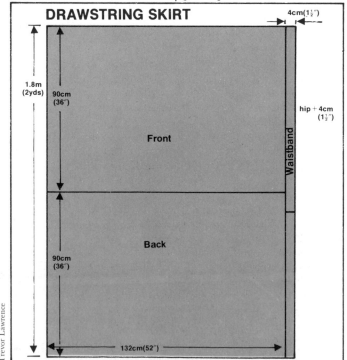

DRAWSTRING SKIRT

- 1.8m (2yds)
- 90cm (36″) — Front
- 90cm (36″) — Back
- 132cm(52″)
- 4cm(1½″)
- hip + 4cm (1½″)
- Waistband

Silk blouse

- Sleeve
- 25cm (10″) armhole
- 25cm (10″) armhole
- 40cm (16″)
- s. seam
- Sleeve
- s. seam
- Back — CB
- 25cm (10″) armhole
- 25cm (10″) armhole
- neck slit — 12cm(5″)
- Front — CF
- 40cm (16″)
- s. seam
- 4cm (1½″)
- sleeve band
- neck band
- sleeve band
- 65cm (25½″)
- 65cm (25½″)
- 65cm (25½″)
- 2.6m (2⅞yds)
- 90cm(36″)

Trevor Lawrence

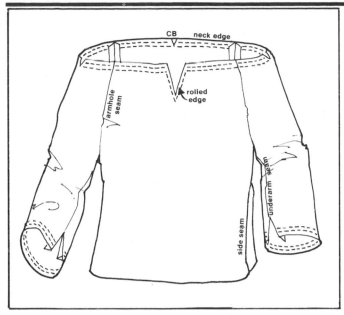

1. Diagram to show how sleeves form part of neck.

□ Do same to wrists and sleeves and pull up to 20cm (7½").

□ Fold neckband in half, mark CB. Make notches 35cm (13½") either side (to be CF) and halfway between CF and CB, to match centres on sleeves. Fig. 1 shows assembly.

□ Fold cuff bands in half and mark centres.

□ Place bands on neck and wrists, RST with matching notches.

□ Pin and sew with 9mm (⅜") seam.

□ Stitch across ends of bands, RST, and along to cuff and neck. Trim seams, turn through to form ties.

□ Fold bands over to WS, turn under, hem raw edge.

□ Neaten bottom of blouse by turning up tiny hem, then turn again and hem by hand.

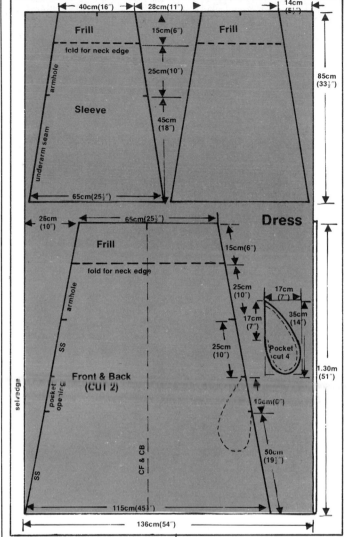

Blue Dress

Hips: 86–107cm (34"–42")
Length: approximately 112cm (44")

MATERIALS

3.6m (4yd) of 136cm (54") – or 115cm (45") wide fabric – which must be reversible
Matching pure silk thread
67cm (26½") length of matching tape, 12mm (½") wide

MAKING

Cut fabric as shown in layout chart.

□ Clip 2cm (¾") notches to mark frill line on sleeves and dress pieces.

□ Mark all other notches in usual way.

□ Join underarm seams on sleeves from wrist to armhole notch.

□ Join SS's on dress from armhole notch to hem, leaving open between pocket notches.

□ Press.

□ Lay each pair of pockets together. Stitch rounded edges, starting at top, 2cm (¾") in from straight edge round to other notch with 9mm (⅜") seam.

□ Working on inside of dress, lay pockets on open sections of SS's RST, with notches matching. Pin and sew, then press pockets to front of dress.

□ Pin sleeves to front of dress, RST from top of SS's to 2cm (¾") notch on frill line. Stitch.

□ Turn sleeves round and do same for back, then press seams open.

□ Make frill seams by placing edges WST (they will be wrong side out), fig. 1.

□ Pin, sew and press seams.

□ Make a chalk line 15cm (6") below frill edge on RS of dress (see fig. 1), and make three rows of gathering stitches round neck edge on chalk line.

□ Pull up to 65cm (25½") and knot ends. Adjust gathers until each side is even.

□ Join tape to make a ring with 9mm (⅜") seam.

□ Put tape on to RS of neck over gathers and pin matching CF, CB and half way across each sleeve.

□ Pin and sew along both edges to hold gathers in place and to form neck edge.

□ Check length of dress. Neaten all edges with narrow zigzag stitch very close to edges. Stretch fabric slightly as you sew, then trim edges.

□ Make small hem on cuffs.

□ Press on WS.

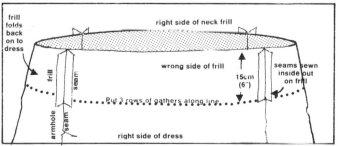

1. The frill folds down over the dress.

Long Yoked Skirt

Waist: 60–70cm (23½″–27½″)
Hips: 90–100cm (35½″–39½″)
Length: up to 100cm (39½″)

MATERIALS
2.4m (2⅝yd) of 140cm (54″) wide fabric
Matching thread
Ribbon for waist tie

MAKING
Cut out fabric as shown in layout chart and mark CF and CB at top and bottom on both yoke pieces.
☐ Mark notches on skirt front and back in the positions indicated in fig. 1.

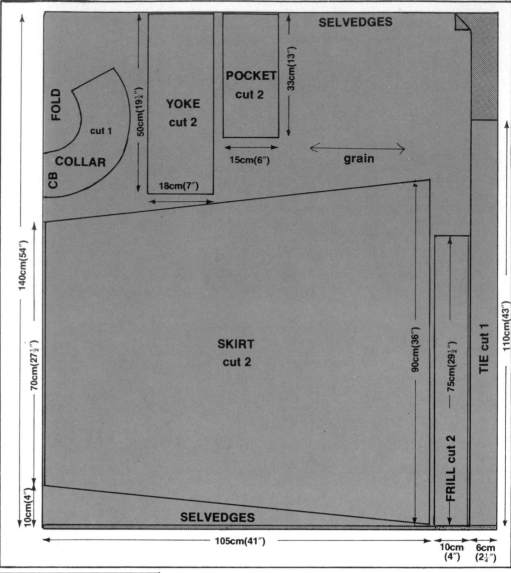

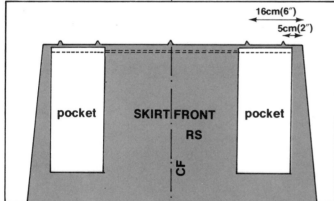

1. Positions of pockets and gathers are shown by notches.

☐ Sew double row of gathering stitches between inner pocket notches on skirt front and position pocket pieces as in fig. 1.
☐ Pin and sew along top of both pockets with a 9mm (⅜″) seam.
☐ Clip notches into stitching line on skirt pieces only, press seam and pocket pieces up and then make a second row of stitches close to seam on RS of pocket pieces. This gives a proper finish to the edges. (The rest of the pocket assembly is done later.
☐ Press pockets down so seam rolls over to wrong side slightly and is hidden.
Buttonholes. On front yoke mark two buttonholes 1.5cm (⅝″) long, 9mm (⅜″) either side of CF and 5cm (2″) below top for tie belt slots.
☐ Cut out a 5cm (2″) square of fabric, neaten all edges and pin centrally under marks for buttonholes on WS.
☐ Make buttonholes and press.
Joining yoke. Join SS's on yoke and skirt pieces with french seams, as shown in fig. 2.

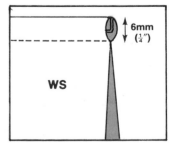

2a. To make a french seam, sew wrong sides of fabric together, 12 mm (½″) from edge. Trim seam allowances.

2b. Trim fabric to encase seam and press down. Then sew another seam to enclose the first one and press again.

☐ Press top edge of yoke down 5cm (2″) to WS. Press raw edge under 3mm (⅛″) and pin down on WS. Stitch close to both folded edges to form a casing.
☐ Lay lower edge of yoke on top edge of skirt RST, matching SS's and CF's.
☐ Adjust gathering to fit yoke at back and front. Pin.
☐ Stitch across front yoke between pockets with a 9mm

(⅜″) seam and from side of pocket round back of skirt to side of other pocket. Take care not to catch sides of pocket bags in this seam.

☐ Fold pockets in half, RST, and pin free edges to free edges of front yoke. Pin in place RST and sew with 9mm (⅜″) seam. Neaten edge of yoke seam and along the top of the pockets.

☐ Sew down sides of pockets and neaten edges.

☐ Turn up hem to required length and press.

☐ Slot tie through button holes and casing.

MAKING THE COLLAR

Cut shaped piece in main fabric and lining.

☐ Cut frill and tie, according to dimensions in cutting layout.

☐ Fold frill in half lengthwise, RST, and sew across ends. Turn inside out and press.

☐ Mark centres and quarters on outer edge of collar and frill. Gather along double raw edge of frill and pull up to fit outer edge of collar.

☐ Pin to collar RST but leave 10mm (½″) of raw front edge of collar free. Sew.

☐ Lay lining on collar, RST, with frill sandwiched in middle. Pin and sew across front and outer edges. Turn through and press.

☐ Sew lining to fabric at neck edge. Lay one edge of tie band to neck of collar, RST, matching CB's. Sew and press seam under band.

☐ Fold band in half RST, stitch across ends and down edges to collar. Turn through and press. Turn under and hem free edge.

Tiered Skirt

Hips: up to 92cm (36″).

For other sizes, only alter width of top band to fit hips. Add or subtract 3cm (1½″) for each larger or smaller size. To alter the length divide the extra length required by three and add that amount to each tier.

MATERIALS

If using one colour, you need 3m (3¼yd) of 90cm (36″) wide fabric.

If using a thick material, such as tweed, use less in middle and bottom tier, e.g. top 95cm (37½″); middle 140cm (54″); bottom 210cm (83″). Work conversely for flimsy fabrics.

MAKING

Cut fabric as in chart.

☐ Join each strip into a ring, RST, and press seams.

☐ Press top edge of top strip down 4.5cm (2″), neaten edge and sew to WS.

☐ Stitch again 2cm (¾″) above first row, to form casing for drawstring, and unpick seam between casing for tie opening.

☐ Gather top edges of middle and bottom tiers. Mark centres and sides on each edge of tiers.

☐ Adjust gathers, match CB and sides, and sew top to middle tier.

☐ Press both seams up and topstitch 9mm (⅜″) above first seam.

☐ Do same to middle and bottom tier. Turn up hem and topstitch 9mm (⅜″) from edge.

☐ Fold the tie in half, RST. Sew one end and long edge, turn through and press. Sew raw edge.

☐ Slot into waist casing.

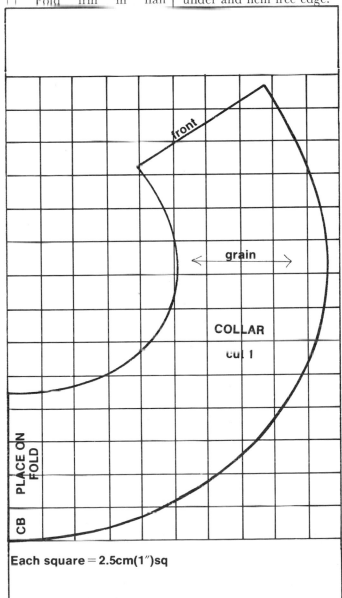

Each square = 2.5cm(1″)sq

PLACE ON FOLD

CB

front

grain

COLLAR

cut 1

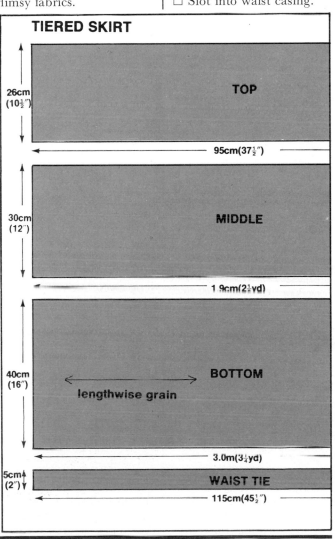

TIERED SKIRT

TOP

26cm (10½″)

95cm(37½″)

MIDDLE

30cm (12″)

1.9cm(2⅛yd)

BOTTOM

40cm (16″)

lengthwise grain

3.0m(3¼yd)

WAIST TIE

5cm (2″)

115cm(45½″)

Trousers

Hips: 89–97cm (35″–38″)
Waist: 64–70cm (25″–27½″)
Finished length of outside leg: 105cm (41½″)
Finished length of inside leg: 76cm (30″)

MATERIALS
2.8m (3⅛yd) of 90cm or 115cm wide fabric (36″, 45″); or 1.8m (2yd) of 140cm (54″) wide fabric.
10cm (⅛yd) matching fabric for waist binding
20cm (8″) zip
Hook and eye

MAKING
Cut fabric out as shown in layout chart.
☐ Shape centre front and back by making free-hand curves with the help of a plate and following measurements given. Or use graph pattern.
☐ Cut strip of thinner, matching fabric 68cm×8cm (27″×3″) for waist binding.
Pockets. Press under 9mm (⅜″) on sides and pointed ends of pocket pieces.
☐ Press and pin pocket tops down 2.5cm (1″) and sew down close to raw edge.
☐ Pin pockets on trouser fronts 12cm (5″) below top edge, and 12cm (5″) in from CF. Topstitch in place.
Trousers. Pin waist tucks as shown in fig. 1 and topstitch 5cm (2″) deep. Press.
Note: for larger sizes (up to waist 70cm (27½″), make tucks smaller to fit.
☐ Sew front crutch with 2cm (¾″) seam, leaving 20cm (8″) open from top edge.
☐ Neaten edges, press.

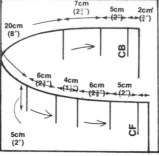

1. Detail of waist pleats.

☐ Put·zip in.
☐ Sew back crutch seam and press open.
☐ Bind waist by marking centre of waist binding and match to CB of trousers, RST and overlapping ends of strip over CF by 2cm (¾″) at each end.
☐ Pin and sew 9mm (⅜″) from top edge, see fig. 2.
☐ Press seam up.

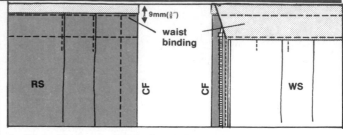

2. Waist binding is visible from RS and forms band on WS.

☐ Fold on to wrong side, fold ends of strip in at CF and press raw edge under.
☐ Pin and sew on WS in place.
☐ Topstitch on RS just below edge of binding. See fig. 2.
☐ Sew hook and eye on band at CF.
Legs. Place inside legs RST, matching at crutch seam. Pin and sew with 2cm (¾″) seam to 6.5cm (2½″) from bottom.
☐ Clip into seam here and continue seam, WST (i.e. make seam inside out) to bottom. Press seam open.
☐ Zigzag lower edge and press up 3cm (1¼″) on RS.
☐ Topstitch close to edge.
☐ Press up another 3cm (1¼″) to form turn-ups and catch stitch at seam and half way round.

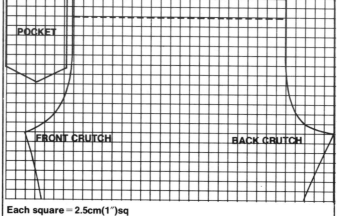

Each square = 2.5cm (1″)sq

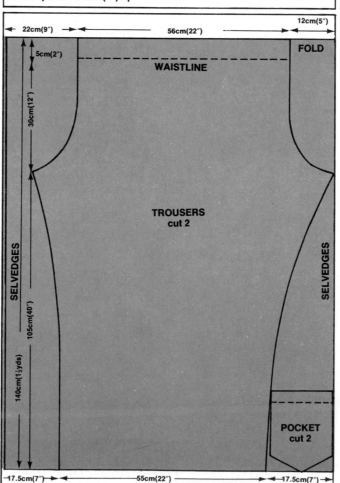

Quilted Poncho

Finished poncho measures 122cm (48″) wide and 132cm (52″) long.

MATERIALS
2.8m (3⅛yd) of 140cm (54″) wide fabric, or 3.75m (4⅛yd) of 90cm (36″) wide fabric, for outer layer. (Choose firmly woven cotton fabric such as good quality curtain lining.)

Barbara Firth

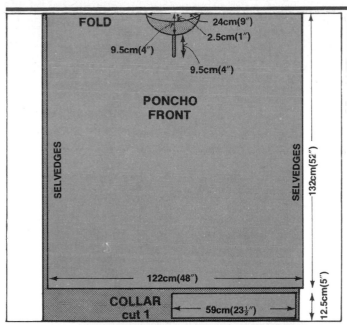

FOLD

24cm(9")

9.5cm(4")

2.5cm(1")

9.5cm(4")

PONCHO
FRONT

SELVEDGES

SELVEDGES

132cm(52")

122cm(48")

12.5cm(5")

COLLAR
cut 1

59cm(23½")

7.5cm(3")

17.5cm
(7")

10cm
(4")

FOLD

1

20cm
(8")

FOLD

2

17.5cm
(7")

add 7.5cm(3")

FOLD

3

1. Three binding patterns which can be used to edge poncho.

**Same amount of fabric
for lining
3.75m (4⅛yd) terylene
wadding 90cm (36") wide
Fabric scraps for
appliqué.** (Look for
interesting textures but all
fabrics must be roughly
same thickness.)
Thread in fabric colours

MAKING

Cut collar, wadding, lining
and top, as in layout.
☐ Cut out appliqué shapes,
using photograph on page
110 as a guide.
☐ Cut binding strips, as in
fig. 1, joining where necessary. (1 and 2 are for sides, 3

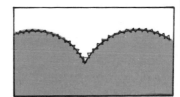

2. How to sew on edging.

is the hem.)
☐ Appliqué curved binding
edge to main fabric, (fig. 2).
Use close, zigzag stitch.

☐ Pin appliqué pieces in position; pin at right angles to
stitching line and sew round
each piece.
☐ If necessary, join wadding
edge to edge with large herringbone stitches.
☐ Mark vertical quilting
lines 15cm(6") apart on
main poncho piece.
☐ Sandwich wadding be-
tween fabric and lining, and
pin together, smoothing out
any fullness from centre to
sides. Remember to pin at
right angles
☐ Stitch along all quilting
lines, sewing in one direction
only.
☐ Trim raw edges and bind
by turning edging over on to
lining and handsewing (fig.
3).
Collar. Apply collar bind-
ings on top collar in similar

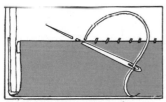

3. Fold edging over and sew.

way as to the sides of the
main poncho.
☐ Sandwich wadding be-
tween top and under collars.
☐ Pin, fold binding round
and hem as for sides.

Little
Girl's Dress

To fit: 2–3 years
Finished length: 66cm
(26")

MATERIALS
**1.7m (1⅞yd) of 90cm
(36") wide fabric
Matching bias binding or
make binding from
matching fabric
30cm (12") zip**

MAKING
Cut out fabric as in chart.
☐ Make and tack pleats on
sleeves.
☐ Make and tack pleats of
dress, then sew them down
for 6.5cm (2½") on wrong

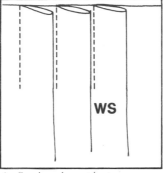

WS

1. Sewing dress pleats.

side as in fig. 1.
☐ Sew centre back seam to
zip notch. Press open. Insert
zip.
☐ Sew shoulder and side
seams.
☐ Make casing at base of
sleeves for elastic. Sew sleeve
seams.
☐ Insert sleeves and sew,
neaten edges.
☐ Bind neck edge. Turn up
hem.
☐ Insert elastic to fit wrists.

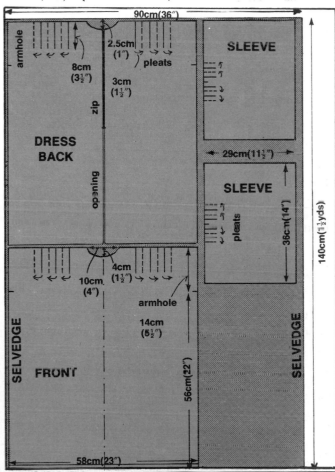

90cm(36")

armhole

8cm
(3½")

2.5cm
(1")

pleats

3cm
(1½")

zip

SLEEVE

DRESS
BACK

opening

29cm(11½")

SLEEVE

pleats

36cm(14")

140cm(1½yds)

4cm
(1½")

10cm
(4")

armhole

SELVEDGE

14cm
(5½")

FRONT

56cm(22")

SELVEDGE

58cm(23")

Pinafore

To fit: 2–3 years
Finished length: 56cm (22″)

MATERIALS
90cm (1yd) of 90cm (36″) wide fabric
2m (2¼yd) of broderie Anglaise trim

MAKING
Cut fabric as shown in layout chart.

☐ Place two bodice pieces RS together and sew all round internal rectangle (i.e. neck edges). Double sew corners, then clip into corners, trim seam, turn through and press well.

☐ Gather waist of skirt back and front to fit width of bodice. Gather broderie Anglaise trim to fit each side of bodice.

☐ Press in 9mm (⅜″) seam allowance down both sides of bodice and lining, and sandwich gathered trim between the two layers. Pin or tack together and sew.

☐ Turn under twice and sew sides and bottom of both skirt pieces.

☐ Place two waistband pieces RST and, matching CF to CF of bodice, mark position of bodice sides. Sew from this point to end of ties, across short ends and back to same point, leaving middle section free.

☐ Turn ends through to RS and press.

☐ Sew one side of waistband to both sections of bodice at the waist, RST.

☐ Sew gathered skirt to lower edge of same waistband, RST. Press seams in. Turn under and hem waistband lining.

☐ Repeat for back.

Duvet Cover

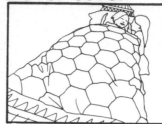

MATERIALS
10m (11yd) of 90cm (36″) wide red and white cotton fabric, patterned with various designs.
(Eight hexagons can be cut from a piece 50cm×90cm (20″×36″.) Each hexagon is 20cm (8″) wide.
Two sheets heavy brown paper 50cm×65cm (20″×26″)
Compass
Red and white thread
Pins, long zip

MAKING
Cut out several hexagon shapes from paper, following instructions and diagrams on the right.

☐ Pin template on wrong side of fabric and cut out shape, leaving a seam allowance of 1cm (⅝″) from edge of template.

☐ Turn seam allowance over template and tack, fig. 1.

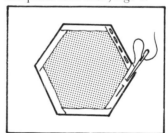

1. Stitching hexagon turning.

☐ Make several hexagons in this way.

☐ Place two hexagons, RST and overcast along one edge (fig. 2).

2. Sewing hexagons together.

☐ Cut out and assemble all the pieces in this way, until you have two huge rectangles the size of your duvet. (Take out cards as you work and flatten seams with iron.)

There are 45½ hexagons on each side of the duvet shown here.

☐ Join the two rectangles, right sides together, to make a giant 'bag', turn right side out and sew in zip.

HOW TO DRAW A HEXAGON

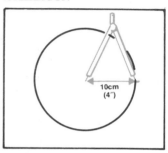

Use a compass to make a circle, 10cm (4″) in radius.

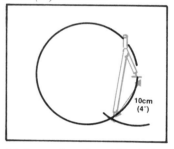

Make another 10cm (4″) circle on perimeter of the first one.

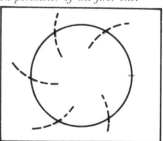

Make another circle where last one intersects; repeat process all round first circle.

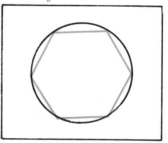

Using a ruler, connect all the intersecting marks and a hexagon is formed.

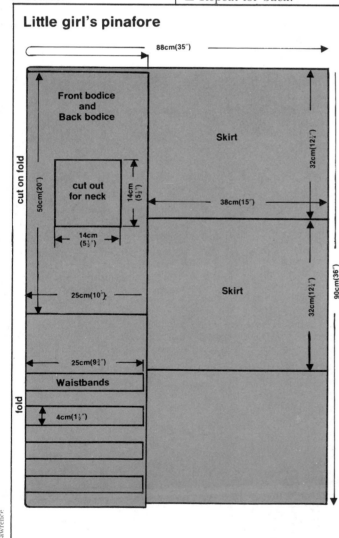

Little girl's pinafore

88cm (35″)

Front bodice and Back bodice

cut on fold

50cm (20″)

cut out for neck

14cm (5½″)

14cm (5½″)

25cm (10″)

25cm (9¾″)

Waistbands

4cm (1½″)

fold

Skirt

38cm (15″)

32cm (12½″)

Skirt

32cm (12½″)

90cm (36″)

Trevor Lawrence

Larry Layabout

Larry Layabout stands 1.83m (6') tall in his bare feet, but he can easily be cut down in size by reducing the measurements proportionately. The pattern is made almost entirely of rectangles, plus a circular head. The only paper pattern required is for the foot (which is one foot (30cm) long).

The pattern can be used to make a female doll by simply omitting the moustache.

MATERIALS
1.40m (1½yd) of 140cm (54") cotton poplin
3 bags of 400gm (13oz) stuffing, preferably washable
20 skeins 18m (20yd) red crewel wool, or tapestry wool, for hair
Needle and thread
Size 20 tapestry needle
2 large buttons
Felt scraps for features
Scissors
Metre (yard) stick, pencil
Compass
Fabric glue
Clothes: jeans with 60cm (24") waist; old shirt and plimsolls.

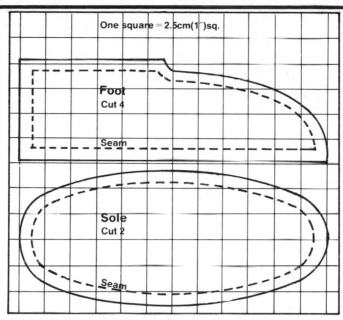

One square = 2.5cm(1")sq.

Foot Cut 4

Seam

Sole Cut 2

Seam

1. Graph of curved foot pieces. Gussets must also be cut.

MAKING THE DOLL
Using metre (yard) stick, mark out dimensions of the rectangular pieces on the fabric and mark 1cm (½") seam allowances all round.
□ Draw head, using compass or large plate.
□ Trace and enlarge foot pattern (fig. 1), following method described at the end of the book.
□ Cut out pattern pieces.
□ Sew up leg and arm seams, leaving about 20cm (8") open in the middle of one side of each piece for stuffing.
□ Tack and sew legs to body pieces, RST, and with leg seams at the back.
□ Tack and sew arms in the same way so that an open ended 'bag' with arms and legs results. Then, topstitch across 'shoulders', leaving 13cm (5") open for head.
□ Sew feet sides to gussets, RST, and sew soles to feet, RST, but leave about 10cm (4") open at 'heels' for stuffing.
□ Sew feet to legs, RST, and turn feet through.
□ Stitch head together, RST, but leave small opening for stuffing.
□ Attach button eyes and cut out and glue on felt features.
Stuffing. Stuff arms and legs first, through openings, and hand stitch seams together.
□ Stuff feet and lower legs from soles and stitch up openings.
□ Stuff head and body and attach together by hand, RST.
Hair. The hair and moustache are attached to the head by one stitch, using tapestry needle and crewel wool (fig. 2).

2. Stitch yarn to head.

□ Attach in rows, starting with short 'fringe' first.
Clothes. Dress doll in old clothes.

Section editor:
Roma Trundle

Designers:
Women's clothes by Sue Thompson; tot's dresses and pinafore, Susan Olave; appliqué quilt is by Linda Brill.

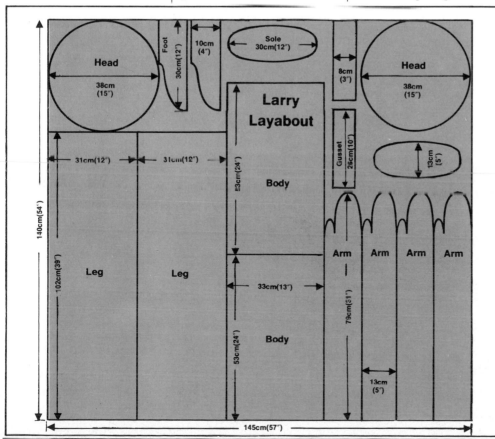

Head 38cm (15")

Foot 30cm(12")

10cm (4")

Sole 30cm(12")

8cm (3")

Head 38cm (15")

Larry Layabout

Gusset 26cm(10")

13cm (5")

140cm(54")

102cm(39")

31cm(12") 31cm(12")

53cm(24")

Body

Leg Leg

33cm(13")

79cm(31")

53cm(24") Body

Arm Arm Arm Arm

13cm (5")

145cm(57")

MACRAMÉ

Macramé is the craft of knotting strands of yarn to make a pattern. Most of the knots are simple to tie and some may be familiar to you already, although you may may not know their macramé names.

Basic knots. Most macramé is worked using two basic knots – the clove hitch (fig. a) and the flat, or square knot (fig. b). Both types are knotted over one or several strands which are called knot bearers, and both knots are fully explained, along with their variations, in the Knot Library on page 138.

Sinnets. A length of knotting is called a sinnet and most macramé patterns are made up of different arrangements of sinnets.

Mounting. Macramé strands must be anchored in order to be worked and this is normally done on a temporary anchor or base. The simplest is a door handle; the strands are tied to it with a piece of string. Alternatively, a pencil tied to a drawer handle (fig. c), or a piece of string pinned at each end to a board (fig. d) can be used. By varying the shape of the anchor, the shape of the macramé alters as well.

MATERIALS

Yarn. Macramé can be worked in most types of yarn, but, traditionally, it is worked in string and rope of all thicknesses and fibres. These are mostly available in natural shades but they can be dyed easily.

Finer yarns, such as crochet cotton may also be used but the knots are very small, and time-consuming – although the effect is beautiful. Knitting wool is not particularly successful because of its resilience and hairiness; it is also very difficult to unpick.

You can also use leather strips or thongs, raffia, piping cord and, of course, special twines which are now being made for macramé.

Macramé board. It is helpful – and in some cases essential – to work macramé on a board marked in squares which form guidelines to keep the work straight and symmetrical. You can buy special boards, already marked out with squares, or you could use a piece of cork board, or similar material which takes pins, and cover it with graph or squared dressmaker's paper.

Other materials you will require are: a tape measure, scissors, pins and rubber bands to hold the strands of twine in bundles.

ESTIMATING YARN

To calculate the length of yarn you will need for a project, multiply the required finished length by eight and multiply this figure by half the number of strands to be used (each strand is folded in half before starting).

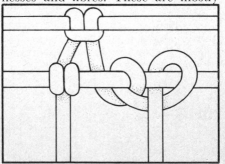

a. Clove hitch (double half hitch).

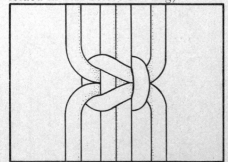

b. Flat knot, sometimes called square knot.

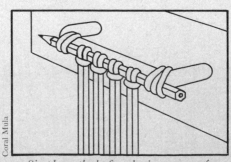

c. Simple method of anchoring macramé.

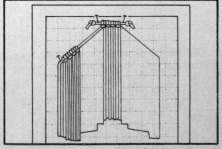

d. Macramé board enables shaping of work.

Theo Bergström

Coral Mula

130

The three belts are examples of diagonal cording and they must be worked on a macramé board. The cording is combined with other knots – sinnets (lengths) of flat knots, alternating flat knots and Josephine knots. Sizing can be done by adjusting the number of pattern repeats.
Instructions are on pages 141–142.

The neck purse is another example of diagonal cording. The strands of shiny Russia braid are knotted round two small dowel rods and the pattern worked on each rod. A loose interlacing forms the centre of the design. The two sections are· sewn together and lined, and long strands attached for the necklace.
Instructions are on page 142.

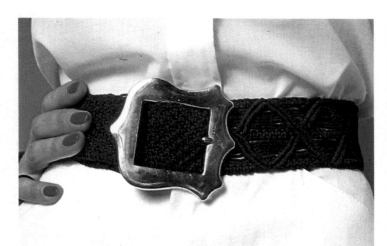

Theo Bergström

Blind. Macramé is an unusual way of dressing a window that does not need a movable blind. Changes in light throw the pattern into relief. The blind is made of alternating Josephine knots and a centre panel of horizontal and diagonal cording. Decorative sash cords complete the design.
Instructions are on page 143.

Once the essentials of macramé have been learned, it is possible to begin designing projects. Picture-making is a good area in which to start. An amazing number of patterns can be produced using a few macramé knots, as each will give its own special texture to the area in which it is used. But how it is used, will also affect the picture.

Choose a subject which has a simple outline and easily recognizable features; think of the subjects children like to draw – houses, trees, animals, fish, ships. Draw the outline on paper, mark in the features, and pin the drawing to a macramé board so that you can work over it.

Then choose knots which you think will give the appropriate texture to the different areas of your shape – horizontal cording for close, firm parts; diagonal cording for leaf shapes and angles; alternating flat knots for large, light areas. Braids of close flat knots, or alternating half hitches, are good for defining outlines, as demonstrated in the house pictured here.

Experimentation of the above kind reveals the true potential of macramé.

House. This imaginative picture should not be undertaken by beginners, but it is an excellent project once the basic macramé technique has been experienced.

Cording is used for the roof and for the porch above the door. An impression of decoration round the roof edges is given by blackberry balls.

The door and windows are shown by leaving the strands straight and unknotted in the appropriate areas, while the 'bricks' are worked in alternating flat knots. Sinnets of flat knots and alternating half hitches frame the sides.

The lampshade below has six panels which are worked in two alternating patterns, but one pattern could be used all round. The design is constructed of bands of flat knots divided by horizontal cording from bands of twisted knots. The centre sections contain alternating flat knots, but are emphasized by a large flat knot in one panel and studdings of blackberry balls in the other.

Instructions for both the house and the lampshade are on page 144.

MOUNTING KNOTS

Lark's head
This knot is used to mount strands for most macramé projects. Fold each strand in half, pass loop over knot anchor and thread ends through. Pull ends to tighten knot.

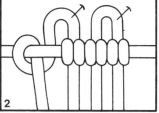

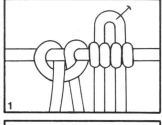

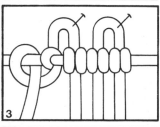

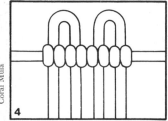

Picots
Another way of mounting strands. Wind one end round knot base as shown (1). Pin the second end in a loop above, to desired height, (2) and wind round knot base as first end (3). 4 shows completed picots.

Coral Mula

FLAT OR SQUARE KNOTS

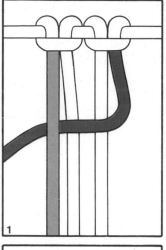

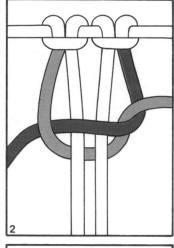

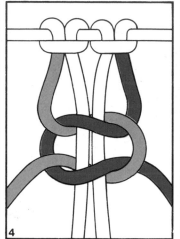

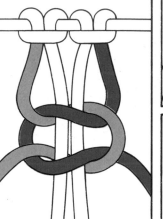

Flat or square knot
This basic knot is usually worked on strands in groups of four, using the outside strands only. Take the right-hand one across the centre and under the left strand, take the left strand under the centre and over the right. Repeat steps 1 and 2, but working from left to right as shown in 3 and 4. Note that centre strands become knot bearers.

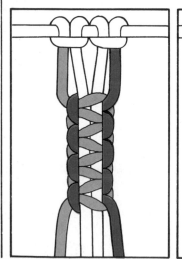

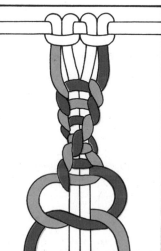

Alternating flat knots
Work groups of four strands. Tie a flat knot on each group, take two strands from each and tie a flat knot in centre; let remaining strands hang. Regroup as before and repeat.

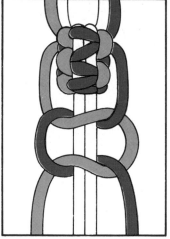

Blackberry ball
Tie a sinnet of flat knots, e.g. 4 or 6, thread centre strands through middle above the first knot as shown. Tie another flat knot below the ball.

Knot Lengths, Sinnets
For a flat knot sinnet, repeat flat knot stages 1–4 for required length. For a twisted knot sinnet, repeat stages 1 and 2 (omit 3 and 4). The sinnet will twist automatically as you progress.

CLOVE HITCH KNOTS

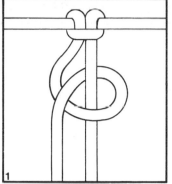

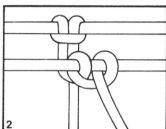

Alternating half hitch
Work with two or four strands divided in two groups. Tie left group over the right in a half hitch, then the right over the left. Repeat to form a sinnet.

Half hitch, Clove hitch
The basis of cording, which gives ridged effects in macramé. Hold, or pin one strand straight and wrap another round it (1). Repeat for a double half hitch or clove hitch (2).

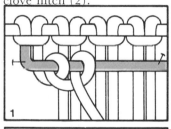

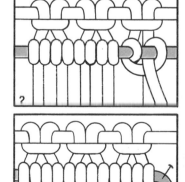

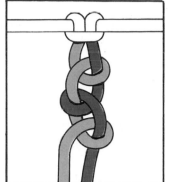

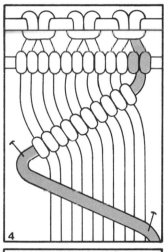

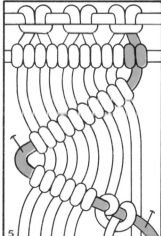

Cording
Horizontal cording: pin first strand across others to form knot bearer and tie hanging strand over it in a clove hitch (1). Work row (2). Bend knot bearer round, pin and tie strands over it from right (3).

Diagonal cording: work as horizontal cording but pin the knot bearer diagonally. Next row: bend knot bearer round and pin diagonally again (4). Tie strands over it, keeping them flat (5). The knot bearer forms the shape.

MISCELLANEOUS KNOTS

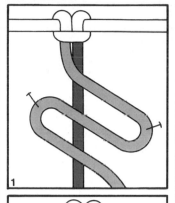

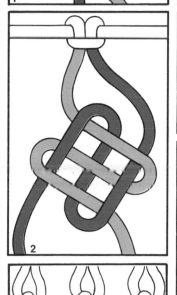

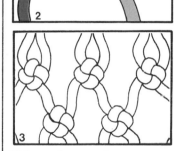

Chinese button knot
Work with two strands. Pin one strand as shown (1) and weave the second strand through (2). Pull firm. Work alternating chinese button knots by regrouping on alternate rows (3).

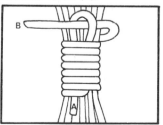

Binding
Make a loop with one end (A) deeper than required depth of binding. Hold in position and bind round with other end from bottom to top (B). Thread B through loop, pull A until B disappears and cut off A.

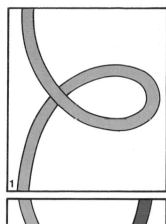

Josephine knot
Work on two, four or six strands. Divide in half and pin one half (1). Interlace second half through first (2), tighten slowly, pulling all ends evenly. Tie a sinnet (3). This completes the knot.

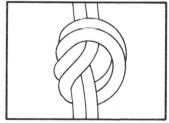

Overhand knot
This is the simplest and the most familiar of all macramé knots. It can be tied with any number of strands by twisting one end round to make a loop and then pulling the other ends through. Useful for beginning sinnets.

POT HANGERS

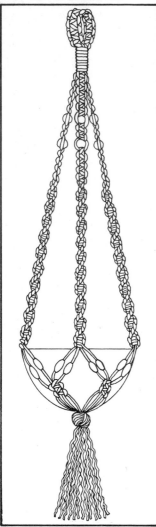

1. Anchoring working strands.

All the pot hangers shown involve the same basic techniques: they are begun by folding the yarn in half and making a loop which is attached to a base (fig. 1).

Then yarn is bound, usually as in fig. 2; sometimes after a few knots.

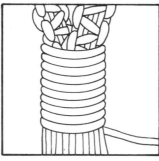

2. Bind with working strand.

The designs are constructed mainly from one easy knot, the flat or square knot, and a variation of it – the twist knot or half knot. Both are diagrammed in the Knot Library.

The designs are made by building lengths of knotting, called sinnets (fig. 3), and you can create your own designs by simply varying the length and placement of the sinnets.

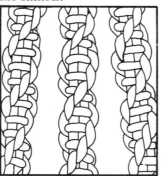

3. Making lengths of knots.

At certain points the strands are re-grouped to make a 'pocket' for the pot (fig. 4).

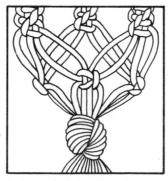

4. Regrouping makes a 'pocket'.

Double Pot Hanger

Length: 1.7m (67″)

MATERIALS
Eight strands thick jute, 13.5. (16yd) long
Two strands thick jute, 45cm (18″) long

WORKING
Hold the long strands of jute together and fold in half. Tie the loop to a door handle (see fig. 1).
☐ Working from the centre of the loop outwards, in both directions, make a total of 16cm (6¼″) flat knots (see Knot Library).
☐ Hold all the strands together and bind for 4cm (1½″) with one of the short strands (see fig. 2).
☐ Divide the strands in groups of four and plait the groups by overlapping, as in fig. 5, for 15cm (6″).

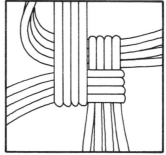

5. Transverse view of method.

☐ Re-form the strands into four groups and work 38cm (15″) twisted knots (see Knot Library), followed by 10cm (4″) flat (square) knots on each.
☐ Re-form the groups by taking two strands from one and two strands from the next. Leave 5cm (2″) and work 30cm (12″) twisted knots and 6cm (2¼″) flat knots on each.
☐ Re-form the groups as before, leave 10cm (4″), and work one flat knot on each group.
☐ Leave another 10cm (4″) and bind the strands together for 5cm (2″) with the remaining short strand.
☐ Trim all ends level and untie from door handle.

Beaded Hanger

Length: 1m (39″)

MATERIALS
8 strands medium-weight piping cord, each 7.5m (25′) long
2 split brass rings of 3cm (1¼″) diameter
8 wooden beads

WORKING
Fold the strands in half and tie to door, as in fig. 1.
☐ Leaving 10cm (4″) from the top of the loop, wind each strand round split brass ring once (fig. 6).

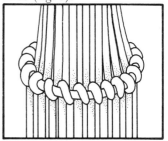

6. Alternative binding method.

☐ Divide the strands into four groups and work 23cm (9″) twisted knots on each.
☐ Leave 3cm (1¼″) and work one flat (square) knot.
☐ Repeat last step three times.
☐ Work 5cm (2″) flat knots on each group immediately below the last knots.
☐ Cut off the two shortest ends in each group, leaving 2.5cm (1″). With the remaining ends, make four half hitches (see Knot Library) to cover the cut ends.
☐ Leaving 4cm (1½″) from the last half hitch, thread a bead on each strand and tie an overhand knot to secure.
☐ Take one strand from each group and tie in an overhand knot with a strand from the next group, about 7.5cm (3″) from last overhand knot.

☐ Repeat all round.
☐ Leaving 7.5cm (3″) after these knots, tie all the strands in an overhand knot.
☐ Trim the strands to within 30cm (12″) of the knot. Comb out the strands to make a tassel.
☐ Untie loop from door handle and insert the other split ring through loop.

Single Hanger

Length: 1.20m (47½″)

MATERIALS
Six strands thick piping cord, each 9.5m (32′) long
Four strands thick piping cord, each 45cm (18″) long
One brass ring, 2cm (¾″) in diameter

WORKING
Thread each long strand through the ring so that all the ends are even and bind the strands together for 4.5cm (1¾″) with one of the short strands (fig. 2).
☐ Work 15cm (6″) twisted knots, tying two strands over all the others. Then, bind all the strands together as before.
☐ Divide the strands into pairs and work 9cm (3½″) alternating half hitches (see Knot Library) on five of the groups.
☐ Work 2.5cm (1″) alternating half hitches on the sixth group.
☐ Bend the longer groups outwards from the short one so that the last knots are level (fig. 7. Bind all the strands.

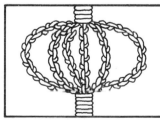

7. Making the 'crown' effect.

☐ Divide the strands into three groups and work 7.5cm (3″) flat knots on each.
☐ Leave 4cm (1½″) from the last knots and work 15cm (6″) flat knots on the same

groups but using the outer strands as the knot bearers.
☐ Leave another 4cm (1½″) and work 11cm (4½″) flat knots using the original strands as knot bearers.
☐ Leave 7.5cm (3″) and reform the groups with two strands from one and two strands from another. Work two flat knots on each group.
☐ Leave another 7.5cm (3″) and bind all the strands together as before.
☐ Trim the ends to finish off.

Cream Belt with Orange Beads

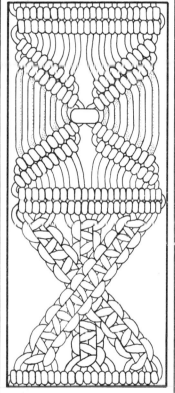

Length: 70cm (27½″) plus 25cm (10″) tassels.
Width: 5cm (2″).
Repeat: each repeat section is 12.5cm (5″) long.

MATERIALS
Six strands parcel string, each 12m (13½yd) long
Six orange beads (with holes large enough for two strands of string)
16 amber beads (with holes large enough to take three strands of string)
Removable knot base
Macramé board

WORKING
Using lark's head knots, mount the strands on a removable knot base so that you have 12 working strands.
☐ Starting 25cm (10″) below the knot base, and using clove hitches, make two rows horizontal cording (see Knot Library). Use the first strand as the knot bearer.
☐ Work two rows diagonal cording (see Knot Library) with the outside strands as knot bearers.
☐ Thread the knot bearers from the last row through an orange bead and work diagonal cording back to the edges, using the same strands as knot bearers.
☐ Work a second diagonal row, using the strands now

Cream Belt with Josephine Knots

Length: 66cm (26″). Alter by adjusting number of pattern repeats.
Repeat: 11cm (4½)″)
Width: 5cm (2″)

MATERIALS
Five strands parcel string, each 4.05m (4½yd) long
Removable knot base

in the middle as bearers.
☐ Work two rows horizontal cording, as before. This completes one section of the repeat.
☐ Divide the strands into three groups and work 6cm (2¼″) flat knots on each.
☐ Cross the first and third groups over the centre group. This completes the repeat pattern.
☐ Continue to work the pattern until the macramé is the correct length, but finish with the *first half* of the repeat pattern so that both ends of the belt match.
☐ Cut tassel and remove knot base.
☐ Divide ends into groups of three, thread an amber bead on each, work a flat knot and add another amber bead.

Two beads (optional)
Fabric glue
Macramé board

WORKING
☐ Mount four of the strands with picots (see Knot Library) on the removable knot base. This makes eight working strands.
☐ Using the remaining strand as the knot bearer throughout the rest of the macramé, centre it across the working strands immediately below the removable base and work two rows of horizontal cording (see Knot Library) using each end in turn as knot bearer.
☐ Leave 2cm (⅝″) unworked, pull the knot bearers down with the other strands and work two more rows of horizontal cording.
☐ To start the repeat pattern,* divide the working strands in half and work diagonal cording towards the centre.
☐ Join the knot bearers together with a chinese knot (see Knot Library), then work diagonal cording from the centre to the edges.
☐ Omitting the knot bearers, tie a Josephine knot with the working strands.
☐ Pulling the knot bearers down on each side of the Josephine knot, work

diagonal cording to make a criss-cross pattern, as before.

☐ Omitting the knot bearers, divide the working strands in half and pin one group diagonally across the board so that the strands lie parallel to each other. Weave the other strands through them (fig. 1). Remove the pins.

1. Interlacing the strands.

Black Belt

Length: 95cm (37½″)
Repeat: 4cm (1½″)
Width: 5cm (2″)

MATERIALS
12 strands fine macramé twine, each 7.60m (8⅓yd)
Buckle with 5cm (2″) wide shank
Macramé board
Darning needle

WORKING
Using the lark's head knot, mount the strands on the buckle shank, placing six on each side of the prong (total of 24 working strands).

☐ Work 2.5cm (1″) flat knots.

☐ Continue repeat pattern (from asterisk) until the belt is 4cm (1½″) shorter than required.

☐ Work two more rows horizontal cording.

☐ Leaving the knot bearers free, divide the working strands in half and work a blackberry ball on each group. (Alternatively, work a flat knot on each group, thread a bead on each and work another flat knot.)

☐ Bring down the knot bearers and work two more rows horizontal cording.

☐ Cut the ends, leaving 6mm (¼″) and glue down the ends on the wrong side to finish off.

☐ Using the first strand as a knot bearer, work one row horizontal cording.

☐ Leaving the centre four strands free, work from the middle outwards on the remaining strands in diagonal cording, using cords 10 and 15 as bearers.

☐ Repeat, using the next strands as knot bearers.

☐ *Work back to the middle from the left only in diagonal cording. (The asterisk marks the beginning of the repeat pattern.)

☐ Work flat knots on the reserved centre four strands to the depth of left-hand cording (A on repeat pattern).

☐ Work diagonal cording from the right across all the strands of the belt (B) *except the last four on the left.*

☐ Pin the cording to your working board to hold it in position.

☐ Work flat knots on the reserved left-hand cords from the cording above them to the depth of the cording held by the pin (C).

☐ Remove the pin and continue diagonal cording with these four strands to the edge.

☐ Work same depth of flat knots on last four strands of right-hand side (E).

☐ Reserving the centre four strands, work diagonal cording from the middle to the right-hand side, using all the strands on this half of the belt (F).

☐ Repeat stages from

asterisk until the macramé is the desired length, minus 12.5cm (5″).

☐ Work close, alternating flat knots (see Knot Library) for 10cm (4″).

☐ Continue in alternating flat knots but omit one knot at the beginning and end of each row to taper the belt.

☐ When only four strands are left in use, darn all the ends into the wrong side of

the belt and cut off any excess to finish it.

Belt loop. Mount the remaining strands on a pencil and work 21cm (8¼″) flat knots.

☐ Remove the pencil, cut through the mounting loops and knot these ends with the strands at the opposite end of the macramé to make a loop.

☐ Cut off the excess and place loop on the belt.

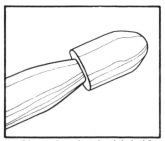

Neck Purse

Size: 11cm×8cm (4⅜″×3⅛″), plus tassel.

MATERIALS
Two dowel rods, 6mm (¼″) diameter×10cm (4″) length
Sharp knife for shaping rods
Stain or paint
20 lengths Russia braid, each 12m (48″) long
Lining fabric, 12.5cm×23cm (5″×9″)
Macramé board

WORKING
Shape the dowel rod as shown in fig. 1 and stain or

1. Shape dowel rod with knife.

paint it to complement braid.

☐ Mount all lengths of braid on one of the rods and tie two outer strands together to make a necklace.

☐ Using the next strands as knot bearers, work two rows horizontal cording into the centre.

☐ Using the four strands now on the edge at each side, work three flat knots.

☐ Leave the two centre strands and work one row diagonal cording on the remaining strands from the middle to the edge.

☐ Work a second row of diagonal cording, using the centre strands as knot bearers.

☐ Interweave all the strands and then work one row diagonal cording from the edge to the centre.

☐ Work three flat knots on each half, using three strands in each knot.

☐ Work another row of diagonal cording.

☐ At the centre, make a blackberry ball of eight flat

Coral Mula

knots using four strands.

☐ Work one row diagonal cording from the sides to the centre, each time picking up the hanging strand from the last knot and adding it to the knot bearer to increase the thickness of the inner core. At the centre, work one flat knot using all the strands. Leave cords to form a fringe.

☐ Work the other side of the purse in the same way, using nine of the remaining cords.

ASSEMBLY

To make up the purse, place the sides with wrong sides together and slip-stitch to within 2.5cm (1″) of the top.

☐ Fold the lining in half and trim folded end to same shape as purse. Machine stitch edges, leaving 2.5cm (1″) open at the top.

☐ Insert lining into purse so that wrong sides are together, fold under raw edges of lining and slip-stitch neatly to macramé.

☐ Adjust length of loops, leaving enough to hang purse around neck.

Macramé Blind

The dimensions of the blind shown are 81cm×91cm (32″×36″) but the size can be adjusted by changing the number of strands and varying the length of the central section.

MATERIALS
Roller blind and fittings
Heavy hemp, cut into enough strands to fill the roller. But the total number of strands used must be divisible by six i.e. 12, 18, 24 etc. Each strand should be eight times the length of the finished blind.
Two wooden rings, 9cm (3½″) diameter

WORKING
Mount the strands with lark's head knots on the roller section of the blind so that the knots are just touching.

☐ Using the first strand as the knot bearer, work one row horizontal cording.

☐ Divide the strands into groups of six and work a Josephine knot on each (see Knot Library).

☐ Leaving three strands free at each edge, regroup the other strands by taking three strands from one group and three from the next and work another row of knots.

☐ Regroup knots and work a third row as the first.

Central panel. Decide the width of the centre panel, using complete groups of Josephine knots.

☐ Pin the first and last strands of the panel to one side to be used in the side panels. Divide the strands into four even groups and work on the two middle groups.

☐ Work two rows horizontal cording.

☐ Divide the two groups into four (A, B, C, D) and work more horizontal cording on the outside groups (A and D), until the blind is about half the required length.

☐ On the inner groups (B and C), and using the outside strand each time as knot bearer, work four rows diagonal cording to the centre.

☐ Work four rows out to the edge again to make an X shape which finishes level with the horizontal cording on the other groups (A and D).

☐ Work two rows horizontal cording across all four groups (A–D) and then continue cording B and C for the same length as worked on A and D previously.

☐ On A and D work diagonal cording in X shapes to the same depth as B and C.

☐ Work two rows horizontal cording across A, B, C and D.

Overall pattern. Return to the strands in outer groups and work rows of Josephine knots as before, but on the inside four strands (beside central panel) work flat knots between each Josephine knot row.

☐ Halfway down the blind, link the last Josephine knot to the middle panel by threading one strand through (fig. 1).

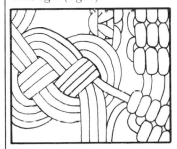

1. Linking knot to panel.

Blind pull. When the knots in the overall pattern are level with the bottom of the middle panel, continue in flat knots on the same four strands as before for several centimetres (inches) and then wind the strands round the wooden rings.

Overall pattern. Work three rows of Josephine knots over all the remaining strands and then two rows horizontal cording.

☐ Tie the ends round the stretcher bar at the bottom of the blind.

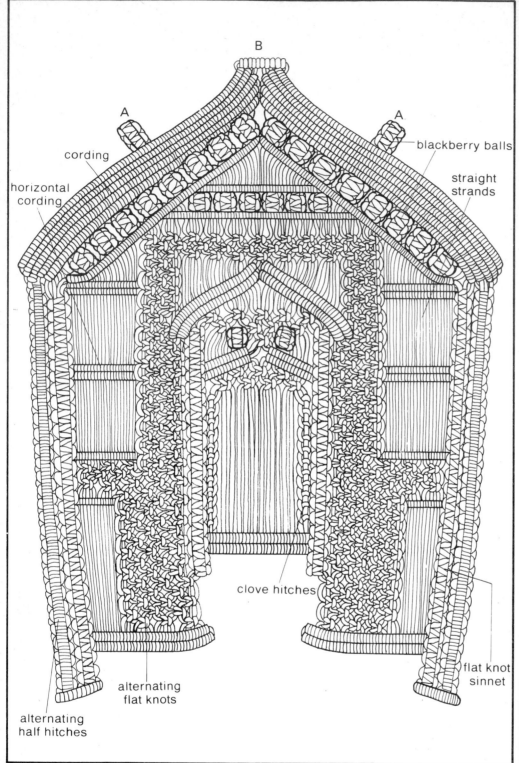

B

A A

cording

horizontal
cording

blackberry balls

straight
strands

clove hitches

flat knot
sinnet

alternating
flat knots

alternating
half hitches

Coral Mula

The dimensions of each panel are 20cm×13cm (5″×8″), but you can adapt the design to requirements.

MATERIALS
Drum lampshade frame
Lightweight twine, cut in to enough strands to fill top ring of frame. The total number must be divisible by four. Each strand should be eight times height of frame.

WORKING
Using a lark's head knot, mount the strands on the top ring with picots.
☐ Divide height of each panel in three.
Solid panel. (fig.1) Work row of horizontal cording.
☐ Tie groups of four strands in flat knot braids for a quarter of depth of first third.
☐ Work one row of horizontal cording.
☐ Tie groups of four strands in twisted knot braids for remaining depth of section.
☐ Work one row horizontal cording.
☐ Regroup strands, using two strands from one group and two from another, and work three flat knots.
☐ Regroup and continue alternating flat knots for one third of panel, adding blackberry balls where indicated.
☐ Add row of horizontal cording followed by twist knots (as earlier) and flat knots, as at beginning.
Open panel (fig. 2). Work first third as solid panel but make twisted sinnets shorter towards centre.
☐ Work a blackberry ball on the centre sinnet.
☐ Work alternating flat knots, leaving more and more central strands free.

Macramé Picture

Size: 47×37cm (18½″ ×14½″)

MATERIALS
40 strands parcel string, each 6m (20′) long
Two strings: one 45cm (18″) and one 10cm (4″) long, for knot bases.
Hardboard, to size of picture

Felt
Fabric glue
Macramé board

WORKING
Pin longer knot base horizontally on board and mount strands with lark's head knots.
☐ Make a blackberry ball on strands 21–24 and 61–64 (A on chart).
☐ Using the shorter knot base, work horizontal cord-
ing on strands 37–44 (B on chart).
☐ Unpin longer base and, using strands 38 and 43 as knot bearers, cord out from centre to ends.
☐ Pin work in arched position and work the sides and then the middle, following the diagram.
☐ Glue felt to the hardboard, and then glue the macramé in position on top.

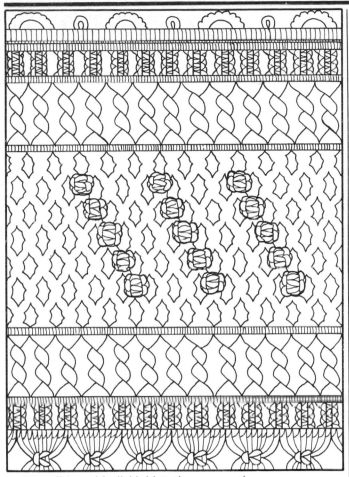

1. The solid panel is divided into three even sections.

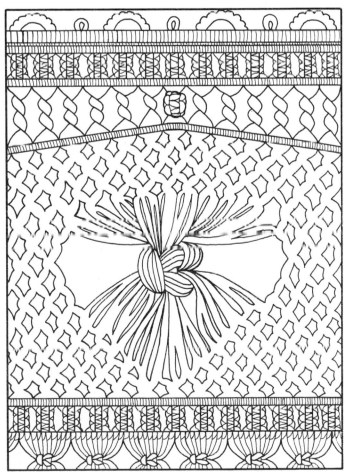

2. The open panel is decorated with a large flat knot.

☐ Tie free strands into a large flat knot, then continue alternating flat knots down into three-quarters of third section.

☐ Work pattern at bottom as for solid panel, and tie strands to ring.

Fringe. Leave a short amount of yarn unworked, then group into six and make two rows of alternating flat knots. Trim ends.

Note: fringes of alternating flat knots of different lengths can also be worked on clothes or linen.

Macramé Hammock

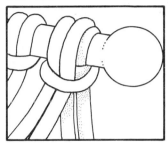

Length: 2m (6′6″)
Width: 90cm (3′)

MATERIALS

28 strands jute cord, 35m (11½yd) long
30 strands jute cord, 3.6m (4yd) long
2 strands jute cord, 7.2m (8yd) long
2 strands jute cord, 18m (20yd) long
2 pieces wood dowelling with 2.5cm (1″) diameter, each 95cm (98″) long
4 wooden balls, drilled with 2.5cm (1″) holes
2 large solid metal rings

WORKING

Using a lark's head knot, mount the 28 lengths of jute on a length of dowelling.

☐ Divide strands in groups of four and work rows of alternate flat knotting, leaving 20cm (8″) after the first row and 10cm (4″) between all other rows, until the hammock is 1.90m (6′4″) long.

☐ Leave 20cm (8″), and tie strands on the second dowel with clove (double half) hitches.

Side braids

Mount one 7.2m (8yd) length of jute on each end of the first dowel and mount the 18m (20yd) lengths over them as in fig. 1.

Tie two flat knots, leave

1. Make new knot over old one.

15cm (6″), and continue in twisted knots until 1.8m (6′) long.

☐ Thread the braids down through the sides of the hammock and adjust the hammock length to about 2m (6′6″).

☐ Leave 15cm (6″) gap in the braids and temporarily tie them to bottom dowel.

End ties

Mount half the remaining 30 strands on each dowel between the knots.

☐ Pass the ends round a metal ring and adjust to required length; tie firmly with a flat knot.

☐ Pull out the hammock to judge the shape. If it is too baggy, lengthen the side braids; if too tight, shorten the braids. Jute tends to stretch, so do not make the hammock too baggy. Bind, then trim ends for fringe.

☐ Insert the ends of the dowelling into the holes in the wooden balls.

Consultant:
Lindsay Vernon

Designers:
White pot hangers, by Bridget O'Reilly; belts by Karina Sterry and Janet Arthur; neckpurse by Jacqueline Short; house, Diane Swanson; hammock by Susan Cook and blind by Christine Hanscomb.

WOODWORK

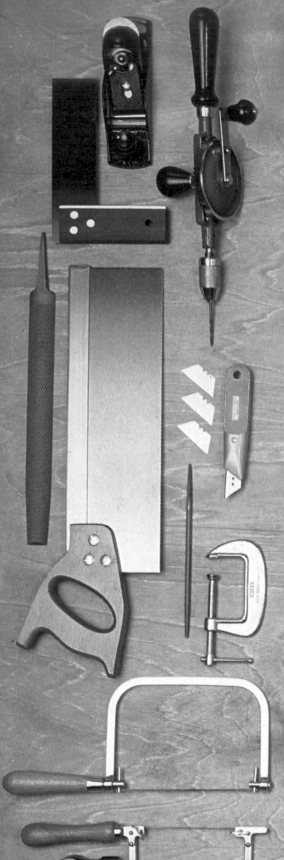

Rex Bamber

Wood is one of the most satisfying mediums in which to work since the grain, colouring and finish are fascinating in their variety and the uses of wood are enormous in scope.

Traditionally, woodwork is a man's task, from felling trees to cutting them to size and using the pieces constructively. But the introduction of modern precision tools and tools with fine cutting edges, plus the rise of DIY shops which will cut timber to size, have made woodcraft increasingly popular with women as well as with men.

Probably no handicraft has such an array of tools at its disposal as woodwork, but for the amateur craftsman, a small collection suffices.

Choose a handsaw, that you find easy to handle, bearing in mind that the more teeth it has, the finer it will saw. For drilling holes, both electric and hand drills are available with a number of bits for producing holes of different sizes.

Files, rasps and planes are useful for removing rough edges and smoothing surfaces; while a craft knife, such as an Xacto or Stanley knife, has several blades and can be used for a number of small tasks, including carving.

A good hammer is essential. Other useful devices are a G-clamp for holding wood while sawing and a carpenter's square for obtaining straight lines or right angles. A retracting tape measure or a segmented carpenter's ruler is also necessary.

CARVING

The woodcarver's art is as versatile as it is old; its uses range from the production of functional, everyday objects such as spoons and bowls to the purely artistic purposes of fine sculpture. At all levels, imagination and experience play their part, but even beginners can produce artifacts of charm and usefulness.

The decoys opposite are a good beginning project. Their shapes need only be suggestive as long as proper proportions are given consideration. The birds can be carved without professional woodcarving tools, and finished either by painting, or by waxing or varnishing.

MATERIALS

Soft wood such as pine is, for obvious reasons, easier to carve than hardwood and is desirable, therefore, for first projects. Balsa wood is even more malleable, but it is often difficult to obtain blocks of suitable size and, consequently, these must be built up by gluing several pieces together. Pine planks can also be glued in this way. Another solution is to carve one part of the sculpture from one plank and the rest from another, then glue the two together. For example, the head and neck of the tall marsh bird shown here were carved from a separate plank and then glued to the body.

TOOLS

Balsa can be carved with an ordinary craft knife such as an Xacto or Stanley knife and, for simple tasks, a potato peeler can be used.

Pine requires more attention, but craft knives can be used for the final shaping, as with balsa.

A hand saw is necessary for removing large areas of wood, or cutting a plank or block to size.

A coping saw must be used when cutting out a pattern or general shape. Its blade bends, allowing the user to cut round curves in the pattern.

Rasps, or Surform tools, are extremely useful for shaving away unwanted wood in areas where some control is required.

Craft knives. The final carving can be accomplished with craft knives, as mentioned previously. All these tools are part of any well-equipped tool-kit.

DECOYS

Many country homes in 18th and 19th century America owned 'decoys', or life-size imitations of wild fowl. These wooden copies were lovingly hand-carved from wood by local craftsmen. The decoys were placed on the bank of a lake or pond, to lure migrant waterfowl to land, and thus provide the farmer with his Sunday dinner. Many of these decoys were such fine sculptures that they have been preserved as ornaments, long after their usefulness came to an end. And it is not difficult to reproduce them, with this modern purpose in mind.

Instructions are on page 152.

CUTTING

In woodworker's parlance, cutting tools include saws, chisels and drills: although to the layman saws are the chief cutting tool. There are several different kinds of saw available for different cutting purposes.

Handsaws come in a number of sizes and are essential for making the initial cuts which bring timber to a workable size. In carpentry, careful cutting is of great importance for proper fit.

Coping saws and fretsaws are U-shaped saws (see photograph on previous page) with removable blades. They are used to cut curves in wood and to remove sections from *within* a piece of wood. Both types are used in the same manner and can cut only as far into a piece of wood as the distance between the blade and the bow. (Of the two, the fretsaw has the deeper cutting facility.)

When a piece of wood has areas within it which must be cut, these areas should be cut out first and the outline left until last.

To start a cut within a piece of wood, drill a small hole in the waste area to be removed, then undo the blade by releasing it from the bow at the end away from the handle. Pass the blade through the hole and clamp it back into position. It is now ready to use. Tension the blade so that it is tight; if it is too loose, the cut is more difficult to keep tidy and there is always the possibility of breaking the blade.

The animal plaques opposite are good projects for developing sawing skill. The shapes are not complex and their outlines are general enough that mistakes can be easily remedied. Plywood is used and the decoration applied with acrylic paints.

The angel is a replica of an early American wooden weathervane, and her celestial trumpetings and simple contours have a charm characteristic of inspired amateur art.

Instructions on pages 152 – 154

Rex Barber

149

CARPENTRY

In many respects carpentry is like dressmaking. The materials are different but the process is the same for each, involving careful measurement, cutting out a pattern and assembling all the pieces. Success depends on the ability to use tools proficiently.

In carpentry, it is advisable to develop one or two basic skills at a time – mastering a particular saw, for example, or learning to hammer nails correctly. Both these actions involve simple movements, but considerable dexterity is required.

Soon, even housebuilding is possible – if it is on the diminutive scale of the doll's house shown here. Most DIY shops will cut plywood to specification; windows and a door can be made with a fretsaw and the house glued and nailed together.

Detailed instructions on page 154

Jerry Tubby

150

Marsh Birds

MATERIALS
Wood: 50mm×100mm (4″ ×2″) wood, 61cm (24″) long. (Alternatively, one piece 30cm (12″) long, and a separate piece of scrap wood for the head and neck.)
100 mm×25 mm (4″×1″) wood, 20cm (8″) long – for the base.
6mm (¼″) dowelling, 23cm (9″) long, for the 'leg'.
Sandpaper: rough, medium and fine grade.
Wood glue
Tracing paper, pencil
Wax, or gloss paint
Hand saw
Coping saw
Surform or rasp
Craft knife
G-clamp
Hand drill with 6mm (¼″) bit
Plastic wood (optional)

CARVING
Trace and enlarge the outline on paper so that the overall length is 45cm (18″), and transfer it to one side of the block (or blocks) of wood. (A special section at the end of the book explains how.)
□ Repeat outline on the opposite side, making sure that the outlines correspond.
□ Put the block in a vice, or use the G-clamp, to secure it to a work top (fig.1).

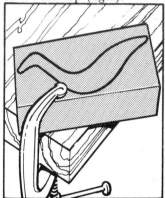

1. G-clamp secures wood block.

□ Use the hand saw to remove as much as possible of the surrounding waste.
□ Cut out the outline with the coping saw, adjusting the wood in the G-clamp as you go.
□ Give the body and neck proper rounded shape with the rasp or Surform tool.
□ Use craft knives to shape

the areas which the Surform cannot. Always be sure to work with the grain.
□ Using coarse, then medium and fine grade sandpaper, smooth the wood till you can see the lines of the grain stand out and the whole surface has a satiny feel.
□ If you have made the bird in sections, try the pieces to ensure a good fit. Glue them together and use plastic wood, if necessary, to fill gaps in the join. Leave to dry, then smooth with sandpaper.
Pedestal. To position the 'leg', balance the bird on your forefinger to find the point of balance – the natural pivot on which it will rest easily.
□ Drill a 6mm (¼″) hole at this point, cutting into the body at an angle which will hold the decoy upright on its stand – unless you want the bird to have its head looking upwards, or down, as though it were feeding.
□ Drill a 6mm (¼″) hole in the centre of the base.
□ Glue one end of dowelling, push it into the stand and leave to dry. Then glue the other end and position the bird.
□ Paint or wax to finish.

Animals

MATERIALS
12mm (½″) plywood
Stick-on tab with ring, for hanging animal
White emulsion paint
Acrylic paints
Paper, pencil
Felt tipped pen
G-clamp
Sandpaper
Wood drill
Sawing pin or bench peg
Fretsaw and blades
Round file

MAKING THE ANIMAL
Draw and enlarge the animal on a piece of paper, using the method described at the end of the book.
□ Draw the shape on the wood with a felt tipped pen.
□ Clamp the sawing pin or bench peg to a work top.
□ Drill a small hole in the waste areas within the design.
□ To cut these out, undo one

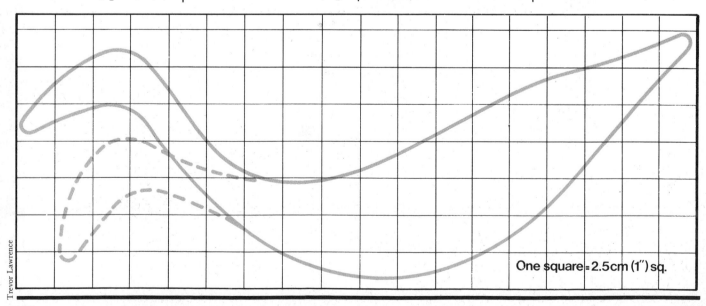

One square = 2.5cm (1″) sq.

Trevor Lawrence

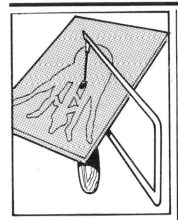

1. Saw handle is underneath.

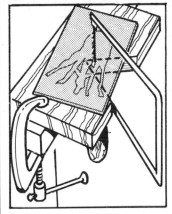

2. Saw on V-shaped bench peg.

end of the blade and thread it through the hole, fix the blade and tighten it. Do this so that the handle is not on the design side (fig.1).

☐ Position the wood so that it rests on the sawing pin, or bench peg, with the blade in the V-shaped notch of the sawing pin (fig.2).

☐ Hold the wood in position with one hand, and with the other, work the saw up and down. Move the wood, *not the saw*, in the direction of the cut.

☐ Once all the inside waste areas have been removed, cut out the outline.

☐ Smooth off all rough edges using the round file. Finish off with sandpaper.

☐ Apply two coats of emulsion paint for undercoat and then proceed to paint the animals with acrylic colours. Do not worry about accuracy of colouring, as a simplified appearance is part of the charm of these figures.

☐ Fix stick-on tab to back.

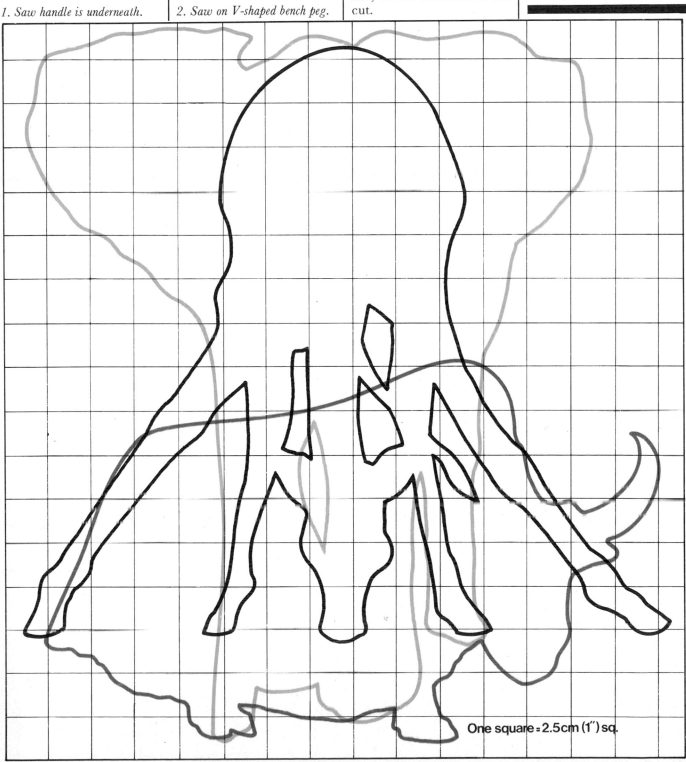

One square = 2.5cm (1″) sq.

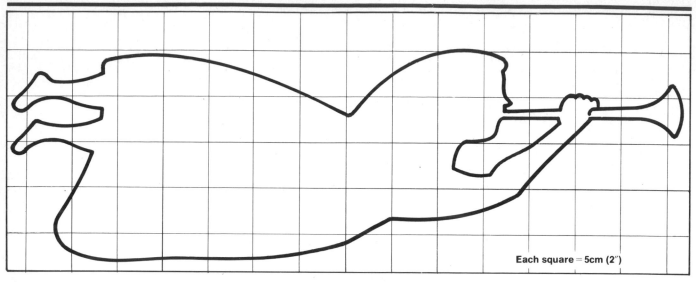

Each square = 5cm (2")

Angel

MATERIALS
25mm (1") plank 99cm (39") long and 25cm (10") wide. (Or glue the pieces together)
Tools (as for animals on previous page)
Acrylic paint, or household gloss paint and undercoat

MAKING
Cut the figure out like the animals described previously (page 152).

☐ Round off the sharp corners and edges of the figure's front with a craft knife, then rub down with a round file and sandpaper.

☐ Paint the figure, using gloss household paint or acrylic paint.

Doll's House

The house is made up like a box, with sections of plywood cut to size, then, glued and nailed together. Afterwards the hinged front is added and the sills and panes are glued in position.

MATERIALS
6mm (¼") plywood, pre-cut to dimensions
Clear acetate, for the windows
Sticky white labels, or paper strips and glue for panes
80cm (30") of 6mm (¼") thick moulding for sills
Picture moulding about 2.5cm (1") wide, 46cm (18") long, for cornice.
61cm (24") piano hinge.
Small 'box' hinges for door
Scrap wood about 3mm (⅛") thick, 8×14cm (3¼"×5½") for door, plus off-cuts for door panels
Sheet of formica for roof covering (optional)
Wood glue
Enamel paint and undercoat
Fretsaw, sandpaper
Drill, compass
Plane, hammer
Panel pins (thin nails)
Carpenter's square
General-purpose glue
Compass

MAKING
Have the DIY shop cut the plywood to size. See fig. 1 and diagram for dimensions.

☐ Plane the edges to make sure they fit evenly.

☐ Assemble the 'box' as shown in the diagram. First glue, then nail together, the top, bottom and sides, checking with the carpenter's square that you have true right-angled joins. Before nailing, allow the glue to set and, if possible, apply pressure with a few books as weights.

☐ Add the back, gluing and nailing as before.

☐ Put in the floors in the same way, following the positions in the diagram.

☐ Rub the box down with sandpaper.

☐ Check the measurement and fit of the house front. Note that it covers the entire box like a lid.

☐ Make a template, or pattern the exact window size, then measure and mark the positions as illustrated, but draw round the template in each position to get a uniform size.

☐ Use the template to draw part of the door, then complete the curve of the fanlight above the door, with a compass.

☐ Cut out the door and windows with the fretsaw, using it as described for the animal plaques on page 152.

☐ Smooth the inside edges with sandpaper.

☐ Using the window template, cut out the window 'glass' from the acetate, adding an extra 6mm (¼") all round for gluing.

☐ Cut out and stick a grid of

2.5cm (1")

46cm (18")

4cm (1½")

9cm (3½")

15cm (6")

7cm (2¾")

Floor line

12mm (½")

71cm (28")

5.5cm (2")

4cm (1½")

Floor line

7cm (2¾")

4cm (5½")

4cm (1½")

8cm (3")

Back = 71cm × 42.8cm (28" × 17½")

1. The dimensions of the doll's house are given above.

Trevor Lawrence

white paper strips on the windows to make panes.
☐ Glue the panes on the inside of the windows with general-purpose glue.
☐ Make up the panelled door by sticking small squares of wood on the door rectangle, then glue a curtain ring on for the knocker.

☐ Glue on the sills and door surround.
☐ Glue or nail the hinges on the door.
☐ Add decorative moulding to the top of the house. Nail with panel pins.
☐ Attach the piano hinge to the 'box' and front of the house.

☐ The roof can be covered with formica, if desired. Glue in place.
☐ Apply undercoat and two coats of enamel paint to the box and front, and the house is complete. If you wish to 'paper' the inside, use contact paper.

Consultant:
Louis Jordaan
Designer:
Carson Ritchie

The diagram below shows an 'exploded' view of the doll's house, illustrating how it is assembled. Have the pieces pre-cut at a local DIY shop.

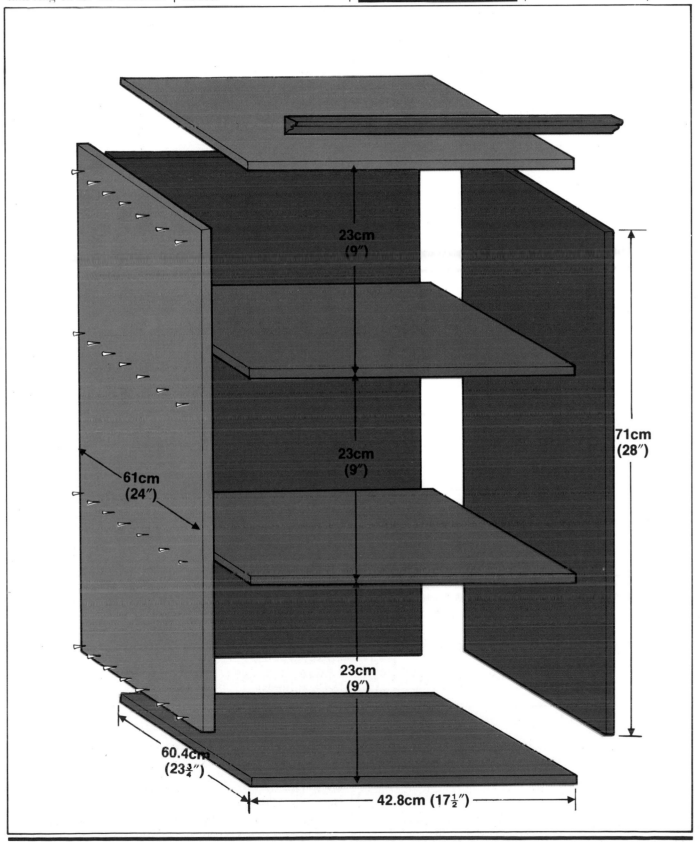

23cm (9")

23cm (9")

23cm (9")

71cm (28")

61cm (24")

60.4cm (23¾")

42.8cm (17½")

EMBROIDERY

Embroidery is the age-old craft of embellishing fabric by stitchery. Practised throughout the world, there are dozens of basic stitches and numerous variations on them. This vast reservoir would take years – if not a lifetime – to absorb, but a multitude of embroidery designs can be worked, using only one or two stitches. The most popular of these are cross stitch, satin stitch and chain stitch. They are diagrammed – along with many others – in the Stitch Library on pages 177–179.

Embroidery falls into two categories – surface and counted thread. In surface embroidery the design depends on the shape of the motif to be executed and the stitches are worked in the direction and in the size most suitable. With counted thread embroidery the motifs and stitches are based on the weave of the fabric. Designs tend to be linear or geometric and stitches are worked over two to six threads (according to the desired effect) and always lie parallel, or at 90° or 45° to the selvedge. Both drawn thread and much embroidery worked in cross stitch are forms of counted thread work.

Over the centuries, various styles of embroidery have developed which are characteristic of particular regions or countries. The traditional embroidery of Mexico, for instance, has a distinctly different character from that worked in Hungary or Czechoslovakia. Crewel work, described later on in the chapter, is an example of an English embroidery style which developed in the 17th century and also became popular in the American colonies.

In Europe and America, skilled needlework was the mark of an accomplished woman; and who is not familiar with the finely worked samplers, often bearing mottoes, which once tested girls' skills much as a maths exam might today?

From traditional styles, modern embroidery has grown new shoots. In picture making, for example, stitches are sometimes combined with paint or dyes, and the subject matter is as often abstract as it is representational, with texture playing as important a part as colour and outline. Machine embroidery is another modern embroidery form which is gaining great popularity, owing to the number of stitches

swing-needle machines can produce.

MATERIALS

Fabrics. There are several fabrics – linen, cotton and mixtures – which are made especially for household linens, or cushions, which are to be embroidered.

For clothing, the fabric must suit the garment, but good dress fabrics for embroidery include calico, sailcloth, flannel, wool, linen and linen types. The fineness or looseness of the weave will, of course, influence the relative fineness or looseness of the stitching. For surface embroidery choose fabric to give desired effect. For counted thread work, buy it with a suitable number of threads per cm (1″).

Threads. The most widely available and versatile embroidery thread is stranded cotton. This is composed of six strands, lightly twisted together, so that two or three strands can be withdrawn to give a lighter effect. For more chunky stitchery, use pearl cotton – a twisted, shiny thread, available in two thicknesses.

For embroidery on wool, use two-ply crewel yarn which is stranded in a similar way to stranded cotton. Tapestry wool – a four-ply yarn – is suitable for heavy effects.

Needles. A crewel needle is needed for most embroidery and, as a general guide, the finer the needle (or higher the number), the better the embroidery – providing the eye of the needle accepts the yarn without chafing. Crewel needles are available in packs of assorted sizes and sizes range from four to 10.

Frames. To maintain an even tension and avoid puckering, it is advisable to mount fabric on a frame – particularly for work in which the stitches are made in two or more movements. (Stitches made in one basic movement are easier to do when the fabric is held in the hand.)

The most useful frame for general use is a ring, hoop or tambour frame. This has an inner and an outer ring, made from wood, plastic or metal, with a screw for adjusting tension. It is available in various sizes.

To mount the fabric in the frame, separate the rings. Bind the inner ring with tape to prevent the fabric from mark-

ing or slipping. Lay the fabric over the inner ring, right side up for hand embroidery, wrong side up for machine embroidery; press the outer ring over it. Tighten the tension screw and pull the fabric taut, checking that the grain is square.

TRANSFERRING DESIGNS

Embroidery motifs should normally be transferred in the following way: draw the motif or design on tissue paper, pin it to the cloth to be embroidered and then stitch along the lines of the design with large running, or basting stitches. Pull the tissue paper off and embroider over the running stitches which can be pulled out later. For some projects, tailor's chalk can be used to mark the positions of the design. (For more information on enlarging and transferring designs, see the special section at the back of the book.)

An alternative method of transferring, which is particularly suitable for small intricate designs, is to use dressmaker's carbon paper. Choose it in a colour which will show up on your fabric and place it shiny side down between the fabric and tracing. Trace over the design firmly so that the outlines are offset onto fabric and then remove the carbon and original tracing.

Embroidery is among the most versatile of decorative forms; there are many stitches and great scope for original design.

The embroidery examples shown opposite serve to illustrate the rich variety of styles which has developed in different parts of the world, using the same reservoir of stitches.

Top left: the Chhi-lin, a traditional, Chinese emblem of good fortune, is worked in glittering gold thread. Opposite it is an example of South American mola work in which the top layers of cloth are cut back and stitched to reveal other layers beneath. It is a form of reversed appliqué and produces particularly colourful results.

The Indian floral design, incorporating white flowers and green birds, is worked in long and short stitch and in chain stitch. Below it is a fine example of 18th century German embroidery, also worked in long and short stitch, yet wholly different in character.

Yugoslavia is the origin of the splendid peasant dress, luxuriantly embroidered with flowers on linen and edged with fine cut work embroidery.

SIMPLE STITCHERY

One of the chief fascinations of embroidery
is its immense versatility; not only are
there broad differences in general style, as illustrated on the previous page, there are also differences
in the application of each stitch. Whether
it is worked minutely or in a large, almost freehand
fashion (like the work shown here), considerably
affects the design results. The latter method has special
appeal for many forms of modern decor-
ation, and for beginners in general, since
the meticulous placement and size
of stitches is not very important, and can even add
charm to the design. Many such patterns
can be worked, using the eye as a
guide, or working from very simple sketches.
Instructions are on page 180.

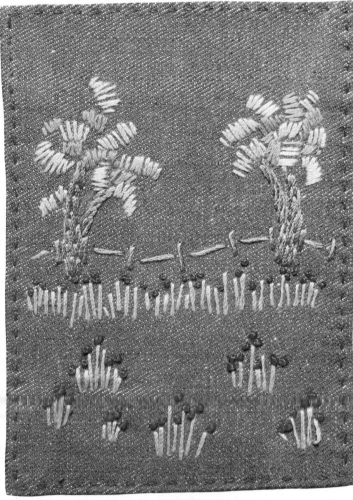

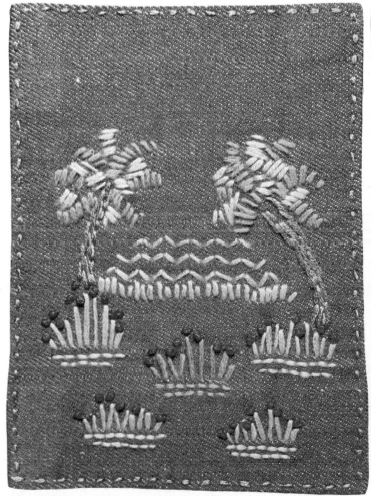

Three simple stitches are used to work this tunic, yet the result is successfully reminiscent of Eastern European or gypsy styles. The white rows are stitched in herringbone, while the stars are worked in two cross stitches, one on top of the other (alternatively, use star stitch). The green and white border lines are whipped back stitch. All are diagrammed in the Stitch Library on pages 177–179. This is not difficult embroidery and can be worked by a beginner using the eye as a guide to stitch size and placement. The tunic is made following instructions for the peasant-style shirt given in the Sewing chapter.

Instructions for applying embroidery appear on page 180

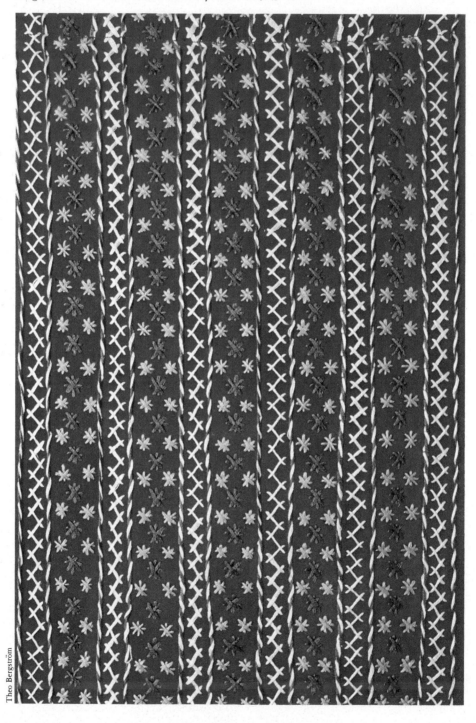

Theo Bergström

The delicate motifs on the bed linen on this page and on the cami-knickers opposite show the effectiveness of fine embroidery worked with a few basic stitches. Virtually the same stitches are used in both instances.

The motifs can be applied to all kinds of articles and to clothing, and, of course, may be worked singly. But fine stitching of this kind is time-consuming and should only be undertaken in small areas until the worker is fairly proficient.

Red flowers. The method is the same for each motif and you should start by tracing the colour drawing and transferring it to your fabric, using the carbon paper method described in the introduction to the chapter and a metre (yard) stick or ruler to measure correct placement of the design on the fabric. Using two lengths of stranded cotton thread in the needle, work stems in whipped back stitch. Satin stitch is used for petals and their centres, and fishbone for leaves.

The following number of flower motifs can be worked per one skein of thread: flower petals, nine; centres of flowers, 15; sepals and streaks on petals, 20; leaves, three; and stems, six. This is a good project for practising fine embroidery.

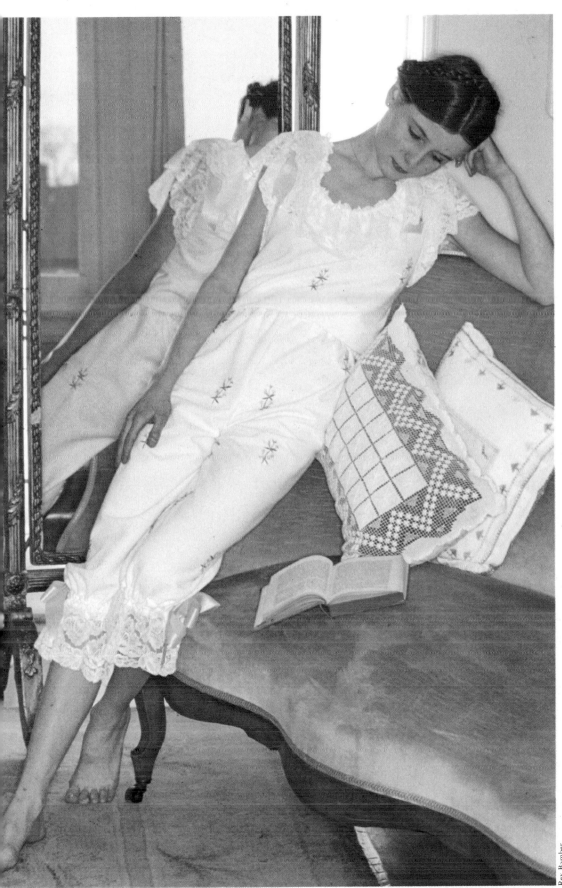

Creamy cami-knicker style lounging pyjamas trimmed in lace and bows are nostalgic reflections of the past. Use soft, woven flannel and work the motif as described for the linen opposite, but use straight stitch for sepals and streaks.

Make the camisole from a sleeveless, commercial pattern and the knickers from the trouser pattern on page 126. Trim leg length to size and do not taper. Gather lace slightly before attaching. Insert elastic in waistband and cuffs.

SAMPLER

Samplers have been used as a method of practising and recording stitches and patterns since the 16th century. Fine needlework was considered an essential accomplishment of every lady, and girls were taught embroidery at an early age – the sampler being one of their first projects.

In the 18th and 19th centuries, samplers became pictorial – often with a domestic or religious theme. They would usually include some form of lettering, perhaps the alphabet or a proverb worked in counted cross stitch, as practice for making household linen. They would also generally be signed with the maker's name, age and the date. Nowadays, although printed reference for stitches is so readily available, the sampler still is useful for practice and to show the texture of stitches. Several basic stitches are used in the sampler shown here, which is also a valuable demonstration of how stitches can suggest texture and different effects when worked in groups. You could easily substitute a proverb for the alphabet if you prefer, and the letters can be used individually for monograms.

The finished sampler could be framed to make a picture or you could use it to form one side of a cushion cover. If you wish to sign it, write your name in pencil in the bottom corner and work over it in stem or chain stitch, adding the date and your age in the same way.

Detailed instructions on page 181.

Theo Bergström

CREWEL WORK

Crewel work is the name given to embroidery worked entirely in woollen crewel yarn. It was a form of embroidery popular in Britain in the 17th century for household decorating when printed fabrics were scarce and fine needlework too time-consuming or inappropriate for such things. It is known also as Jacobean embroidery, after the period of its development.

The traditional themes combine a vivid Eastern influence (derived from increasing Oriental trade) with the more familiar, floral motifs typical of Tudor embroidery. The result is a colourful variety of plants, animals and birds, often depicted as 'growing' from one source – the Tree of Life. This appears in different forms in embroidery throughout the world.

The cushion below incorporates part of the traditional crewel motif, the Tree of Life (shown in detail right). The colours are typical of Jacobean crewel work which was done with total disregard for proportion and reality. Many of the objects were included as symbols – Christian and Oriental – and are a glorious mixture of the familiar and the exotic.

The large flower on the cushion is worked four times, with slight variation in detail and filling stitches – heavier stitches being used on the left-hand side. It illustrates how different fillings can alter the whole appearance and 'feel' of a design. Because of its free-flowing style, elements of the design can be re-arranged or used separately on a smaller cushion or other surface.

Instructions on page 182

Jerry Tubby

The cushion on this page is worked with a simpler, more modern approach than the example opposite. The rectangular house motif is repeated at right angles and the filling is slightly varied in the two versions to add interest. A tiny floral edging frames the whole, while central focus is created by the imaginative tree motif.

Buttonhole stitch is used for the roof tiles and scalloped window blind edging, while Jacobean couching creates the window grilles. The central tree is worked in bunches of straight stitch interspersed with french knots for berries; this also applies to the flowers round the edge of the cushion.

The house outline is herringbone stitch and the whole design is integrated by the four chain stitched 'trunks' radiating from the central motif in an original interpretation of the traditional Tree of Life.

Illustrations on page 184

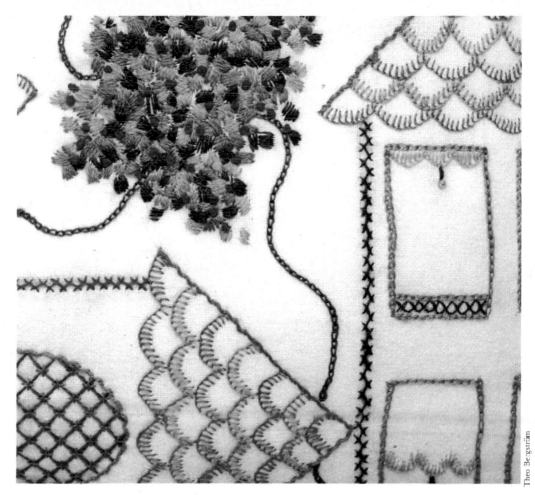

Theo Bergström

Jerry Tubby

CUT WORK

Cutwork is a form of lace-making much used in Italy and Scandinavia in the 18th and 19th centuries. It is worked by outlining a simple motif with running stitch and then buttonhole stitch, and cutting away the fabric inside the motif. This area may then be filled with more stitchery.

Blind. The flowers on the blind below have special appeal because the cut areas allow light to filter in. The motif is reversed alternately along the blind to give more interest. It could be worked in the same colour as the blind, using light and texture for effect. *Instructions are on page 184.*

DRAWN THREAD

Drawn thread work is one of the most delicate of embroidery styles. As the name implies, in drawn thread embroidery, threads are pulled out in bands from the fabric and certain stitches are worked to pull some of the remaining threads in the band together, while separating others. This gives a delicate, lacy effect which is well illustrated in the mat shown below. Drawn thread embroidery is of peasant origin and was popular in Europe during the 16th century as a decorative device on costumes. Today it can be used to make insets and fringes on household linens such as tablecloths and face towels, or it can be used to ornament lingerie and linen or fine cotton blouses and skirts.

The most suitable fabrics are of a fairly loose, even weave, such as linen or cotton. Thread of the same colour as the base fabric should be used in the stitches to create a proper effect. A thread with a darker or lighter shade could also be used, but avoid contrasting thread as it tends to spoil the effect. The thread should be of a similar thickness to the individual threads in the fabric: mercerized cotton or stranded cotton, for example.

Stitches. Most of the stitches suitable for drawn thread embroidery are based on hemstitch and back stitch, and combinations of them give different effects. Several typical stitches are illustrated in the Stitch Library on page 178.

Place mat. The mat below is a veritable drawn thread sampler in that six different stitches – each one traditional to drawn thread work – are used and serve to illustrate the visual variety the technique presents. The mat could be made with only one or two stitches repeated throughout.

Use a fine, woven cotton or linen and one strand of stranded cotton thread. Cut the fabric to size, allowing for a fringe and decide the positions and widths of the bands to be withdrawn. In marking these out on the fabric, use a ruler and tailor's chalk to work out proportions before you begin to withdraw threads.

To withdraw threads, cut each one in the centre of the band, then pull it out from the edge until the withdrawn thread is about 2.5cm (1″) from the edge of the fringe line. Darn this end into the border so that both ends protrude, then cut off excess ends.

Work chosen stitches on remaining threads in each band (the threads which were at right angles to the withdrawn threads).

Work a row of simple hemstitch round the mat's edges at the desired depth of the fringe. Then fray out remaining threads to form fringe.

The stitches which are used to make the mat are as follows from left to right: hemstitch, wave stitch filling, ladder hemstitch, double or Italian hemstitch, ladder hemstitch, wave stitch filling and hemstitch. This completes the first section.

The middle section is worked in hem stitch, wave stitch filling, zigzag hemstitch, interlaced hemstitch, zigzag hemstitch, then wave stitch filling and hemstitch.

The third section is worked like the first one. All the stitches which are used are diagrammed in the Stitch Library.

The dimensions of the mat can vary.

MACHINE EMBROIDERY

Machine embroidery is a relatively new technique which has been made possible by the development of the swing needle sewing machine. Using this machine, it is possible to produce comparatively quickly a number of embroidery stitches which mimic hand stitches, as well as several stitches which are peculiar to machine embroidery.

The main pre-requisite is ability to control your machine, since this determines the extent of textural and decorative explorations you can pursue successfully.

The tablecloth shown here is a good example of the simpe use of zigzag stitches to create decoration, and it is a suitable project for beginners since the contours of the design are not difficult and make a good exercise in machine control.

First divide your cloth into an even number of squares for 'place settings' and mark them with tailor's chalk.

In each square lay a place and draw round the plate and cutlery with the chalk (or work from a paper template), then sew round outlines using contrasting thread.

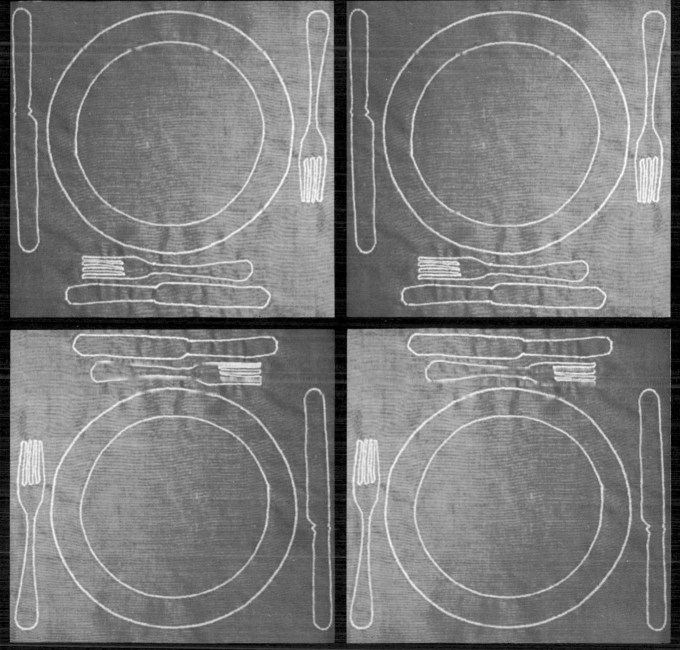

Machine embroidery falls into two categories – automatic and free. Automatic machine embroidery depends on the potential of the machine for the number of patterns it will produce: all you have to do is set the machine and guide the fabric through.

With free machine embroidery, you simply use the two most basic machine stitches – straight and zigzag – and the results depend on your own skill. To obtain maximum manoeuvrability, the feed teeth and foot, which hold the fabric firmly and feed it through evenly in normal sewing, are dropped or removed (your machine manual will tell you how). The fabric is put into a frame (as described on page 156) which provides the tautness necessary for the top thread to link with the bottom thread as you guide the fabric through, quickly for long stitches and slowly for close ones. This takes practice, particularly with zigzag stitch because of the sideways movement.

One limitation of machine embroidery in comparison with hand embroidery is the type of thread that can be used, since only normal sewing thread can be used in the machine. If you use a different colour in the bobbin from that of the top thread, and tighten the top tension so that the bobbin thread is pulled up on to the right side, an effective speckled look will result. You can use heavier thread, providing you wind it on the bobbin by hand (adjust tension accordingly). The embroidery then has to be worked with the wrong side facing up so that the heavy thread appears on the right side.

The dolls on this page can be worked freely or by feeding fabric through in the usual way.

Trace the outlines from photographs opposite and overleaf, enlarge them following instructions at back of book and transfer to fabric with carbon paper. Machine stitch outlines in contrasting thread.

Detailed doll instructions, page 185

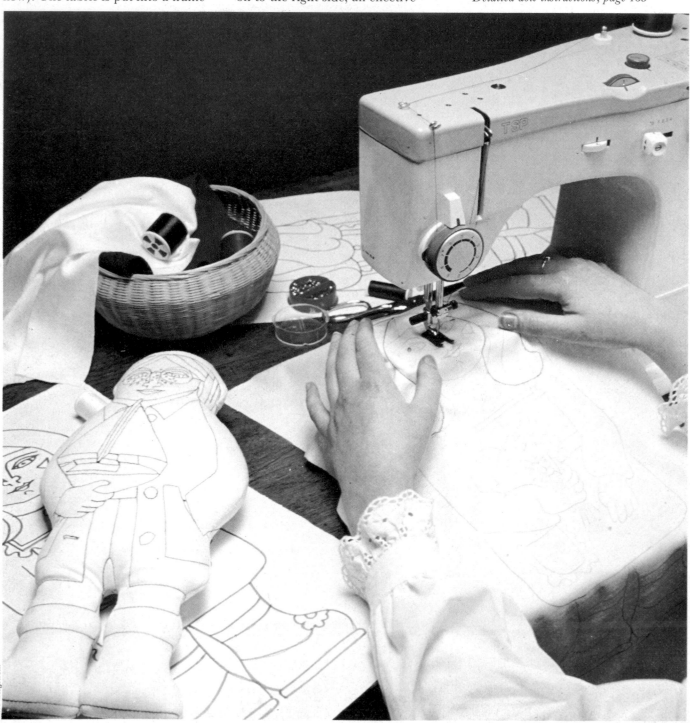

Theo Bergström

STITCH LIBRARY

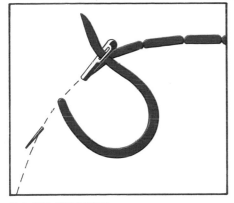

BACK STITCH

Working from right to left (if right-handed), take a back stitch and bring out needle the same distance on the line ahead. Work next stitch to touch first. Use for lines.

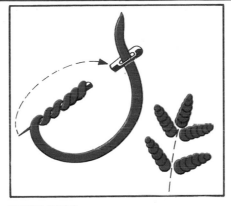

BULLION

Make a loose back stitch, bringing out needle at starting place; before pulling through, twist thread round needle several times. Use this stitch for filling areas.

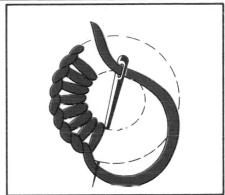

BUTTONHOLE OR BLANKET

Use as outlining stitch. Working from left to right, take straight stitches between double lines, or from edge, looping thread under needle. Work stitches closely for buttonholing.

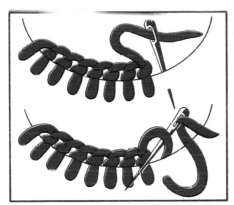

BUTTONHOLE, HEDEBO

Use as an edging or filling stitch for cut work. Work in two movements as shown with the edge pointing away from you. Pull tight, if edging, but leave loose for filling.

CHAIN

Use as outlining or filling stitch. Work along line of design, looping thread under needle as shown. Do not pull too tight or chain effect is spoiled. This is a basic embroidery stitch.

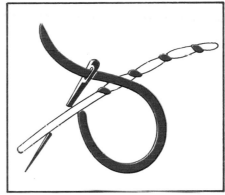

COUCHING

Use for outlining. Lay thread along line and catch down with small stitches as shown. Catching thread may match or contrast with the basic line thread of the design.

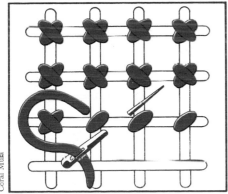

Coral Mula

COUCHING, JACOBEAN; OR TRELLIS

Use for filling. Work the foundation in long stitches to form a trellis pattern and catch down at intersections with cross stitch. Cross stitches may match or contrast with trellis thread.

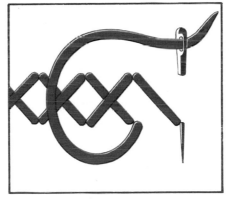

CROSS STITCH

Use for lines, outlining or for filling. Work even-sized diagonal stitches to cross as shown. Stitches may touch or be spaced but you must ensure that the top stitch of each cross lies in same direction.

DAISY

Use individual stitches at random or in groups for filling. Work individual chain stitches, catching down the loop with a small stitch and moving to next stitch as shown. Also known as detached chain stitch.

FEATHER STITCH

Use for outlining. Work downwards on the line of the design alternately to left and right with needle pointing to the line and looping the thread under it as shown.

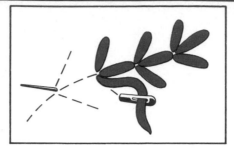

FERN

Use, as the name suggests, for filling sprays and leaves, or in a line as shown. Work by taking three even-sized straight stitches radiating from a centre hole.

FISHBONE

Use for filling. Work close, slanting stitches from centre line of shape alternately to left and right, thus forming a plaited effect in the centre. An open-worked version is also possible.

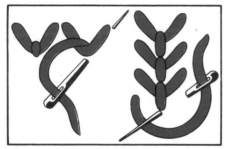

FLY

Use for filling. Make a loose straight stitch and hold down in a V. Return needle to centre and catch down with a tiny stitch. Stitches may touch or be spaced.

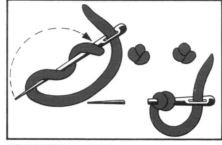

FRENCH KNOT

Work at random, or closely as filling. Bring thread through and hold taut, twisting needle round it two or three times. Re-insert needle at starting point and pull tight.

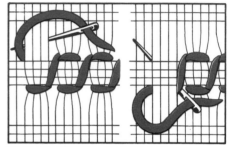

HEMSTITCH, ITALIAN

Use for drawn thread work to link two drawn bands. Working from right to left, pass the needle round threads of one band and bring out to repeat on second band.

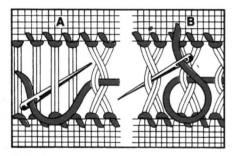

HEMSTITCH, INTERLACED

Use for drawn thread work. Join thread to fabric at end of band, pass needle as shown over two groups and pull thread taut so that the groups twist.

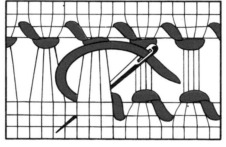

HEMSTITCH, LADDER

Use for drawn thread work. Stitch edge of drawn band, passing needle round threads in band as shown. Work opposite edge to match. Bands are separated into regular groups.

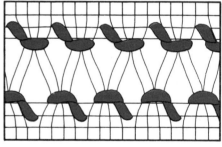

HEMSTITCH, ZIGZAG

Work one edge as ladder hemstitch. Along opposite edge of band reform the groups by taking half the threads from one group and half those from next. This creates the zigzag effect.

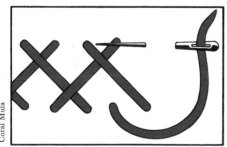

HERRINGBONE

Use for lines. Work from left to right taking regular back stitch between two lines of the design alternately to form a criss-cross pattern. Stitches may also be worked closely. Use either a matching or a contrasting thread.

LEAF

Use for filling, particularly leaf shapes, as the name suggests. Work close stitches alternately to left and right edges of the shape from a double centre line to form a ribbed or plaited effect. Often used with an outline stitch.

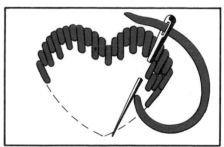

LONG AND SHORT

Use for filling. Outline the shape with alternate long and short straight stitches and then fill remaining area with straight stitches to touch base of previous row. Adjust stitch size to fill as required.

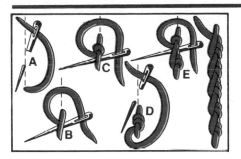

PORTUGUESE STEM

Use to form a thick line (E). Work as shown in steps A-C and start the next stitch as shown at D. The needle should pass under the stitches without penetrating the fabric.

RUNNING

This is the simplest of all stitches. Use as a basic stitch by itself for outlining, or as a basis for more complex stitches. Keep stitches an even size with smaller spaces between them.

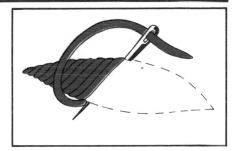

SATIN

Use for filling. Work by taking straight close stitches across the shape. Keep stitches parallel and take care not to pull thread too tight or work will pucker.

SCROLL

Use for lines and outlining. Take small slanting stitches across the line of design, twisting thread round needle as shown, before pulling tight. Work from left to right.

SPLIT

Use for lines, outlining or for filling. Using a soft thread, take small back stitches on the line of design, splitting thread with needle as shown in the design.

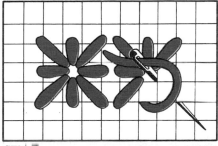

STAR

Use as a counted thread or surface stitch worked at random on design. Work eight stitches into centre hole so that a square outline is formed as shown.

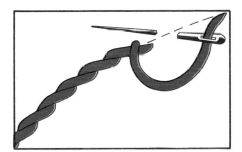

STEM

Use for lines and for outlining. Working from left to right (if righthanded), take short, slanting back stitches across design line, always keeping thread below the needle.

STRAIGHT

Use as a loose, filling stitch or work at random on design. Form by taking straight stitches in the position and direction required. Also known as stroke stitch.

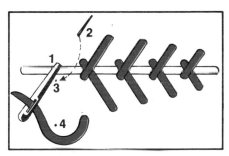

THORN

Use, as name suggests, to make thorny effects. Make a long centre stitch first, then work stitches over it, following numbered order shown in the diagram. Useful in pictorial embroidery.

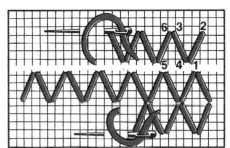

WAVE FILLING

Use this stitch for filling on both counted and drawn thread work. Work stitches in the order shown – in rows from right to left and left to right alternately, to form diamond shapes. Pull the stitches firmly.

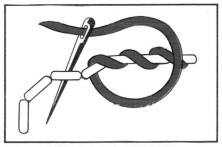

WHIPPED BACK STITCH

Use for lines. Work a row of back stitch and then, in contrasting thread, work over stitches as shown. To avoid penetrating fabric or splitting thread, use a round ended needle or bodkin. Note: wrapping stitch does not enter fabric.

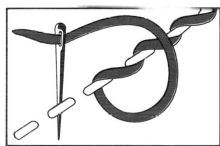

WHIPPED RUNNING

Use for lines. Work a row of running stitch and then, in contrasting thread, work over it as shown. To avoid penetrating fabric or splitting thread, use a round ended needle or bodkin. Note: wrapping stitch does not enter fabric.

Gloves

MATERIALS
Woollen gloves
Oddments of knitting yarn
Crewel needle
Cardboard, scissors
Pencil

WORKING
Place a glove flat on the cardboard and draw round it with the pencil.
☐ Cut out cardboard and insert the hand shape in one of the gloves.
☐ Work the embroidery, using the photograph on page 158 as a general guide for positioning. There is no need to be precise. Use the following stitches – all of which are diagrammed in the Stitch Library – and take care not to pull the stitches too tight. Work the flowers first in 'lazy daisy', or chain stitch, with French knots in the centres. Stitch the wavy stems in backstitch.
☐ Repeat embroidery on other glove.

Denim Pockets

MATERIALS
Stranded embroidery cotton: light green, dark green, brown, red, yellow, turquoise, blue.
Tissue paper
Sewing cotton
Tailor's chalk

WORKING
Trace the design from the photograph on page 159 to the tissue paper, and transfer to fabric, as described in the introduction to the chapter. It is not necessary to mark the position of every French knot as these can be judged with the eye.
☐ Using six strands of embroidery cotton for a bold line, and three strands of cotton for a thinner line of stitching, work the design following the stitch guide on the left.

Tunic

MATERIALS
Tunic: for fabric requirements, pattern and instructions for making up, peasant-style shirt in the Sewing Chapter.
Stranded embroidery cotton: five skeins each of white and two shades of green.
Crewel needle
Tailor's chalk, ruler

WORKING
Cut out the tunic, following Sewing chapter recipe.
☐ Mark the required position of the embroidery by

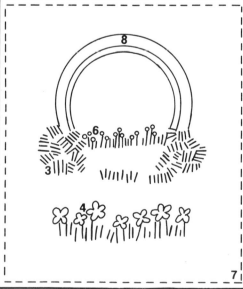

Paul Williams

| The chart shows which stitches are used to create each of the denim designs. All are diagrammed in the Stitch Library. | 1. Buttonhole/blanket stitch 2. Back stitch 3. Straight stitch 4. Daisy stitch | 5. Stem stitch 6. French knots 7. Running stitch 8. Chain stitch |

marking vertical lines with the chalk. In the version shown, the total width of the embroidered panel on the front is 21cm (8½"). The green 'stripes' are 2.5cm (1") wide and the white 'stripes' are 2.5cm (1") wide. The design is slightly narrower on the collar and cuffs.

□ Use all six strands of cotton in the needle and work along each row, spacing the stitches by eye.

□ Work the white stitches in herringbone and the 'stars' in star stitch or in two cross stitches, one on top of the other.

□ The green and white design is worked in whipped backstitch. All stitches are diagrammed in the Stitch Library.

□ When embroidery has been completed, press lightly on wrong side, then make up tunic according to instructions given previously.

Sampler

The details of the sampler on pages 164 and 165 are shown in full size and the house design can be traced directly from the photograph.

The cross stitch alphabet is given here on a graph, so that letters can be rearranged to spell out a motto, if desired.

MATERIALS
Stranded embroidery cotton in four shades of green, three of brown, two of yellow, three of pink, two of red, plus blue and orange.
Evenweave linen or linen-type cloth, or wool
Crewel needle
Tissue paper

WORKING
Transfer the house design, using the tissue paper method described in the chapter introduction.

□ Work the stitches, following the stitch guide. All stitches are diagrammed in the Stitch Library.

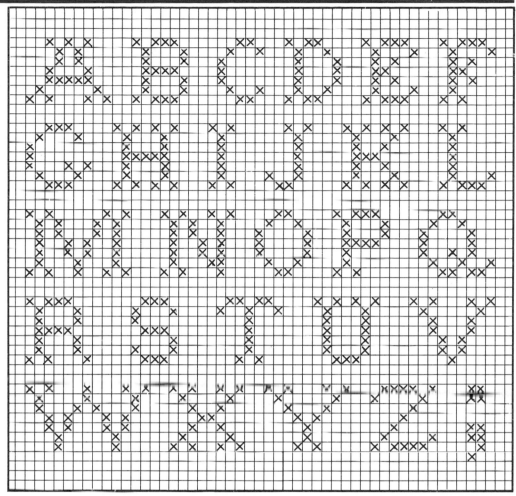

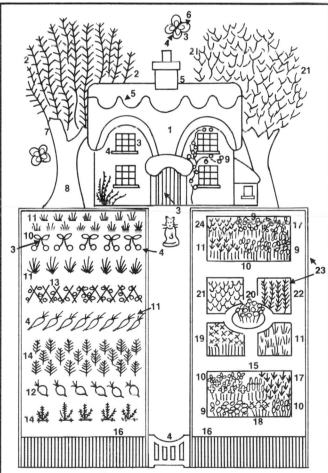

Above: counted cross stitch for alphabet.

Below: guide to stitches used to work sampler.

1. Long and short stitch
2. Fern stitch
3. Back stitch
4. Satin stitch
5. Stem stitch
6. Several straight stitches, couched
7. Scroll
8. Running stitch
9. French knots
10. Detached chain stitch
11. Straight stitch
12. Satin stitch with straight stitch leaves
13. Herringbone with detached chain stitch leaves
14. Thorn stitch
15. Bullion stitch
16. Chain stitch
17. Detached chain stitch held down with 3 straight stitches
18. Cross stitch
19. Cross stitch and straight stitch
20. French knots and straight stitches
21. Feather stitch
22. Fern stitch
23. Fly stitch

Embroidered Picture

Pictorial embroidery has a long tradition and the example on pages 166 and 167 illustrates how it can be used in combination with dyes and simple stitchery to make a modern, 'primitive' portrait.

The picture was inspired by a photograph. The outlines were retained but the details have been simplified. Note how the various stitches create a textural, as well as a visual pattern throughout. The finished size of the picture is 84×61cm (2'9"×2'), but this can be modified.

MATERIALS
Welsh flannel and calico (for backing), 15cm (6") larger than required size.
Fabric dyes (such as Dylon Color-fun) in red, yellow, green, black and blue, brown and purple.
Pearl embroidery thread in pink, red, yellow, white, black, blue, lilac and four shades of green.
Frame
Tissue papers and tracing paper, the size of picture
Tailor's chalk
Artist's brushes
Needle

WORKING
Trace the design from the photograph and enlarge to required size, following directions at the back of the book.
☐ Trace the outlines of the couple and the objects on the flannel (the stitched patterns will be added later).
☐ Following dye manufacturer's instructions, paint the flannel, covering the broad areas with solid, unshaded colour (dilute or mix colour as appropriate).
☐ When the dye has dried, iron the fabric to fix colour.
☐ Using tailor's chalk to mark the lines, sketch in the linear patterns. For more detailed patterns, use the tissue paper method described in the introduction to the chapter.
☐ Baste calico backing to the flannel back and mount cloth on a frame, when working.
☐ Work the embroidery following the stitch guide given below.

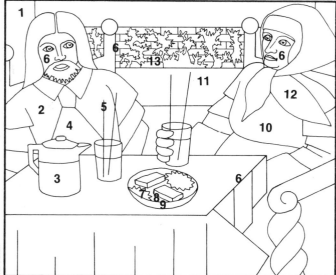

Coral Mula

Work embroidery as indicated. Large simple stitches are used to work the picture. The numbers indicate stitch positions. The shapes are outlined in split stitch which is also used to fill the faces. Feather stitch and French knots form the pattern on the woman's dress, while the man's shirt is French knots and split stitch.

1. Buttonhole/blanket stitch; 2. Split with French knots; 3. Star stitch with fern; 4. Fern; 5. Couching; 6. Split stitch; 7. French knots; 8. Fly stitch; 9. Star stitch; 10. Feather stitch with French knots; 11. Straight with cross stitch; 12. Cross with split; 13. Daisy with French knots.

Tree-of-Life Cushion

Size: the finished dimensions of the cushion cover are 44×86cm (17½"×34").

MATERIALS
Evenweave linen, or linen type fabric, 90×100cm double (36"×40"), plus 20cm (8") for piping
Crewel wool in four shades

The cushion is worked predominantly in long and short stitch and satin stitch (leaves, flowers, acorns), with stem stitch for stems and outlining. Numbers indicate main positions and other stitches.

1. Long and short stitch (shaded on leaves).
2. French knots both spaced and clustered.
3. Stem stitch. Main plant, stems and round leaves to form outer edges.
4. Buttonhole/blanket stitch.

5. Satin stitch on small buds, also variation over stitched acorns with back stitch.
6. Couching.
7. Portuguese stem stitch.
8. Jacobean couching with variations. Satin stitch over stitched with crossbars; decorated in spaces with French knots, cross stitch and satin stitch.
9. Back stitch worked in zigzag lines, separated by lines of stem stitch.
10. Star stitch.

of brown, blue and pink; five shades of green and one shade of grey and buff.
Crewel needles
Tissue paper
3m (3yd) piping cord (optional)

Frame, tailor's chalk
Cushion pad, or terylene stuffing

WORKING
Cut out the fabric and baste the outlines of the design, using the tissue paper method described in the chapter introduction. For the filling stitches within sections of the design, it is in some cases easier to use tailor's chalk to mark guidelines as you work.
☐ Stitch the pattern using the stitch guide opposite. All stitches are diagrammed in the Stitch Library.
☐ Make up the cover as described on page 32.

One square = 2.5cm (1″) sq.

House Motif Cushion

MATERIALS
50cm (½yd) evenweave fabric, such as linen or fine woollen fabric, 90cm (36″) wide.
Cushion pad 40cm (16″) square
Crewel wool: 1 skein each of blue in two shades; red; brown in three shades; green in three shades.
Crewel needle
Tacking cotton
Tissue paper
Graph or squared paper

MAKING
Trace the enlarged design on tissue paper. (For instructions on enlarging designs, see section at the end of the book.)

☐ Cut the evenweave fabric into two pieces 45cm×45cm (18″×18″), to form the back and front of the cushion cover, plus turnings.

☐ On one piece, pin and baste the tissue paper with the enlarged design so that the edge of the design is parallel to the straight grain of the fabric, leaving a border of fabric around each side of the design.

☐ Baste with medium-sized running stitches along all the design lines, through both the tissue paper and the fabric. Then carefully tear away all the paper leaving the stitched outline of the design intact.

☐ Using the stitch plan opposite, work the embroidery. Use short lengths of wool, as friction during stitching will cause the wool to wear thin. When whipping the running stitches, use two lengths of wool at a time to give a bolder line. Use the lines of the fabric as guides when stitching straight lines.

Take care not to pull the stitching too tight when working embroidery freely in the hand, otherwise puckering will occur and the overall shape of the fabric will become distorted.

☐ When all the embroidery

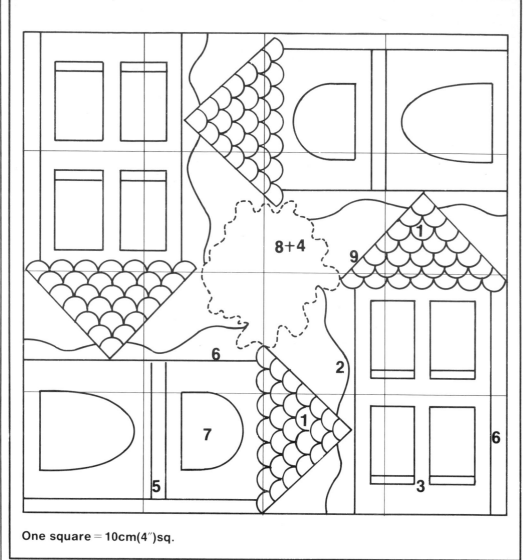

One square = 10cm(4″)sq.

The house design can be enlarged using graph lines or using a ruler to mark the outline of each house. The stitches which are used are numbered to show their placement

in the design.
1. Blanket/buttonhole
2. Chain stitch
3. Cross stitch
4. French knots

5. Fly stitch
6. Herringbone stitch
7. Jacobean couching
8. Straight stitch
9. Whipped running stitch

is complete, remove all the basted lines except those which represent the seam lines.

☐ Press on the wrong side, using a damp cloth, and carefully easing out any slight puckering which may have occurred.

☐ Make up the cushion cover in the usual way (see page 32).

Cut Work Blind

MATERIALS
Firmly-woven fabric such as linen, or linen types, the required size of blind.

Pearl embroidery cotton in four shades of rose pink, three shades of orange/yellow, two shades of green, one shade of lilac.
Hoop frame
Crewel needle
Bias binding for scalloped edge

WORKING
Trace the motif opposite and transfer to fabric, repeating as required to fit the width of the blind, and leaving room along the bottom edge for scallops. Reverse every other motif.

☐ Draw the scallops using a side plate or dessert plate to give a curved line.

☐ Work two rows of running

stitch between the double lines of the design.

☐ On the shapes to be cut out, slash the fabric at intervals from the centre of the shape to the edge.

☐ Work round the edge in Hedebo buttonhole stitch, turning the fabric to the wrong side with the needle as you progress (fig.1.)

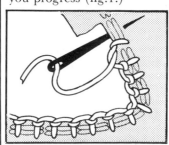

1. Turn fabric to wrong side.

184

□ As you complete the shape, cut away the excess fabric from the wrong side.
□ Work two rows round the other shapes in the same stitch, placing the second row so that the looped edge is on the opposite side from the first row (fig.2).

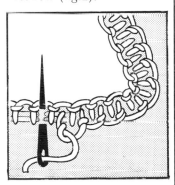

2. Work second row over first.

□ Work a second row round the cut edges.
□ To work the fillings of cut shapes, mount the fabric in a frame and work round in rows of Hedebo buttonhole stitch, placing the stitches in the loops of the previous row (fig.3). Keep the work flat by

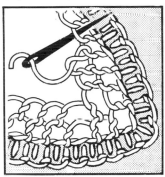

3. Making lacy filling stitch.

omitting stitches at even intervals in each row.
□ Cut out the scallops and finish with bias binding (fig.4).

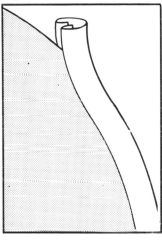

4. Stitch bias binding to edge.

Dolls

Size: the height of each doll is 38cm (15″).

MATERIALS (for one doll)
Light-weight, stretchy fabric such as cotton jersey, 40cm (16″) square
Matching thread
Black sewing thread
Terylene stuffing
Embroidery frame (optional)
Carbon paper, pencil

WORKING
The patterns are made using the photographs on pages 175 and 176. Trace the designs for the front and back of the doll, then transfer to the fabric. (A special section at the back of the book explains how to enlarge designs.)
□ Using a regular stitch on your machine, stitch along the solid lines of the design. Alternatively, drop the machine feed, mount the fabric in a frame and work the design by free machine stitching (it may be easier to do the curves this way), but remember to work with the fabric right side up.
□ Cut out, leaving a seam turning of 1cm (⅜″) from the dotted lines of the design.
□ Place halves of the doll together, with right sides facing, and stitch along the dotted lines, leaving an opening at the side.
□ Turn right side out through the opening, stuff the doll firmly, legs first, and sew up the opening by hand.

Consultant:
Lindsay Vernon
Designers:
Gloves, cami-knickers, bed linen and tunic embroidery are by Catherine Kay. Sampler stitches by Catherine Kay after a design by Jannat Houston; denim pocket motifs, crewel house cushion and mat by Jane Iles; embroidered picture by Julia Sorrell; dolls by Margaret Smitten.

RUG MAKING

The various methods of making rugs, using different materials and ways of binding them together, are a tribute to the ingenuity of man. Rugs can be braided, knotted, hooked, woven, knitted, crocheted and stitched. Rug materials range from grass to pure silk, embodying enormous textural and pattern-making possibilities. This chapter explains some of the simplest and most straightforward forms of home rug-making, and examples can also be found in the Needlepoint and Crochet chapters.

BRAIDING

This is a very old method of making rugs from rags. The rags are cut into strips, folded and then braided together. The braid is coiled into the required shape and laced to hold it together.

MATERIALS

The most hard-wearing braided rugs are made from woollen rags, but most types of fabric can be used. For uniform wear, however, it is advisable to use the same type of rags throughout.

For stitching the rug together, you will need a bodkin (a large, flat needle),

and some carpet thread. As a general guide, allow about 1m (40″) of fabric 137cm (54″) wide for an area 30cm (12″) square.

METHOD

Preparing strips. Cut or tear the fabric on the straight grain into strips about 4cm (1½″) wide. (If you are using some fabrics which are lighter in weight than others, cut them into strips 5.5cm (2¼″) wide.)

Prepare 4cm (1¼″) strips by folding the long raw edges to the centre, and then in half, lengthwise, to enclose the raw edges completely (fig.1).

To make strands of similar bulk and width with 5.5cm (2¼″) strips, fold them in three, and then in half, lengthwise (fig.2).

Roll the strips up on card and secure with pins. It will be easier to braid them this way, unwinding as you work.

Braiding. To begin braiding, seam the ends of two strands together on the bias (fig.3). Re-fold and lay the join flat with open side facing down, and insert the end of the third strip (fig.4). Oversew in place.

Turn the strands so that they are all hanging down and tie the joined end to a door handle or table leg.

Start braiding in the conventional way (fig.5). To keep the braid compact and

firm, pull the strands firmly sideways, not down, and take care not to twist the strands.

Joining new lengths. Avoid making joins in more than one strip at the same place or the braid will be lumpy. Join on the bias as shown in fig.3.

Lacing. When you have braided several metres (yards), you can start coiling, and lacing them together. Work on a flat surface – the table or floor.

Oval rugs. Decide the width and length of the oval and lay the braid flat for the *difference* between the measurements. Loop braid back for the same amount, keeping it flat, and begin lacing the two lengths together (fig.6). Coil the braid round this centre strip, or core, and continue lacing. To keep the rug flat, omit lacing a few of the loops on the curves of the outside coils.

Round rugs. Coil the braid round and round, lacing as you progress. To keep the rug flat, miss lacing loops on the outside coils at regular intervals.

Finishing off. Trim the ends of the strands to different lengths and taper each one. Turn in the edges and slip-stitch with matching thread. Continue braiding and coiling as far as possible. Sew the shortest strand under its neighbour and wrap this one with the remaining one; work the ends into the rug and sew neatly in place.

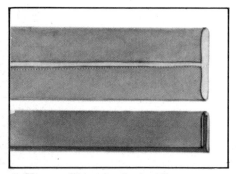
1. How to fold strips for braiding.

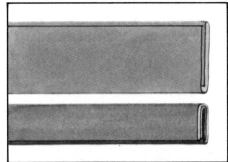
2. Folding method for wider strips.

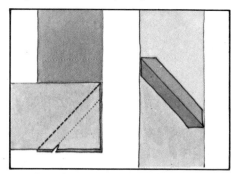
3. Join strips on the bias as shown.

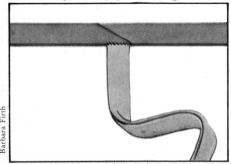
4. Start braids by joining three strips.

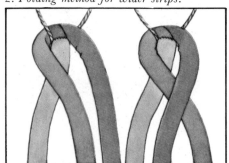
5. Braid strips in the conventional way.

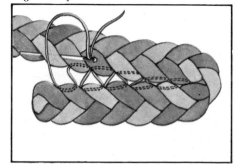
6. Lace braid together with a flat needle.

HOOKING

This is an old country method of making a rag rug by hooking strips of rag through hessian, in loops, to form a pile. Originally sacks were used as the backing but today hessian (burlap), bought by the piece, forms a more usual base.

MATERIALS

Rags. Use similar kinds of rags to those used for braided rugs, already described, and allow about 50g (2oz) per 12cm (5″) square.

Hook. You will also need a rug hook which has a steel barb so that the strips can be hooked through hessian easily.

Frame. A frame is necessary in order to provide a taut surface for the stabbing action of the hook. A needlepoint frame (fig. 1) which enables the rug to be rolled up as it is worked, is advisable but an improvised rectangular frame could also be used for a small rug.

Hessian (burlap) can be bought in furnishing or upholstery shops, and some craft shops. Choose a width suitable to the rug or wall-hanging you are making and allow 10cm (4″) all round for turnings.

If you are hooking a *rug* then it is advisable to back it with another piece of hessian of the same size.

Linen carpet thread and a carpet needle are needed to turn under the edges of the hessian.

METHOD

Trace the design, enlarge to size and transfer it to the hessian. (See instructions at the back of the book for tracing and enlarging.) Then, mount the hessian on a frame.

Cut the rags into strips on the straight grain 15mm (½″) wide and as long as possible.

To hook the strips into the hessian, loop the end of one strip over for about 2.5cm (1″) and hold it underneath the hessian in the appropriate area of the design.

Detail of a painting by Seurat which was the inspiration for rug opposite.

Poke the hook through the hessian from the top, insert it through the loop (fig.2) and draw up the loop through the hessian for about 15mm (½″).

Still holding the strip below the hessian, poke the hook through, about 5mm (¼″) from the first loop, and pull through a second loop to the same height (fig.3).

Continue like this until the shape is filled with loops of colour, blending shades on the background to produce a subtle effect. Work all areas in the same way, using solid colour on the definite parts of the design, such as the figure shown here.

To finish the rug, remove from the frame and fold the turnings to the wrong side. Then fold under the turnings on the second piece of hessian and oversew to the rug with wrong sides together.

Bath mat. The design opposite comes from the painting above. It is transferred by projecting a transparency of the painting on to hessian (burlap). (This method is described at the end of the book and coloured slides of the painting are available from The National Gallery, London.) The flecked effect produced by the rags cleverly suggests the 'pointillistic' technique of the painting. The mat is made following the hooking method described here.

Barbara Firth

1. A needlepoint frame is recommended.

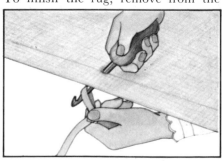

2. Hook the rag from underneath.

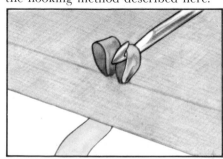

3. Draw loops through hessian (burlap).

188

LATCHET HOOKING

Many rugs are traditionally made by weaving an open mesh canvas and then knotting bits of wool on it to make a pile. It is a laborious process, but the results are incredibly fine, and rightly famous. The most notable examples are Oriental.

Latchet-hooking is a highly simplified way of making a knotted, pile rug. The action of the hook knots the yarn on the weft (horizontal threads) of the rug canvas.

The most popular form of latchet-hooked rugs is the rya rug. Rya (pronounced reeah) is Finnish for shaggy and originally referred to rugs with lengths of unspun sheep's wool knotted on a mesh. Like their prototypes, modern rya rugs are also characterized by a long pile and because of its length, every meshed row in the canvas does not need covering.

MATERIALS

Canvas. Special canvas is sold for rya rugs. The mesh has 10 knots to 7.5cm (3"), on each horizontal row, but only five rows of knots vertically. This is because, on rya canvas, every row is not open mesh (see photograph). Rya canvas is obtainable in several widths. When buying, allow 10cm (4") for turnings of 5cm (2") at each end.

Standard rug canvas can also be used for rya rugs, and the knots worked on alternate weft rows only.

Latchet hook. This looks like a crochet hook but has a wooden handle and a hinged latchet which closes the hook to prevent it from being caught in the canvas.

Wool. Two-ply woollen yarn suitable for rya rugs is sold in packs containing 168 pre-cut pieces, 18cm (7") long. Three lengths are used in each knot, so one pack covers slightly more than 7.5cm (3") square.

Turkey rug wool, which is sold in skeins, can also be used for latch-hooking, and the pile cut to the desired length.

METHOD

Leaving 5cm (2") for turnings at each end, mark the pattern on the canvas, then fold up the nearest end so that the holes in the turning match those in the canvas underneath.

Using three strands of yarn for each knot, insert the pile in the first weft row, through the edge of the double canvas, starting at the left-hand side and working to the right.

Figs.1—4 show how to make the knot. As each knot is made, pull the ends of the pile tightly to secure it.

Continue this process, working rows of knots, and following the pattern, until 15cm (6") from the end; then fold up the turning and work the last rows of knots through the double canvas, as at the beginning.

Geometric rug. The bold, geometric design shown opposite is copied from a 19th century patchwork quilt made by the Amish, an American religious sect. The rug measures 115cm (45") square and requires rya canvas of that width, 125cm (50") long. 207 packs of cut, rya yarn is also needed in the amounts per colour listed in fig.5.

Rya rug canvas (left) and ordinary rug canvas (right), plus wool and hook.

The rug is worked as described previously, using three strands per knot — one strand in one shade and two strands in another, to give a subtly, mottled effect. The pattern can be drawn on the canvas using a ruler and pencil, or felt tipped pen.

The geometric pattern used in the latchet-hooked rug opposite is based on a 19th century American patchwork quilt. Each of the knots consists of three strands of yarn and two different shades.

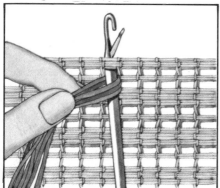

1. Insert latchet hook as shown.

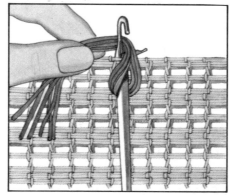

2. Put yarn into open hook.

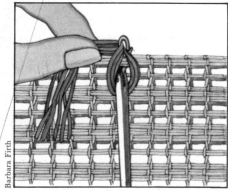

3. Draw hook back through hole.

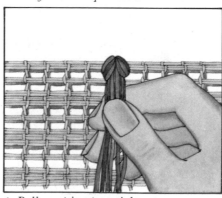

4. Pull resulting knot tight.

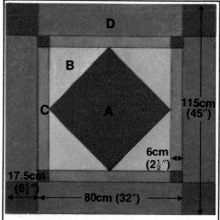

Quantities of rya packs needed:
39 scarlet, 20 tomato
23 turquoise, 12 sky blue
29 royal blue, 58 medium blue
9 jade green, 17 pale jade

Colours used in each area and number of threads per knot:
A = 2 scarlet, 1 tomato
B = 2 turquoise, 1 sky blue
C = 2 pale jade, 1 jade
D = 2 medium blue, 1 royal

5. Colour and yarn chart for rug.

Barbara Firth

UNIT WEAVING

These are rugs with a woollen pile on a mesh base, made in units 20cm (8″) square. The base is jute string darned on a rectangle of nails, and luxurious pile is produced by latchet-hooking lengths of wool into it. The squares are then laced together. Advantages of making rugs in unit form are that each square is a convenient size and not too heavy for a lap. Also, it is possible for several people to work on squares at a time.

MATERIALS
The pile may be made from strips of woollen cloth, tapestry wool or two-ply rug wool. Allow approximately 200gm (8oz) per square.
Mesh. Four-ply twisted jute string is needed for the base – allow 100gm (4oz) per square and work with six strands, or balls of string.
A frame on which to darn the base mesh can be made from a square of blockboard or chipboard 2cm (¾″) thick, and 25cm (10″) square. 48 oval nails, 4cm (4½″) long are also needed, plus a hammer.
Miscellaneous. A packing needle for darning the base and a latchet rug hook for knotting the pile on the base are necessary.

METHOD
Making the frame. Mark a 23cm (9″) square on the board and hammer nails in so that they are vertical and protruding about half their depth at 2cm (¾″) intervals round the square (fig.1).
The mesh base. Using a strand of string from each of six balls, attach the ends to one corner nail with a temporary knot and leave a tail of 23cm (9″). Wind the strands backwards and forwards around the nails to form the warp (fig.2). Measure an extra 3m (10′) and then cut off. Thread the packing needle and darn in and out of warp threads to form the weft (fig.3). When complete, undo the temporary knot at the beginning, divide the threads in two and darn along the edge in each direction (fig.4). Cut off and

repeat with the end tails, then slip the square off the nails.
The pile. Cut the yarn into pieces, 30cm (12″) long with 10 strands per knot. Tie the knots round the junctions of warp and weft as shown in fig.5, working in rows from right to left and left to right alternately, to keep the square shape. The square will become firmer as you progress.
Lacing squares together. Place the completed squares, pile-side down, and lace together, as for braided rugs, using three strands of jute, (fig.6).
For large areas it is easier if you make two 'rugs' and lay them side by side – the join is covered by the pile.

1. Making the 'loom' frame.

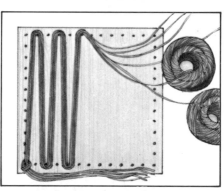
2. Creating the base warp.

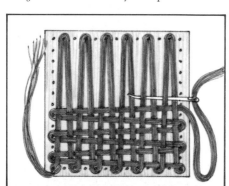
3. Creating the weft on the frame.

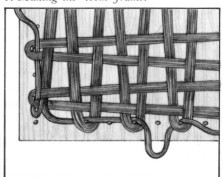
4. Darning edges of the base.

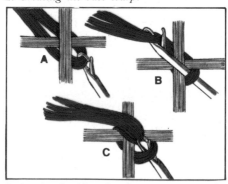
5. Latchet-hooking the pile on the base.

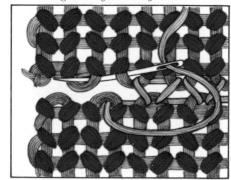
6. Lacing the squares together.

Barbara Firth

192

Brilliantly coloured
squares and a rich, deep
pile characterize this splendid
rug. The squares are made separately
by an easy method of weaving and the
pile is hooked on to them. Finally, all
the squares are laced together. For a different, or more subdued feeling, use
contrasting shades of one colour
such as brown, or use one
colour throughout.
Design by Ann Sutton

CROCHET

Crochet is a way of constructing fabric by making chains of loops with a hook, fig. a. Each new row (or round) is worked into the previous one, fig. b – and so the fabric builds up, fig. c.

There are only half a dozen crochet stitches and they differ from one another in two ways: the number of times (if any) that yarn is wound round the hook before it is inserted in the previous row (or round), and the number of loops the hook is drawn through at a time. Diagrams of the stitches appear on pages 212 and 213. Unfortunately, the names of crochet stitches in Britain and America cause considerable confusion because the same names are used in both countries, but they refer to *different* stitches. To avoid mistakes, therefore, two separate sets of instructions are given in this chapter for most of the patterns.

MATERIALS

Traditionally, crochet emulated the fine laces of the Middle Ages, and minute and intricate designs were worked with minuscule hooks and very fine cottons. Nowadays, a vast number of materials is used and most of them can be worked relatively quickly.

Yarns. The most popular crochet material is knitting yarn and most knitting yarns on the market are suitable for crochet. Other materials such as raffia, macramé twine and various threads can also be used successfully, depending on the desired result. For example, a kitchen table mat made from parcel string is more practical than one made from wool. As long as the yarn is pliable, it is usable.

When working from a pattern, always try to buy the type of yarn recommended. If a substitute must be made, choose a yarn of similar thickness and test tension (gauge) before you begin.

Hooks. The only tool needed for crochet is a hook. This consists of a shaft with a hooked end which enables you to draw yarn through the looped stitches. The diameter of the shaft determines the size of the stitch and hook sizes are graded according to shaft diameters. But all crochet hooks are similar in shape and length because, unlike knitting, there is seldom more than one loop on the hook. A list of hook sizes appears in the Gen-

eral Guide on page 211 but, as a rule, the size of the hook relates to the quality of the yarn you are using; a large hook is needed for thick yarn and a small hook for fine yarn. However, you can get fascinating results by experimenting with yarn and different hooks.

TENSION (GAUGE)

This means the number of stitches and rows per centimetre, inch or given measurement obtainable with a particular yarn and hook size. When working from a pattern it is vital to use the

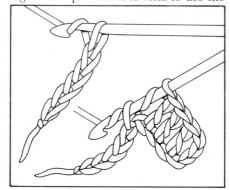

a. Looped chains are the basis of crochet.

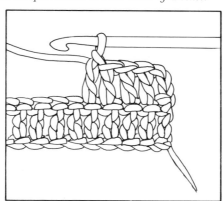

b. New loops are attached to previous rows.

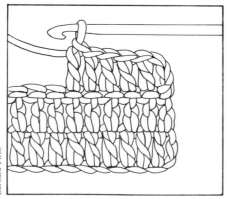

c. The looped chains build up into fabric.

tension (gauge) stated or the finished item will not be the correct size.

Always check tension (gauge) by working a test sample using the correct yarn and needle size before beginning work on any pattern. Work a 10cm (4″) square: if you have too few stitches and rows to the centimetre (inch), then your tension (gauge) is too loose and you should try one size smaller hook. Too many stitches and rows in the sample mean that your tension (gauge) is too tight and you need a larger hook. Change the hook as often as necessary, as long as the end result is the same tension (gauge) as specified.

Take into account that tension (gauge) will vary according to how relaxed you are as you work; reassess your work frequently to see that it is not becoming too tight or loose.

MAKING UP

Take care in making up and finishing a crocheted garment.

Blocking. Lay the finished pieces on a padded ironing surface and shape them to the measurements given in the instructions by placing pins at frequent intervals, at right angles to the edge of the crochet. Press and allow the work to dry. When blocking synthetics, do not iron, but spray with water and allow to dry before removing pins.

Pressing. Always follow the directions given with the yarn. As a general rule, wool requires pressing under a damp cloth with a warm iron: many synthetics need no pressing or only a cool iron over a dry cloth.

Joining pieces of crochet. You can do this unobtrusively or make a decorative feature of the join; either way it must be fairly loose. If the crochet stitches are very large, you can slip stitch the pieces together using the same yarn, or matching thread if the original yarn is unsuitable. A backstitched seam is preferable if the crochet stitches are small.

On the right side of the work, use double crochet (American single crochet) to join pieces; a contrasting colour can be very effective.

The rug opposite illustrates one of the most popular of all crochet patterns, Granny squares. The technique is described in more detail overleaf; instructions are on page 214.

Barbara Firth

GRANNY SQUARES

These multi-coloured squares are based on a traditional pattern also called Old America. They are easy for a beginner to learn to crochet and a thrifty way to turn scraps of yarn into pretty patchworks. Choose a colour scheme carefully, either for a random effect or a sophisticated, planned version.

Granny squares are useful and colourful examples of working in rounds rather than rows. Initially you need to start with a circle.

Making a circle. Start with a short length of chain (described in the General Guide). Join the chain to form a circle by slip stitching into first chain worked. Work stitches in the first round actually into the centre of the circle. Remember, you still need 'turning chains' to represent the first stitch. (These are also explained in the General Guide.) On completion of a round, join the last stitch to the first with a slip stitch. Different shapes form out of this basic circle according to the position of increased stitches on subsequent rounds.

Making a square. Granny squares comprise blocks of stitches with chain spaces between. The first round has four blocks – one for each side of the square; and four spaces – one for each corner. On each round you increase four blocks by working two blocks separated by a space, into each corner.

The blanket shown on the previous page is a random selection of colours. A black border on each square has a dramatic effect.

The woman's jacket is a simple, buttoned cover-up based on a T-square design. It has a drawstring tie at the waist threaded through a panel of double crochet (American single crochet). Outer edgings match the borders round each square.

The child's poncho has squares in alternating colours with a twisted cord tie at the neck.

The bag consists of 18 squares crocheted together on the right side for an unusual ridged effect. The handle is a plait of the different coloured strands of yarn.

More detailed instruction for the Granny square designs begin on page 214.

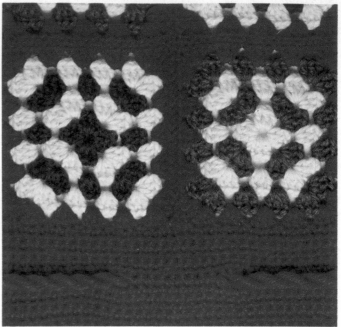

ON
THE BEACH

These cool, cotton beach
tops are made in crochet fabrics
constructed by repeating one simple
stitch throughout the pattern.
Instructions on pages 215–217

CROCHET LACE

There are a number of forms of crochet lace of which filet is the most popular. Filet work consists of a mesh background made by joining trebles (American double crochet) with chain stitches. Patterns are formed by blocking in the spaces with stitches corresponding in number to the chain separating them. Traditionally, designs were in very fine cotton for delicate lace curtains, tablecloths and edgings.

The beautiful filet crochet edging seen here surrounds a tablecloth in drawn thread work (a technique described in the Embroidery chapter). Similar to a lot of filet work, it is a geometrically-based design featuring diamonds positioned to create a scalloped edge. Work the edging separately in rows along the width of the design, then sew it on the tablecloth when it is complete.

Instructions for edging on page 218

Crochet is an excellent medium for making many different trimmings, borders and edgings. Lace patterns are especially popular and these range from simple openwork stitches which give a lacy look (such as the mesh designs of filet crochet described on the previous page) to the intricate, painstaking motifs and backgrounds which are typical of traditional Irish crochet.

Many lacy designs feature the 'shell' which is a group of stitches, variable in number, all worked into the same place in the previous row. Stitches before and after the shell act as anchors to make the group of stitches fan out to give its distinctive appearance. Other simple backgrounds comprise arch stitches – see the collar, cuffs and garter on these pages – which are various arrangements of chain stitches. Often patterns are enhanced with picots: these are another characteristic of lace in which a small loop of chain stitches, either within a mesh background or embellishing the outer edge of a border, give a cob-web effect.

Instructions for the petticoat, edging, collar, cuffs and garter are on pages 218 and 219.

John Carter

Crochet lace originally developed as an imitation of fine bobbin lace and the art of making it reached its peak in Ireland in the 19th century. At its most elaborate, it is worked in very fine cotton using delicate steel hooks; but less finely wrought work, using larger needles and coarser cotton which can be worked more quickly and easily, has outdistanced traditional forms in popularity.

But crochet edgings need not be confined to lace, as the cherry edging below proves. Following the basic stitches of the pattern the motif can be worked to any length and used to ornament clothing as an alternative to shelves. *Instructions are on page 219.*

CROCHETING RAGS

Clothes are not the only use to which crochet fabric can be put; and wool and cotton yarn are not the only materials which can be used. Both these points are amply illustrated by the rag rugs shown. The economic attraction of crocheting rags is obvious and the recycling potential will be satisfying to many. Bear in mind that the type of fabric you choose will affect the feel and wearability of the finished rug. Cotton fabrics are hard-wearing, silky ones more glamorous; but one type should be used throughout the design. The type of design may be dictated by the availability of a good supply of rags, but in any case, rag rug making consumes a great deal of fabric. You also need a very large crochet hook, a No. 5.00 (H–8 American) at least. Its size depends on the rags used. For very thick fabrics, try making your own hook from a stick of wood or large twig. Tear rags into strips about 2cm to 2.5cm (⅝″–1″) wide. Join strips using method described in the Rug Making chapter (braided rugs), or use a reef knot to keep joins flat. An accurate guide to tension is impossible as this depends on the thickness of the materials. Each square is 75cm (30″). Instructions and materials for a three-square rug (as above) appear on page 220. Add 33% for rug opposite.

205

The rose motif coat shown here (and the falcon coat on the following page) are works of high fashion to tempt the more experienced crocheter. The design looks deceptively difficult: the style of the coat is basically very simple – a straight main section topped with sleeves and yoke worked from cuff edge to cuff edge with minimum neck shaping. The eight rose motifs (close-up in the picture below) are appliquéd on at a later stage. The coat is fastened by buttons and embroidered loops. In the main fabric, single row stripes of trebles (American double crochet) in subtle colours are emphasized with a horizontal chain effect added in a different colour. Bordering the striped sections are multi-coloured, semi-circular and shell patterns. A special lining, ironed on, ensures that the coat keeps its shape.
Instructions on page 220

Rex Bamber

206

An imposing falcon with wings out-
spread so that they form a design
on the front makes a magnificent
appliqué motif for this simple coat
shape. The motif is derived from
the ancient Egyptian god, Horus.
Only attempt this design if you are a
competent and imaginative crocheter,
as it entails working to measurements and shapes rather than the
usual detailed row-by-row directions. First you need to make a
paper pattern of the coat, according
to the dimensions given in the
instructions. Draw the falcon on
this pattern so that you have a
template to follow. The coat is in
a shell pattern fabric and the various sections of the falcon are
crocheted in simple stitches. To
keep the coat in perfect shape, use
the same iron-on lining as the rose
coat on the previous page.
Instructions on page 221

Simply striped baby
bootees and top are worked
in easy half trebles (American half
double crochet) with picot edging.
Instructions are on page 223.

Jerry Tubby

STARTING NEW ROWS

Crochet stitches vary in depth and require an extra number of chains at the beginning of each row so that the hook is at the correct height for the stitch being used. These extra chains are 'turning chains'; the chart indicates how many you require for the stitch you are using. American stitches are in italics.

TYPE OF STITCH	CHAINS
Double	1
Single	
Half Treble	2
Half Double	
Treble	3
Double	
Double Treble	4
Treble	
Triple Treble	5
Double Treble	

Note that the turning chain forms the first stitch of a new row; work the first pattern stitch into the second stitch of the previous row, fig. 1. At

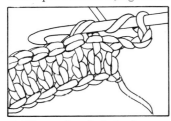

1. The turning chain is also the first stitch in a new row.

the end of a row, work the last stitch into the top of the turning chain of the previous row, fig. 2.

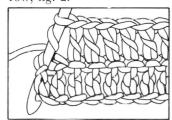

2. Work last stitch as shown.

Placing hook on subsequent rows. At the end of each row, turn your work so that the yarn is again in position at the beginning of the

row. Work the necessary number of turning chains. To work the next stitch, insert hook from front to back under top two horizontal loops of stitch in previous row, fig. 3.

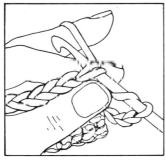

3. Beginning a new row.

SHAPING

Increasing. You must increase to widen the shape you are working. The simplest way to do this is to work twice into a stitch either at the beginning or the end of a row, or in the middle. Working twice into the first and last stitches creates an ugly edge which is difficult to seam because crochet stitches are so deep. Work the increase after the turning chains at the beginning of a row and immediately before the last stitch at the end of a row.

The instructions usually state the point at which you increase; see that in the middle of a row the increases are not on top of each other as this creates bumps in the work.

Extra chain stitches are the neatest method of increasing multiples of stitches at the beginning or end of rows.

Decreasing. This narrows the shape you are working.

The most professional method of decreasing is to work two stitches together either after the turning chains at the beginning of a row or immediately before the last stitch at the end of a row.

Work the stitch until you have two loops on the hook; insert the hook into the next stitch and work that in the same way until there are three loops on the hook. Wind the yarn round the hook and draw through all three loops so making one stitch out of the original two.

To decrease a multiple of stitches at the beginning of a row, slip stitch to the position you require. Simply turn your work at the end of a row leaving the multiple of stitches unworked.

JOINING IN NEW YARN

Loop the new yarn round the hook and draw a loop through the loop on the hook. Continue working as normal.

FASTENING OFF

Cut the yarn about 10cm (4") from your work and pull the cut end through the loop on the hook. Draw the end up tightly to secure the stitch. Use a blunt-ended wool needle to weave in the end of yarn on the wrong side of your work.

WORKING TIPS

Work from right to left if you are right-handed and left to right if you are left-handed. Always bring yarn over and

around the hook from the back.

The hook should always be inserted under the two top loops in the previous row (unless otherwise directed).

READING A PATTERN

Crochet patterns are given in abbreviated form, see list below. Asterisks (*) are used in pattern rows to show you must repeat stitches from that point. Whole sections may be marked with double or triple asterisks for reference further on in pattern.

Alternative garment sizes and number of stitches required to make them are in brackets ( ).

alt = alternate
beg = begin(ning)
ch = chain(s)
cm = centimetre(s)
cont = continu(e) (ing)
dc = double crochet
dec = decreas(e) (ing)
dtr = double treble
foll = following
gm = gram(s)
hdc = half double crochet
htr = half treble
inc = increas(e) (ing)
oz = ounce(s)
patt = pattern
rem = remain(ing)
rep = repeat
RS = right side
sc = single crochet
sp = space(s)
sl st = slip stitch
ss = slip stitch
st(s) = stitch(es)
tog = together
tr = treble
tr tr = triple treble
WS = wrong side
yrh = yarn round hook

CROCHET HOOK SIZES

												STEEL HOOKS					
METRIC	7	6·5	6	5·5	5	4·5	4	3·5	3	2·5	2	1·75	1·5	1·25	1	0·75	0·6
AMERICAN	10½ -K	10-J	9-I	0-H	8 H	6 G	5-F	4-F	3-D	2-C	1-B	8	9	10	12	13	14

CROCHET STITCHES

The basic crochet stitches are quick and easy to learn, once you understand the simple principle for making loops. The foundation chain is, as the name suggests, the basis of all stitches and, although the same stitches have differing American and British terms, the name 'foundation chain' is common to both terminologies. Many beginners have difficulty holding the yarn and hook and co-ordinating their use; with practice, these skills soon come naturally. It is even more frustrating if you are left-handed and prefer to hold the hook in the left hand and the yarn in your right. To give yourself a left-handed version of these diagrams, prop the book open in front of a mirror and study the reflection.

MAKING FOUNDATION CHAIN

Make a slip loop about 15cm (6″) from end of ball of yarn: place on hook (1) and pull to

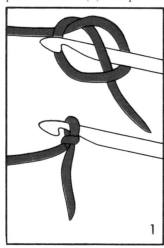

tighten it.

Hold the hook in your right hand as you would a pencil (2). If you are left-handed, remember to look at

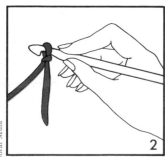

reflected version of diagrams.

Wind yarn round fingers of your left hand (3); looping yarn round the little finger helps to control flow of yarn

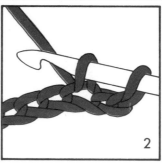

and keep your tension even. Take the hook with the slip loop in right hand and hold yarn with your left hand. Holding the slip loop between thumb and index finger, wind yarn once round hook in an anti-clockwise

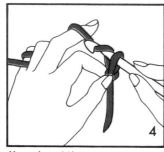

direction (4).

Draw yarn through the slip loop to make one chain (5). The working loop on hook

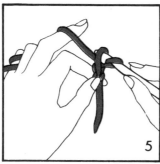

never counts as a stitch.

Make more chains, moving left hand along chain to hold stitch just made.

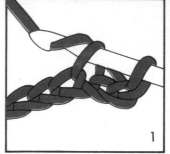

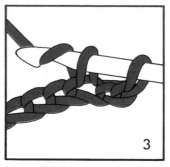

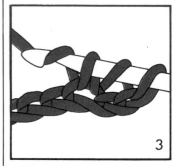

British
DOUBLE CROCHET – DC
American
SINGLE CROCHET – SC

Insert hook from front to back into third chain from hook. Wind yarn once round hook (1).

Draw yarn through chain, making two loops (2).

Wind yarn once round hook again (3); draw yarn through loops on hook (4).

One double crochet (American single crochet) is complete; only the working loop remains on the hook. Repeat these actions into each chain. Turn work so that last stitch becomes first one of next row.

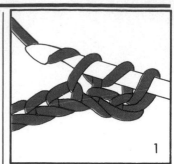

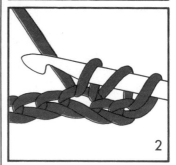

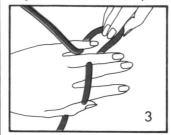

British
HALF TREBLE – IITR
American
HALF DOUBLE CROCHET – HDC

Wind yarn round hook; insert hook from front to back into third chain from hook (1). Wind yarn once round hook.

Draw yarn through chain, making three loops (2).

Wind yarn once round hook again (3); draw yarn through all three loops on hook (4).

One half treble (American half double crochet) is complete and only working loop remains on the hook. Repeat these actions into each chain.

Coral Mula

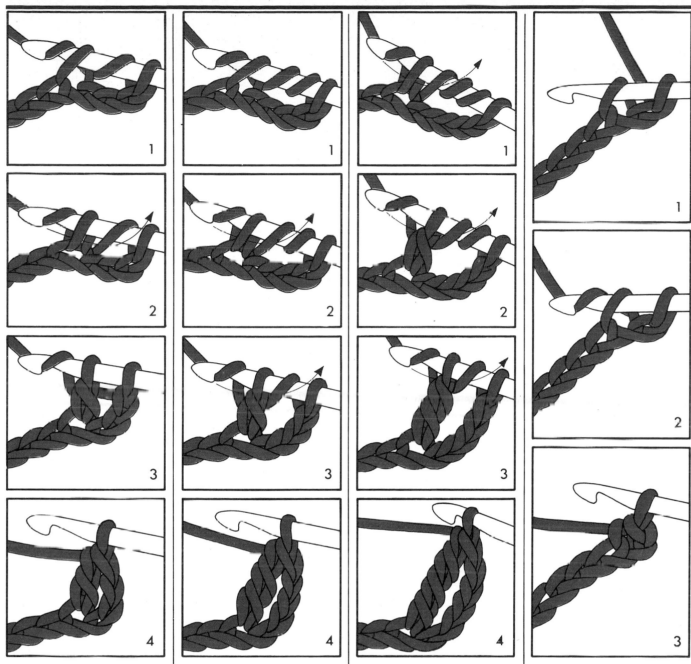

British
TREBLE – TR
American
DOUBLE CROCHET – DC

Wind yarn round the hook; insert hook from the front to the back into fourth chain from hook. Wind the yarn once round hook (1).

Draw the yarn through chain (2), making three loops on hook. Wind the yarn round hook and draw yarn through first two loops. Two loops remain on the hook. Wind yarn once round hook again (3) and draw yarn through both loops.

One treble (American double crochet) is now complete (4). Repeat into each chain.

British
DOUBLE TREBLE – DTR
American
TREBLE CROCHET – TR

Wind yarn twice round hook; insert hook from front to back into fifth chain from hook. Wind yarn once round hook (1); draw through chain, making four loops (2). Wind yarn round hook; draw through first two loops on hook, leaving three loops on hook.

Wind yarn round hook; draw through first two loops on hook (3), leaving two loops on hook.

Wind yarn round hook; draw through both loops to complete (4).

British
TRIPLE TREBLE – TR TR
American
DOUBLE TREBLE – DTR

Wind yarn three times round hook; insert into sixth chain from hook.

Wind yarn round hook (1); draw through chain to make five loops on hook. Wind yarn round hook again; draw through first two loops, leaving four loops on hook.

Wind yarn round hook; draw through first two loops. Three loops remain (2).

Wind yarn round hook; draw through first two loops (3). Two loops remain.

Wind yarn round hook; draw through both loops (4).

British
SLIP STITCH – SS
American
SLIP STITCH – SL ST

This stitch has virtually no depth and is never used for making a complete fabric. Instead it is invaluable in shaping for invisibly moving from one position to another, and for linking the last stitch in a round to the first.

Insert hook from front to back into second chain from hook (1).

Wind yarn once round the hook (2).

Draw yarn through both chain and loop on hook in one movement, leaving one loop on hook (3). This completes the stitch.

Note: American and British patterns are given separately unless the difference is minimal, in which case the American stitches appear in brackets [ ]. American hook sizes are also given in brackets.

Basic Granny Square

BRITISH PATTERN

Using any colour, make 5ch. Join with a ss to first ch to form a circle.

1st round. 3ch to count as first tr, 2tr into circle, 2ch, *3tr, 2ch, rep from * twice more. Join with a ss to 3rd of 3ch. Break off colour in use. Join next colour to any 2ch sp.

2nd round. (3ch, 2tr, 2ch, 3tr) into first 2ch sp, *1ch, (3tr, 2ch, 3tr) into next 2ch sp, rep from * twice more, 1ch. Join with a ss to 3rd of 3ch. Brcak off colour in use. Join next colour to any 2ch sp.

3rd round. (3ch, 2tr, 2ch, 3tr) into first 2ch sp, *1ch, 3tr into next 1ch sp, 1ch, (3tr, 2ch, 3tr) into 2ch sp at corner, rep from * twice more, 1ch, 3tr into next 1ch sp, 1ch. Join with a ss to 3rd of 3ch. Break off colour in use. Join next colour to any 2ch sp.

4th round. (3ch, 2tr, 2ch, 3tr) into first 2ch sp, *1ch, 3tr into next 1ch sp) twice, 1ch, (3tr, 2ch, 3tr) into 2ch sp, rep from * twice more, (1ch, 3tr into next 1ch sp) twice, 1ch. Join with a ss to

3rd of 3ch. Break off colour in use. Join next colour to any 2ch sp.

5th round. (3ch, 2tr, 2ch, 3tr) into first 2ch sp, *(1ch, 3tr into next 1ch sp) 3 times, 1ch, (3tr, 2ch, 3tr) into 2ch sp, rep from * twice more, (1ch, 3tr into next 1ch sp) 3 times, 1ch. Join with a ss to 3rd of 3ch. Break off colour in use. Join next colour to any 2ch sp.

6th round. (3ch, 2tr, 2ch, 3tr) into first 2ch sp, *(1ch, 3tr into next 1ch sp) 4 times, 1ch, (3tr, 2ch, 3tr) into 2ch sp, rep from * twice more, (1ch, 3tr into next 1ch sp) 4 times, 1ch. Join with a ss to 3rd of 3ch. Fasten off.

AMERICAN PATTERN

Using any color, make 5ch. Join with a sl st to first ch to form a circle.

1st round. 3ch to count as first dc, 2dc into circle, 2ch, *3dc, 2ch, rep from * twice more. Join with a sl st to 3rd of 3ch. Break off color in use. Join next color to any 2ch sp.

2nd round. (3ch, 2dc, 2ch, 3dc) into first 2ch sp, *1ch, (3dc, 2ch, 3dc) into next 2ch sp, rep from * twice more, 1ch. Join with a sl st to 3rd of 3ch. Break off color in use. Join next color to any 2ch sp.

3rd round. (3ch, 2dc, 2ch, 3dc) into first 2ch sp, *1ch, 3dc into next 1ch sp, 1ch, (3dc, 2ch, 3dc) into 2ch sp at corner, rep from * twice more, 1ch, 3dc into next 1ch sp, 1ch. Join with a sl st to 3rd of 3ch. Break off color in use. Join next color to any 2ch sp.

4th round. (3ch, 2dc, 2ch, 3dc) into first 2ch sp, *(1ch, 3dc into next 1ch sp) twice, 1ch, (3dc, 2ch, 3dc) into 2ch sp, rep from * twice more, (1ch, 3dc into next 1ch sp) twice, 1ch. Join with a sl st to 3rd of 3ch. Break off colour in usc. Join as before.

5th round. (3ch, 2dc, 2ch, 3dc) into first 2ch sp, *(1ch, 3dc into next 1ch sp) 3 times,

1ch, (3dc, 2ch, 3dc) into 2ch sp, rep from * twice more, (1ch, 3dc into next 1ch sp) 3 times, 1ch. Join with a sl st to 3rd of 3ch. Break off color in use. Join next color to any 2ch sp.

6th round. (3ch, 2dc, 2ch, 3dc) into first 2ch sp, *(1ch, 3dc into next 1ch sp) 4 times, 1ch, (3dc, 2ch, 3dc) into 2ch sp, rep from * twice more, (1ch, 3dc into next 1ch sp) 4 times, 1ch. Join with a sl st to 3rd of 3ch. Fasten off.

Rug

Size: 122cm (48") square

TENSION (GAUGE)

One motif measures 15cm (6") square

MATERIALS

Yarn: 250gm (9oz) of double knitting yarn in colour A; 125gm (4½oz) in each of five other colours.
No.4.00 [F-5] crochet hook

PATTERN

Follow instructions for basic granny square motif, (given previously) and work each of first five rounds in varying combinations of five different colours. Always work 6th (final) round in colour A. Make 64 squares in all. Scw squares tog on WS. Using A, work one row dc [sc] all round outer edge of blanket.

Jacket

Size: to fit 81/86cm (34/36") bust. (Make coat smaller or larger by using one size smal-

ler or larger hook.)
Length: 72cm (28")
Sleeve seam: 35cm (14")

TENSION (GAUGE)

One motif measures 10cm (4") square

MATERIALS

Yarn: 350gm (12oz) of double knitting yarn in colour A; 250gm (9oz) in colour B; 175gm (6oz) in colour C; 125gm (4½oz) in colour D.
No.3.50 [E-4] crochet hook
7 buttons

PATTERN

Follow instructions for first five rounds of basic granny square motif and make 98 squares in all – 49 in each of two colour schemes as foll:
Colour scheme 1. One round each of B, D, B, D and A.
Colour scheme 2. One round each of C, B, C, B and A.
Join top jacket and lower jacket as shown in diagram.

WAIST

Using A, work 171 dc [American sc] (17 from each square plus 1 extra) along top edge of lower jacket. Work 6 rows dc [sc].
Eyelet-hole row. 6dc [sc], *3ch, miss 3dc [sc], 9dc [sc], rep from * 12 times more, 3ch, 6dc [sc]. Work 5 more rows. Fasten off. Sew to top of jacket. Set sleeves into armholes as indicated in diagram. Join XX to XX and YY to YY to form sleeve seams.

EDGING

Work 4 rows dc [sc] all round outer edge, inc 2 sts at each outer corner on every round and dec at inner corners of neck on alt rounds, *at the same time* make buttonholes on second row as foll: 3dc [sc] into corner at neck, *2ch, miss 2dc [sc], 10dc [sc], rep from * 6 times more, work in

Coral Mula

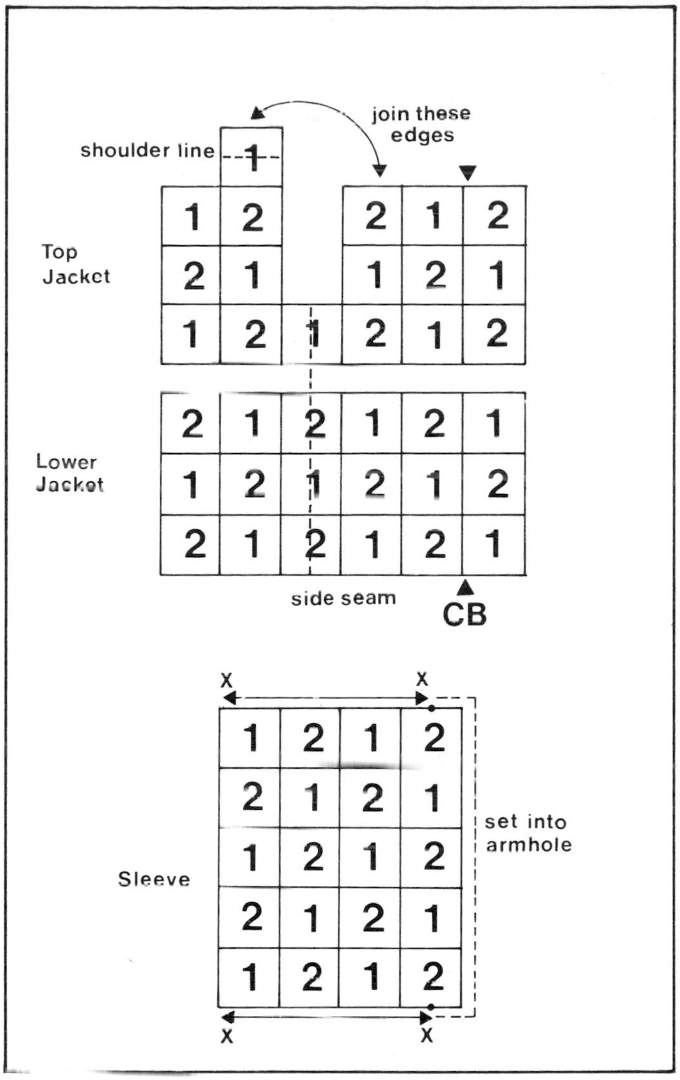
shoulder line
join these edges
Top Jacket
Lower Jacket
side seam
CB
Sleeve
set into armhole
X
X
X
X

Diagram shows how to assemble the granny square jacket.

dc [sc] to end.
Work a similar edging on sleeves.
Make a twisted cord to thread through eyelets at waist using 10 strands of yarn each approximately 450cm (178″) long.

Poncho

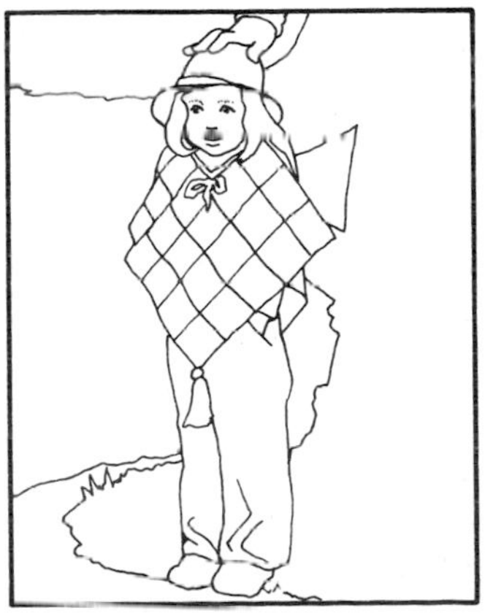

Size: length at centre front, 38cm (15″)

TENSION (GAUGE)
One motif measures 7.5cm (3″) square

Trevor Lawrence

MATERIALS
Yarn: 75gm (3oz) of double knitting yarn in each of two colours, A and B; 50gm (2oz) in colour C.
No.4.50 [G-6] crochet hook

PATTERN
Follow instructions for first three rounds of basic granny square motif and make 42 squares in all – 21 in each of two colour schemes as foll:
Colour scheme 1. One round each of C, B and A.
Colour scheme 2. One round each of C, A and B.
Join as shown in diagram, sewing XX to XX and YY to YY to form seams.

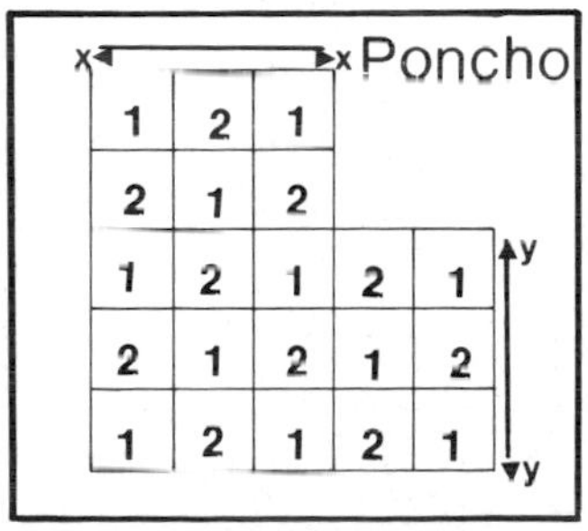
Poncho
x
x
y
y

Poncho assembly diagram.

EDGING
Using C, work 2 rows dc [sc] all round outer edge, inc 2 sts at back and front points.
Using C, work 3 rows dc [sc] round neck edge, dec 2 sts at front and back corners.
Eyelet-hole round. 1dc [sc], 1ch, all round, dec as before.
Make a twisted cord to thread through eyelets using 2 strands of each colour.
Make 2 tassels in each colour and attach 3 (1 in each colour) to front and back points.

Tote Bag

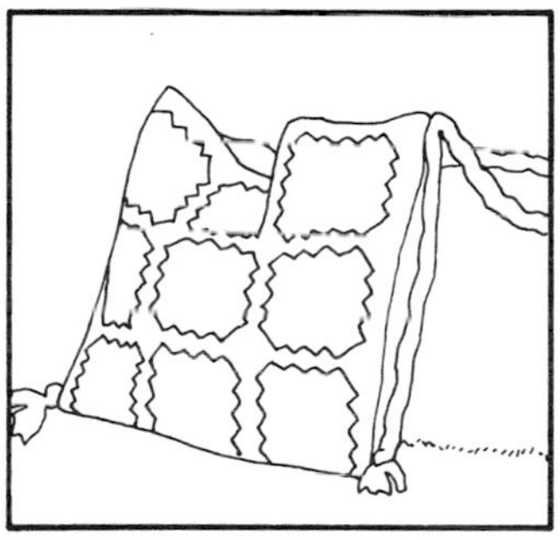

Size: 30cm (12″) square

TENSION (GAUGE)
One motif measures 10cm (4″) square

MATERIALS
Yarn: 100gm (3½oz) of double knitting yarn in colour A; 50gm (2oz) in each of two colours B and C; 25gm (1oz) in colour D.
No.3.50 [E-4] crochet hook
1 button

PATTERN
Follow instructions for first five rounds of basic granny square motif and make 18 squares in all in colour scheme as foll: one round each of A, D, B, C and A.
Using A, crochet 9 squares tog on RS to form bag back and front. Crochet lower edges tog.

GUSSET
Using A, make 54ch.
1st row. 1tr [dc] into 4th ch from hook, 1tr [dc] into each ch to end, 3tr [dc] into last ch, cont along other side of ch working 1tr [dc] into each st to end. Turn.
2nd row. 3ch, 1tr [dc] in to each tr [dc] to end, 3tr [dc] into last tr [dc], 1tr [dc] into each tr [dc] along other side, do not turn, but work in dc [sc] along top edge of gusset. Fasten off.
Crochet gusset in position along front and back side seams. Using A, work in dc [sc] round top edge, making chain button loop at centre back.

STRAP
Make plait using six strands of each colour 80cm (32″) long, leaving tassel at each end. Attach to bag, securing top of tassels to lower edge of gusset at each side. Secure plait at top of gusset. Sew on button for fastening.

Beach Sweater

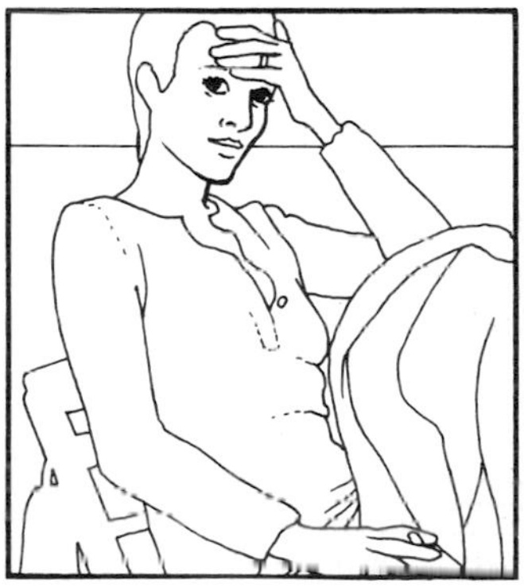

Bust: 81[86:91]cm (32[34:36]″)
Length: 66[68:70]cm (26[26¾:27¾]″)
Sleeve seam: 44[45:46]cm (17¼[17¾:18]″)
Note: The figures in brackets [ ] refer to the 2nd and 3rd sizes respectively.

TENSION (GAUGE)
14 sts and 8 rows to 10cm (4″) over tr worked on No.5.00 hook
[14 sts and 8 rows to 4″ over dc worked on Size H-8 hook]

MATERIALS
Yarn: 475[500:525]gm (17 [18:19]oz) of medium crochet cotton such as Twilleys Tutu.
No.5.00 [H-8] crochet hook
4 buttons
Fabric for facing, if required

BRITISH PATTERN
BACK
Make 68[73:78] ch.
1st row. 1tr into 4th ch from hook, 1tr into each ch to end. Turn. 66[71:76] sts.
2nd row. 3ch to count as first tr, 1tr into each tr to end. Turn.
Cont in tr, dec one st at each end of 11th and every foll 4th row until 56[61:66] sts rem, then cont without shaping until work measures 48cm from beg.
Shape armholes
Next row. Ss over first 3tr, 3ch, patt to last 3tr, turn. Dec one st at each end of next 2[3:4] rows. 46[49:52] tr. Cont without shaping until armholes measure 18[20:22] cm.
Shape neck and shoulders
Next row. Patt 17[18:20], turn.
Next row. 3ch, work 2tr tog, patt to last 5 sts, turn.
Next row. Ss over first 5 sts, patt to last 2 sts, work 2tr tog.
5[6:7] tr rem. Fasten off.
Miss centre 12[13:14] sts, rejoin yarn and patt to end. Turn.
Next row. Ss over first 5 sts, patt to last 2 sts, work 2tr tog. Turn.
Next row. 3ch, work 2tr tog, patt to last 5 sts. 5[6:7] tr rem. Fasten off.

FRONT
Work as given for back until work measures 38cm from beg.
Divide for front opening.
Next row. Patt 26[28:30], make 6[7:8] ch, turn.
Next row. 1tr into 4th ch from hook, 1tr into each of next 2[3:4] ch, 1tr into each tr to end. Turn. 30[33:36] sts.
Cont without shaping until work measures same as back

to armholes, ending at side edge.
Shape armhole
Work to match back armhole shaping. 25[27:29] sts. Cont without shaping until armhole measures 10[12:14] cm, ending at armhole edge.
Shape neck
Next row. Patt to last 4[5:6] sts, turn.
Next row. Ss over first 2 sts, patt to end. Turn. Dec one st at neck edge on next 4 rows, then work one row, ending at neck edge. 15[16:17] sts.
Shape shoulder
Next row. Patt to last 5 sts, turn.
Next row. Ss over first 5 sts, patt to end.
5[6:7] sts rem. Fasten off.
Return to where work was divided, with RS facing rejoin yarn and patt to end. Turn.
Cont on these 30[33:36] sts to match first side.

SLEEVES
Make 34[35:38] ch and work first row as given for back. 32[34:36] tr. Cont in tr, inc one st at each end of 7th and every foll 7th row until there are 40[42:44] sts, then cont without shaping until sleeve seam measures 44[45:46] cm.
Shape top
Next row. Ss over first 3 sts, 3ch, patt to last 3 sts, turn. Dec one st at each end of next 5[6:7] rows, then 2 sts at each end of next 3 rows. 12 sts rem. Fasten off.

MAKING UP
Join shoulder seams. Sew in sleeves. Join side and sleeve seams. Work a row of dc all round neck edge OR bind with a narrow bias strip. Face edges of front opening if required. Cut 4 buttonholes in facing and stitch round. Sew down edge of under flap. Press seams. Sew on buttons.

AMERICAN PATTERN
BACK
Make 68[73:78] ch.
1st row. 1dc into 4th ch from hook, 1dc into each ch to end. Turn. 66[71:76] sts.
2nd row. 3ch to count as

first dc, 1dc into each dc to end. Turn.
Cont in dc, dec one st at each end of 11th and every foll 4th row until 56[61:66] sts rem, then cont without shaping until 19" from beg.
Shape armholes
Next row. Sl st over first 3dc, 3ch, patt to last 3dc, turn. Dec one st at each end of next 2[3:4] rows. 46[49:52] dc. Cont without shaping until armholes measure 7[7¾:8¾]".
Shape neck and shoulders
Next row. Patt 17[18:20], turn.
Next row. 3ch, work 2dc tog, patt to last 5 sts, turn.
Next row. Sl st over first 5 sts, patt to last 2 sts, work 2dc tog.
5[6:7] dc rem. Fasten off.
Miss center 12[13:14] sts, rejoin yarn and patt to end. Turn.
Next row. Sl st over first 5 sts, patt to last 2 sts, work 2dc tog. Turn.
Next row. 3ch, work 2dc tog, patt to last 5 sts. 5[6:7] dc rem. Fasten off.

FRONT
Work as given for back until work measures 15" from beg.
Divide for front opening.
Next row. Patt 26[28:30], make 6[7:8] ch, turn.
Next row. 1dc into 4th ch from hook, 1dc into each of next 2[3:4] ch, 1dc into each dc to end. Turn. 30[33:36] sts.
Cont without shaping until work measures same as back to armholes, ending at side.
Shape armhole
Work to match back armhole shaping. 25[27:29] sts. Cont without shaping until armhole measures 4[4¾:5½]", ending at armhole edge.
Shape neck
Next row. Patt to last 4[5:6] sts, turn.
Next row. Sl st over first 2 sts, patt to end. Turn. Dec one st at neck edge on next 4 rows, then work one row, ending at neck edge. 15[16:17] sts.
Shape shoulder
Next row. Patt to last 5 sts, turn.

Next row. Sl st over first 5 sts, patt to end. 5[6:7] sts rem. Fasten off.
Return to where work was divided, with RS facing rejoin yarn and patt to end. Turn.
Cont on these 30[33:36] sts to match first side.

SLEEVES
Make 34[35:38] ch and work first row as given for back. 32[34:36] dc. Cont in dc, inc one st at each end of 7th and every foll 7th row until there are 40[42:44] sts, then cont without shaping until sleeve seam measures 17¼[17¾: 18]".
Shape top
Next row. Sl st over first 3 sts, 3ch, patt to last 3 sts, turn. Dec one st at each end of next 5[6:7] rows, then 2 sts at each end of next 3 rows. 12 sts rem. Fasten off.

MAKING UP
Join shoulder seams. Sew in sleeves. Join side and sleeve seams. Work a row of sc all round neck edge OR bind with a narrow bias strip. Face edges of front opening if required. Cut 4 buttonholes in facing and stitch round. Sew down edge of underflap. Press seams. Sew on buttons.

Beach Jacket

Bust: 81[86:91:97] cm (32 [34:36:38]")
Length: 72cm (28")
Sleeve seam: 49[50:51:52] cm (19¼[19¾:20:20½]")
The figures in brackets [ ] refer to the 2nd, 3rd and 4th sizes respectively.

TENSION (GAUGE)
16 sts and 16 rows to 10cm

(4″) over patt worked on No. 4.00 hook

[16 sts and 16 rows to 4″ over patt worked on size F-5 hook]

MATERIALS

Yarn: 900[950:1000:1050] gm (32[34:36:38] oz, of medium crochet cotton such as Twilleys Handicraft Cotton No.1

No.4.00 [F-5] crochet hook
66cm (26″) open-ended zip fastener
2×15cm (6″) zips for pockets
25cm (¼yd) lining for pockets

BRITISH PATTERN

BACK

Make 69[73:77:81] ch.

1st row. 1dc into 3rd ch from hook, 1dc into each ch to end. Turn. 68[72:76:80] sts.

2nd row. 1ch to count as first dc, working into front loop only of each st, 1dc into each dc to end. Turn.

Rep the 2nd row until work measures 72cm from beg.

Shape shoulders and neck

Next row. Patt 27[28:30:31] sts, turn.

Next row. 1ch, work 2dc tog, patt to last 6[6:7:7] sts, turn.

Next row. Ss over first 6[6:7:7] sts, patt to last 2 sts, work 2dc tog. Turn.

Next row. 1ch, work 2dc tog, patt to last 6[6:7:7] sts. 6[7:6:7] sts rem. Fasten off.

Miss centre 14[16:16:18] sts, rejoin yarn and patt to end. Cont to match first side.

LEFT FRONT

Make 34[36:38:40] ch and work first 2 rows as given for back. 33[35:37:39] sts.

Rep the 2nd row until work measures 12cm from beg.

Pocket

Next row. Patt 10 sts, turn and cont on these sts.

Next row. Patt to end. Turn.

Next row. Patt to last st, work 2dc into last st. Turn.

Rep the last 2 rows 8 times more. 19 sts. Break off yarn and leave these sts.

Return to where work was left, miss 3 sts, rejoin yarn and patt to end. Turn.

Next row. Patt to last 2 sts,

work 2dc tog. Turn.

Next row. Patt to end. Turn.

Rep the last 2 rows 8 times more.

Next row. Patt across these sts, make 3ch, then patt across the other 19 sts. Turn.

Next row. Patt across first 19 sts, work 1dc into each of the 3ch, then patt to end. Turn.

Cont without shaping until work measures 66cm (26″) from beg, ending at side edge.

Shape neck

Next row. Patt to last 6[7:7:8] sts, work 2dc tog, turn.

Dec one st at neck edge on next 3 rows, then cont without shaping until work measures same as back to shoulders, ending at side edge.

Shape shoulder

Next row. Ss over first 6[6:7:7] sts, patt to end. Turn.

Next row. Patt to last 6[6:7:7] sts, turn.

Next row. Ss over first 6[6:7:7] sts, patt to end. 6[7:6:7] sts rem. Fasten off.

RIGHT FRONT

Work to match left front. Note that pocket starts with patt 20[22:24:26] sts, turn. Dec at pocket edge on every alt row 9 times, then miss 3 sts, patt across other 10 sts and inc at pocket edge on every alt row 9 times.

SLEEVES

Make 51[53:55:57] ch and work first 2 rows as given for back. 50[52:54:56] sts

Cont without shaping until sleeve measures 47[48:49:50] cm. Inc one st at each end of next and foll 2 alt rows, then on every row twice. Fasten off.

HOOD

Make 105ch and work first 2 rows as given for back. 104dc.

Cont without shaping until work measures 20cm from beg.

Next row. 1ch, 48dc, work 2dc tog, 2dc, work 2dc tog, patt to end. Turn.

Next row. Patt to end. Turn.

Next row. 1ch, 47dc, work 2dc tog, 2dc, work 2dc tog, patt to end. Turn. Cont to dec in this way on foll alt row, then on foll 2 rows. Fasten off.

MAKING UP

Join shoulder seams. Pin sleeves in position with centre of sleeve to shoulder seam. Join seams with a row of dc [sc]. Join side and sleeve seams in the same way. Join top seam of hood, then join hood to neck edge with a row of dc [sc]. Work a row of dc [sc] along front edges, hood and pocket edges. Sew in zips. Using 10 strands of yarn make one twisted cord approximately 150cm (60″) long and thread through lower edge, then two cords approximately 60cm (24″) long and thread through sleeve edges. Cut pockets from lining and sew in place.

AMERICAN PATTERN

BACK

Make 69[73:77:81] ch.

1st row. 1sc into 3rd ch from hook, 1sc into each ch to end. Turn. 68[72:76:80] sts.

2nd row. 1ch to count as first sc, working into front loop only of each st, 1sc into each sc to end. Turn.

Rep the 2nd row until work measures 28″ from beg.

Shape shoulders and neck

Next row. Patt 27[28:30:31] sts, turn.

Next row. 1ch, work 2sc tog, patt to last 6[6:7:7] sts, turn.

Next row. Sl st over first 6[6:7:7] sts, patt to last 2 sts, work 2sc tog. Turn.

Next row. 1ch, work 2sc tog, patt to last 6[6:7:7] sts. 6[7:6:7] sts rem. Fasten off.

Miss centre 14[16:16:18] sts, rejoin yarn and patt to end. Cont to match first side.

LEFT FRONT

Make 34[36:38:40] ch and work first 2 rows as given for back. 33[35:37:39] sts.

Rep the 2nd row until work measures 4¾″ from beg.

Pocket.

Next row. Patt 10 sts, turn

and cont on these sts.

Next row. Patt to end. Turn.

Next row. Patt to last st, work 2sc into last st. Turn.

Rep the last 2 rows 8 times more. 19 sts. Break off yarn and leave these sts.

Return to where work was left, miss 3 sts, rejoin yarn and patt to end. Turn.

Next row. Patt to last 2 sts. work 2sc tog. Turn.

Next row. Patt to end. Turn.

Rep the last 2 rows 8 times more.

Next row. Patt across these sts, make 3ch, then patt across the other 19 sts. Turn.

Next row. Patt across first 19 sts, work 1sc into each of the 3ch, then patt to end. Turn.

Cont without shaping until work measures 26″ from beg, ending at side edge.

Shape neck

Next row. Patt to last 6[7:7:8] sts, work 2sc tog, turn.

Dec one st at neck edge on next 3 rows, then cont without shaping until work measures same as back to shoulders, ending at side edge.

Shape shoulder

Next row. Sl st over first 6[6:7:7] sts, patt to end. Turn.

Next row. Patt to last 6[6:7:7] sts, turn.

Next row. Sl st over first 6[6:7:7] sts, patt to end. 6[7:6:7] sts rem. Fasten off.

RIGHT FRONT

Work to match left front. Note that pocket starts with patt 20[22:24:26] sts, turn. Dec at pocket edge on every alt row 9 times, then miss 3 sts, patt across other 10 sts and inc at pocket edge on every alt row 9 times.

SLEEVES

Make 51[53:55:57] ch and work first 2 rows as given for back. 50[52:54:56] sts.

Cont without shaping until sleeve measures 18½[19: 19¼:19¾]″. Inc one st at each end of next and foll 2 alt rows, then on every row twice. Fasten off.

HOOD

Make 105ch and work first 2 rows as given for back. 104sc.

Cont without shaping until work measures 8″ from beg.
Next row. 1ch, 48sc, work 2sc tog, 2sc, work 2sc tog, patt to end. Turn.
Next row.
Patt to end. Turn.
Next row. 1ch, 47sc, work 2sc tog, 2sc, work 2sc tog, patt to end. Turn. Cont to dec in this way on foll alt row, then on foll 2 rows. Fasten off.
Note: for making up instructions see British Pattern.

Tablecloth Edging

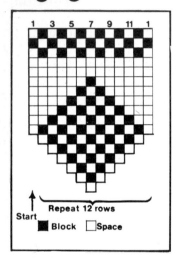

| | 1 | 3 | 5 | 7 | 9 | 11 | 1 |

Repeat 12 rows
Start
■ Block □ Space

Width at widest, 10cm (4″).

MATERIALS

Yarn: Any very fine cotton such as No. 20. – one ball should make about 73cm (29″).
Hook: No. 1.00 [12] steel crochet hook.

TENSION (GAUGE)

17 blocks or spaces and 20 rows to 10cm (4″).

PATTERN

Make 38ch
Row 1. 1tr [dc] into 8th ch from hook, * 2ch, miss 2ch, 1tr [dc] into next ch, rep from * to last 6ch, 1tr [dc] into each of next 3ch, 2ch, miss 2ch, 1tr [dc] into last ch.
Row 2. 3ch, 2tr [dc] into 2ch sp, 1tr [dc] into next tr [dc], 2ch, miss 2tr [dc], 1tr [dc] into

next tr [dc], 2tr [dc] into 2ch sp, 1tr [dc] into next tr [dc] seven times, 2tr [dc] into 2ch sp, 1tr [dc] into 5th of 7ch, 6ch, 1dtr [tr] into base of last tr [dc], then ss [sl st] back along 3ch (thus inc one space) OR 1 block, 1sp, 1 block, 7sts, 1 block, inc 1sp.
Row 3. 7ch, 1tr [dc] into last ss [sl st] (thus inc one space), 2tr [dc] into 2ch sp, 1tr [dc] into next tr [dc], (2ch, 1tr [dc] into next tr [dc]) six times, 2ch, miss 2tr [dc], 1tr [dc] in to next tr [dc], 2tr [dc] into 2ch sp, 1tr [dc] into next tr [dc], 2ch, miss 2tr [dc], 1tr [dc] into 3rd of first 3ch OR inc 1sp, then 1 block, 1sp, 1 block, 7sp, 1 block, 1sp.
Cont in this way, working in patt from chart, until required length. Fasten off.

Collar and Cuffs

Depth: 5cm (2″)
Collar length: 38cm (15″), adjustable
Cuff length: 19cm (7½″), adjustable

TENSION (GAUGE)

15dc to 5cm (2″)
[15sc to 2″]

MATERIALS

Yarn: 40gm (1½oz) of very fine (No.10) crochet cotton
No.1.50 [9] crochet hook

BRITISH PATTERN
COLLAR

Make 116ch or length required with a multiple of 4 sts plus 4 extra ch.
1st row. 1dc into 3rd ch from hook, 1dc into each ch to end. Turn. 115dc.
2nd row. 1ch to count as

first dc, 1dc into each dc to end. Turn.
3rd row. *3ch, miss next dc, 1dc into next dc, rep from * to end. Turn. 57 loops.
4th row. *5ch, 1dc into loop, rep from * to end. Turn.
5th–6th rows. As 4th.
7th row. *7ch, 1dc into loop, rep from * to last loop, 3ch, 1dtr into last loop. Turn.
8th row. 1ch, *(4tr, 3ch, 4tr) into next loop, 1dc into next loop, rep from * to end. Turn.
9th row. *3ch, (4tr, 3ch, 4tr) into 3ch sp, 3ch, 1ss into dc, rep from * to end, working last ss into first ch. Fasten.
☐ Work a row of dc along each short edge if required.

CUFFS

Make 60ch and work as given for collar. Note that there are 59dc after working the first row and 29 loops after working the 3rd row.
☐ Instead of working dc along short edges, join cuffs into a circle.

AMERICAN PATTERN
COLLAR

Make 116ch or length required with a multiple of 4 sts plus 4 extra ch.
1st row. 1sc into 3rd ch from hook, 1sc into each ch to end. Turn. 115sc.
2nd row. 1ch to count as first sc, 1sc into each sc to end. Turn.
3rd row. *3ch, miss next sc, 1sc into next sc, rep from * to end. Turn. 57 loops.
4th row. 5ch, 1sc into loop, rep from * to end. Turn.
5th–6th rows. As 4th.
7th row. *7ch, 1sc into loop, rep from * to last loop, 3ch, 1tr into last loop. Turn.
8th row. 1ch, *(4dc, 3ch, 4dc) into next loop, 1sc into next loop, rep from * to end. Turn.
9th row. *3ch, (4dc, 3ch, 4dc) into 3ch sp, 3ch, 1sl st into sc, rep from * to end, working last sl st into first ch. Fasten off.
☐ Work a row of sc along each short edge if required.

CUFFS

Make 60ch and work as given for collar. Note that

there are 59sc after working the first row and 29 loops after working the 3rd row.
☐ Instead of working sc along short edges, join cuffs into a circle.

Petticoat Edging

Depth: 6cm (2¼″)

TENSION (GAUGE)

Approximately 17tr and 8 rows to 5cm (2″)
[Approximately 17dc and 8 rows to 2″]

MATERIALS

Yarn: 20gm (¾oz) of very fine (No.10) crochet cotton makes approximately 65cm (25½″) of edging.
No.1.50 [9] crochet hook

BRITISH PATTERN

Make 18ch.
1st row. 1tr into 8th ch from hook, 2ch, miss 2ch, (2tr, 2ch, 2tr) into next ch, 2ch, miss 2ch, 1tr into each of next 5ch. Turn.
2nd row. 3ch, 1tr into each of next 4tr, 2ch, miss next sp, (2tr, 2ch, 2tr) into next sp, 1tr into each of next 2tr, 2ch, 1tr into next tr, 2ch, 1tr into turning ch. Turn.
3rd row. 5ch, 1tr into next tr, 2ch, 1tr into each of next 4tr, (2tr, 2ch, 2tr) into sp, 2ch, miss next sp, 1tr into each of next 5tr. Turn.
4th row. 3ch, 1tr into each of next 4tr, 2ch, miss next sp, (2tr, 2ch, 2tr) into next sp, 1tr into each of next 6tr, 2ch, 1tr into next tr, (2ch, 1tr) 7 times into last sp, 2ch, 1dc into base of last tr on 2nd row. Turn.
5th row. 3ch, 1dc into first

sp, (1dc, 3ch, 1dc) in to each of next 8 sps, 1ch, miss 2tr, (1tr into next tr, 2ch, miss 2tr) twice, (2tr, 2ch, 2tr) into sp, 2ch, miss next sp, 1tr into each of next 5tr. Turn.

6th row. 3ch, 1tr into each of next 4tr, 2ch, miss next sp, (2tr, 2ch, 2tr) into next sp, 1tr into each of next 2tr, (2ch, 1tr into next tr) twice. Turn.

Rep 3rd–6th rows for length required, ending with a 4th row.

Last row. 3ch, 1dc into first sp, (1dc, 3ch, 1dc) into each of next 8 sps. Fasten off.

AMERICAN PATTERN
Make 18ch.

1st row. 1dc into 8th ch from hook, 2ch, miss 2ch, (2dc, 2ch, 2dc) into next ch, 2ch, miss 2ch, 1dc into each of next 5ch. Turn.

2nd row. 3ch, 1dc into each of next 4dc, 2ch, miss next sp, (2dc, 2ch, 2dc) into next sp, 1dc into each of next 2dc, 2ch, 1dc into next dc, 2ch, 1dc into turning ch. Turn.

3rd row. 5ch, 1dc into next dc, 2ch, 1dc into each of next 4dc, (2dc, 2ch, 2dc) into sp, 2ch, miss next sp, 1dc into each of next 5dc. Turn.

4th row. 3ch, 1dc into each of next 4dc, 2ch, miss next sp, (2dc, 2ch, 2dc) into next sp, 1dc into each of next 6dc, 2ch, 1dc into next dc, (2ch, 1dc) 7 times into last sp, 2ch, 1sc into base of last dc on 2nd row. Turn.

5th row. 3ch, 1sc into first sp, (1sc, 3ch, 1sc) into each of next 8 sps, 1ch, miss 2dc, (1dc into next dc, 2ch, miss 2dc) twice, (2dc, 2ch, 2dc) into sp, 2ch, miss next sp, 1dc into each of next 5dc. Turn.

6th row. 3ch, 1dc into each of next 4dc, 2ch, miss next sp, (2dc, 2ch, 2dc) into next sp, 1dc into each of next 2dc, (2ch, 1dc into next tr) twice. Turn.

Rep 3rd–6th rows for length required, ending with a 4th row.

Last row. 3ch, 1sc into first sp, (1sc, 3ch, 1sc) into each of next 8 sps. Fasten off.

Garter

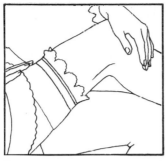

Length: 40cm (16"), adjustable

TENSION (GAUGE)
17dc to 5cm (2")
[*17sc to 2"*]

MATERIALS
Yarn: 20gm (¾oz) of very fine (No.10) crochet cotton.
No.1.00 [12] crochet hook

BRITISH PATTERN
Make 135ch or a multiple of 12 sts plus 3 extra ch.

1st row. 1htr into 5th ch from hook, *1ch, miss 1ch, 1htr into next ch, rep from * to end. Turn.

2nd row. 1ch to count as 1st dc, *1dc into 1ch sp, 1dc into htr, rep from *, ending with 1dc into last sp, 1dc into 3rd of 1st 4ch. Turn.

3rd row. 1ch, 1dc into each dc to end. Turn.

Rep 3rd row 3 times more or for the width required.

7th row. 4ch to count as 1st tr and ch, miss next dc, 1tr into next dc, *1ch, miss 1dc, 1tr into next dc, rep from * to end. Turn.

8th row. 1ch, 2dc into 1ch sp, 1dc into next tr, *5ch, miss 1tr, (1tr, 3ch, 1tr) into next tr, 5ch, miss 1tr, 1dc into next tr, (2dc into 1ch sp, 1dc into next tr) twice, rep from *, ending with 1dc into tr, 2dc into last sp, 1dc into 3rd of first 4ch. Turn.

9th row. 1ch, 1dc into each of next 2dc, *5ch, 1tr into tr, 2ch, (1tr, 2ch, 1tr) into 2ch sp, 2ch, 1tr into tr, 5ch, miss 1dc, 1dc into each of next 5dc, rep from *, ending with 3dc instead of 5. Turn.

10th row. 1ch, 1dc into next dc, *5ch, 1tr into tr, 2ch, 1tr into 2ch sp, 2ch, (1tr, 2ch, 1tr) into next 2ch sp, 2ch, 1tr into next 2ch sp, 2ch, 1tr into

tr, 5ch, miss 1dc, 1dc into each of next 3dc, rep from *, ending with 2dc instead of 3. Turn.

11th row. 1ch, *5ch, 1tr into tr, (2ch, 1tr into 2ch sp) twice, 2ch, (1tr, 2ch, 1tr) into next 2ch sp, (2ch, 1tr into next 2ch sp) twice, 2ch, 1tr into tr, 5ch, miss 1dc, 1dc into next dc, rep from * to end. Turn.

12th row. 1dc into 5ch loop, (3ch, 1dc) twice into same loop, *(1dc, 3ch, 1dc) into each of next seven 2ch sps, (1dc, 3ch, 1dc) into each of next two 5ch loops, rep from *, ending with (1dc, 3ch, 1dc) twice into last 5ch loop. Fasten off.
□ Join into a circle.
□ Stitch elastic behind the dc rows if required.

AMERICAN PATTERN
Make 135ch or a multiple of 12 sts plus 3 extra ch.

1st row. 1hdc into 5th ch from hook, *1ch, miss 1ch, 1hdc into next ch, rep from * to end. Turn.

2nd row. 1ch to count as 1st sc, *1sc into 1ch sp, 1sc into hdc, rep from * ending with 1sc into last sp, 1sc into 3rd of first 4ch. Turn.

3rd row. 1ch, 1sc into each sc to end. Turn.

Rep 3rd row 3 times more or for width required.

7th row. 4ch to count as 1st dc and ch, miss next sc, 1dc into next sc, *1ch, miss 1sc, 1dc into next sc, rep from * to end. Turn.

8th row. 1ch, 2sc into 1ch sp, 1sc into next dc, *5ch, miss 1dc, (1dc, 3ch, 1dc) into next dc, 5ch, miss 1dc, 1sc into next dc, (2sc into 1ch sp, 1sc into next dc) twice, rep from *, ending with 1sc into dc, 2sc into last sp, 1sc into 3rd of first 4ch. Turn.

9th row. 1ch, 1sc into each of next 2sc, *5ch, 1dc into dc, 2ch, (1dc, 2ch, 1dc) into 2ch sp, 2ch, 1dc into dc, 5ch, miss 1sc, 1sc into each of next 5sc, rep from *, ending with 3sc instead of 5. Turn.

10th row. 1ch, 1sc into next sc, *5ch, 1dc into dc, 2ch, 1dc into 2ch sp, 2ch, (1dc, 2ch, 1dc) into next 2ch sp,

2ch, 1dc into dc, 5ch, miss 1sc, 1sc into each of next 3sc, rep from *, ending with 2sc instead of 3. Turn.

11th row. 1ch, *5ch, 1dc into dc, (2ch, 1dc into 2ch sp) twice, 2ch, (1dc, 2ch, 1dc) into next 2ch sp, (2ch, 1dc into next 2ch sp) twice, 2ch, 1dc into dc, 5ch, miss 1sc, 1sc into next sc, rep from * to end. Turn.

12th row. 1sc into 5ch loop, (3ch, 1sc) twice into same loop, *(1sc, 3ch, 1sc) into each of next seven 2ch sps, (1sc, 3ch, 1sc) into each of next two 5ch loops, rep from *, ending with (1sc, 3ch, 1sc) twice into last 5ch loop. Fasten off.
□ Join into a circle.
□ Stitch elastic behind the sc rows with a herringbone casing if required.

Cherry Edging

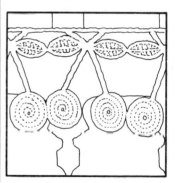

Size: Each pair of cherries is approximately 7.5cm (3") across and 10cm (4") deep.

TENSION (GAUGE)
1 cherry measures approximately 3cm (1¼") across diameter

MATERIALS
Yarn: 11m (12½yd) of fine (No.5) crochet cotton makes 3 cherries or 4 leaves and stems
No.2.00 [B-1] crochet hook

BRITISH PATTERN
CHERRIES
Make 3ch. Join with a ss into first ch to form a circle.

1st round. 7dc into circle. Do not join, but work round continuously.

2nd round. 2dc into each dc. 14 sts.

3rd round. *2dc into first dc, 1dc into next dc, rep from * to end. 21 sts.
4th round. *2dc into first dc, 1dc into each of next 2dc, rep from * to end. 28 sts.
5th round. 1dc into each dc to end. Join with a ss to beg of round. Fasten off.

STEMS.
Join yarn with a ss to one cherry, 3ch, 1tr into next st, turn, (3ch, 1tr into turning ch) 7 times, 6ch, turn, 1dc into 2nd ch from hook, 1dc into each of next 4ch. Fasten off.

LEAVES
Makes 12ch.
1dc into 2nd ch from hook, 1htr into next ch, 1tr into each of next 3ch, 1dtr into next ch, 1tr into each of next 3ch, 1htr in to next ch, 1dc into last ch, turn work and cont in the same way along other side of chain. Fasten off.

MAKING UP
Make a length of chain to fit the shelf, then sew stems, leaves and cherries in pairs as in picture. Note that the leaves are sewn to the same place as the stems are fastened off after the 5dc [sc].

AMERICAN PATTERN
CHERRIES
Make 3ch. Join with a sl st into first ch to form a circle.
1st round. 7sc into circle. Do not join, but work round continuously.
2nd round. 2sc into each sc. 14 sts.
3rd round. *2sc into first sc, 1sc into next sc, rep from * to end. 21 sts.
4th round. *2sc into first sc, 1sc into each of next 2sc, rep from * to end. 28 sts.
5th round. 1sc into each sc to end. Join with a sl st to beg of round. Fasten off.

STEMS
Join yarn with a sl st to one cherry, 3ch, 1dc into next st, turn, (3ch, 1dc into turning ch) 7 times, 6ch, turn, 1sc into 2nd ch from hook, 1sc into each of next 4ch. Fasten off.

LEAVES
Make 12ch.
1sc into 2nd ch from hook, 1hdc into next ch, 1dc into each of next 3ch, 1tr into next ch, 1dc into next 3ch, 1hdc into next ch, 1sc into last ch, turn work and cont in the same way along other side of chain. Fasten off.

MAKING UP
See British pattern.

Rug

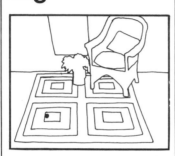

Length: 225cm (90")
Width: 75cm (30")

TENSION (GAUGE)
1 square measures 75cm (30"): this varies according to type of materials used.

MATERIALS
Yarn: approximately 1000 gm (35oz) of rags in each of 5 colours.
No5.00 [H–8] hook

BRITISH PATTERN
Tear or cut rags into strips approximately 2 – 2.5cm (⅝"–1") wide.

SQUARE
With first colour make 8ch. Join with a ss into first ch to form a circle.
1st round. *2ch, 3dc into circle, rep from * 3 times more. Join with a ss to 2nd of 2ch.
2nd round. Ss into 2ch sp, 3ch, 1dc into same sp, *1dc into each of next 3dc, (1dc, 2ch, 1dc) into 2ch sp, rep from * twice more, 1dc into each of next 3dc. Join with a ss to first of 3ch.
3rd round. Ss into 2ch sp, 3ch, 1dc into same sp, *1dc into each of next 5dc, (1dc, 2ch, 1dc) into 2ch sp, rep from * twice more, 1dc into each of next 5dc. Join with a

ss to first of 3ch.
Continuing in this way, working 2 more dc along each side in every round, work 3 more rounds in first colour, then 6 rounds in each of other 4 colours (or vary colours as required). Fasten off.
Make 2 more squares in the same way and join into a strip.

AMERICAN PATTERN
Tear or cut rags into strips approximately ⅝" wide.

SQUARE
With first color make 8ch. Join with a sl st into first ch to form a circle.
1st round. *2ch, 3sc into circle, rep from * 3 times more. Join with a sl st to 2nd of 2ch.

Rose Coat

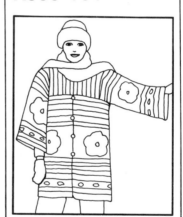

Bust: 81–91cm (32–36")
All round: coat measures 112cm (44")
Length: 82cm (32½")
Sleeve seam: 36cm (14")

TENSION (GAUGE)
16 sts to 10cm (4") over patt worked on 4.50 hook
[16 sts to 4" over patt worked on G-6 hook]

MATERIALS
Yarn: 300gm (10½oz) of double knitting yarn in colour A; 250gm (9oz) in colour B; 200gm (7oz) each in colours C and D; 150gm (5½oz) in colour E; 50gm (2oz) in colour F.
No.4.50 [G-6] crochet hook
6 buttons
Iron-on lining (optional)

2nd round. Sl st into 2ch sp, 3ch, 1sc into same sp, *1sc into each of next 3sc, (1sc, 2ch, 1sc) into 2ch sp, rep from * twice more, 1sc into each of next 5sc. Join with a sl st to first of 3ch.
3rd round. Sl st into 2ch sp, 3ch, 1sc into same sp, *1sc into each of next 5sc, (1sc, 2ch, 1sc) into 2ch sp, rep from * twice more, 1sc into each of next 5sc. Join with a sl st to first of 3ch.
Continuing in this way, working 2 more sc along each side in every round, work 3 more rounds in first color, then 6 rounds in each of other 4 colors (or vary colors as required). Fasten off.
Make 2 more squares in the same way and join into a strip.

PATTERN
MAIN PART
Using A, make 182ch.
1st row. 1tr [dc] into 4th ch from hook, 1tr [dc] into each ch to end. 180 sts. Fasten off. Work horizontal chain effect loosely to prevent puckering; hold E at right-hand edge of row just worked, insert hook from front to back between first two tr [dc] and draw through a loop of E, * insert hook between next two tr [dc] and draw a loop through gap and loop on hook, rep from * to end. Fasten off.
2nd row. Join C at right-hand edge of previous row, 3ch to count as first tr [dc], 1tr [dc] into each tr [dc] to end. Fasten off. Work chain effect (always on RS of work) in D.
Work 8 more rows in stripes as foll: D with C chain; E with A chain; B with F chain; C with D chain; D with C chain; F with B chain; A with E chain; C with D chain. ** Using B, work 12 rows in tr [dc] – there is no need to fasten off after each row; make chain effect on RS of each row in A. Rep first 10 rows in stripe sequence as before. Fasten off.
Next row. With RS of work facing, join D to right-hand edge, miss 2 sts, *4 tr [dc] – 1 diamond shell – into next st,

miss next st, ss into next st, miss next st, rep from * to last 3 sts, 1 shell into next st, miss next st, ss into last st. Fasten off.
Next row. Join E to right-hand edge, 3ch, 2tr [*dc*] into st at base of ch, ss to centre of shell, *1 shell into next ss, ss to centre of next shell, rep from * ending with 3tr [*dc*] into last ss. Fasten off.
Using B, work another row of shells. Fasten off. **.

SEMI-CIRCULAR EDGING

With RS of work facing, make one semi-circle over every 15 sts along lower edge of main part as foll. Join D with a ss into 5th st from right-hand edge, miss 2 sts, 5tr [*dc*] into next st, miss one st, ss into next st. Fasten off. Join B to 2nd st from right-hand edge, 2tr [*dc*] into each of previous 5tr [*dc*], ss into 13th st. Fasten off. Join C to first st, 1dc [*sc*] into each of previous 10 sts, ss into 15th st. Fasten off.
Fill in sp between semi-circles with shells as foll. Join A with a ss to 5th st up on left-hand side of first semi-circle, 4tr [*dc*] into sp between semi-circles, ss into 5th st up on right-hand side of next semi-circle. Fasten off. Make half shell at each end of row.
Using D, pick up and tr [*dc*] 180 sts along top of semi-circles and shells.
Chain with C. Work 3 rows in stripes as foll. C with D chain; E with A chain; A with E chain. Fasten off.

SLEEVES AND YOKE

Using A, make 92ch. Work first row as given for main part. 90 sts. Work 3 rows in stripes as foll. C with D chain; D with C chain; E with A chain. Rep from ** to ** as given for main part. Using C, pick up 90 sts along top of shells and work 6 rows in stripes as foll: C with D chain; D with C chain; F with B chain; A with E chain; C with D chain; D with C chain.
Shape neck
With RS of work facing,

work each row from right to left. Using E, work diamond shells over 45 sts of left half for back. Work 5 more rows of shells in B, C, D, F, C. Use same colour sequence to work shell over 30 sts of right half for front. Work semi-circular edging and stripe sequence as given for main part on cuff edge of sleeve. Make another sleeve and yoke in the same way with neck shaping reversed.

ROSES

Centre. Using D, make 3ch. Join with a ss into first ch to form a circle.
1st round. 1ch, 6dc [*sc*] into circle. Join with a ss into first dc [*sc*].
2nd round. 3ch, 1dtr [*tr*] into next dc [*sc*], ss into same st, *ss into next st, 3ch, 1dtr [*tr*] into same st, ss into same st, rep from * to end. 6 points. Fasten off.
3rd round. Join A with a ss to top of one dtr [*tr*], *1tr [*dc*] into ss between points, 1dc [*dc*] into each of 2 sts to top of next point, rep from * to end. Join with a ss into first ss. Fasten off.

PETALS

(Make 5 for each rose.)
Using B, make 5ch.
1st row. 7tr [*dc*] into 3rd ch from hook, ss into last ch to form a semi-circle. Fasten off.
2nd row. Join C to right-hand edge of semi-circle, 3ch, 2tr [*dc*] into each st of previous row. Turn.
3rd row. Work in tr [*dc*], inc 1tr [*dc*] in every 3rd st. Fasten off.
4th row. Join D to right-hand edge, 1dc [*sc*] into each st round outer edge of semi-circle. Note that reverse side of this dc [*sc*] is RS of petal. Make 3 more roses in C with centres in D; also 4 roses in D with centres in C. Sections of rose in A and B rem in same colours. Sew petals to centre (see detail, page 206).

MAKING UP

Appliqué eight roses to coat on the main part and 2 on each sleeve.
Sew to panels in B with chain

effect in A, alternating colours. Darn in ends of yarn unless you are lining coat. Sew main part to yoke, matching centre front opening. Join sleeve seams. Using A, work diamond shells all round outer edge. Sew on buttons about 10cm (4") apart. Make embroidered button loops.

LINING

Turn coat to WS. Lay in correct shape with back facing upwards on a blanket-covered flat surface (eg. floor).
☐ Iron on rectangle of lining over back; trim edges to 10cm (4").
☐ Turn coat with front facing. Iron down 5cm (2") of back lining onto sides and shoulders. Leave neck and hem edge free to trim as required.
☐ Iron lining on to front of coat, repeating overlaps at shoulders and side seams.
☐ Beginning at side seam, iron a rectangle of lining onto each sleeve. Iron onto one side of sleeve first, turn coat over and iron down other side. Overlap body lining at shoulder (if necessary, trim lining for good fit at underarms).
☐ Finish raw edges; pull lining away slightly at side, shoulder and sleeve overlaps, turn in raw edges and hem.
☐ Finish outer edges in same way, cutting off any excess lining.

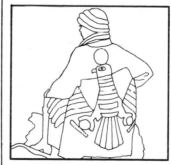

Falcon Coat

Bust: 81–91cm (32–36")
All round: 112cm (44")
Length: 80cm (31½")
Sleeve seam: 40cm (15½")

TENSION (GAUGE)
3 shells and 10 rows to 10cm (4") over patt worked on 4.50 hook
[*3 shells and 10 rows to 4" over patt worked on G-6 hook*]

MATERIALS
Yarn: 350gm (12½oz) each of double knitting yarn in colours A and B; 100gm (3½oz) each of colours C and D; 50gm (2oz) each of colours E and F.
Oddments of dark brown yarn to embroider eye and beak.
No.4.50 [C 6] crochet hook
Brown paper for pattern, pencil
3 buttons
Iron-on lining, optional

PAPER PATTERN
Draw out on paper back, right and left front, sleeves as shown in diagram overleaf.
☐ Join side seams with sellotape (scotch tape) so that body of coat is in one piece.
☐ Draw falcon as foll: Mark centre vertical line of coat back. Draw neckline along straight line joining inner corners of armholes; from this draw in bird's head and circle above head.
☐ To draw arc of upper wing where it meets body, cut a piece of string 40cm (16") long. Secure one end at centre back neck and swing other end outwards in a circle from where it touches body of bird: base for wing feather is 24cm (9½") along circumference of arc. Draw in upper wings as shown in diagram.
☐ To find edge for wing tips, cut another piece of string 71cm (28") long. Secure one end at centre back and swing other end inwards in a circle from joining of A and B on front edge: inner edge of feathers is 35cm (14") along circumference of arc formed.
☐ Divide join of upper wing and feathers in five equal sections each 3cm (1¼"): divide arc of wing tips into five equal sections each 7cm (2¾"). Join corresponding points on upper wing and tips to form feather pattern.

□ Draw in tail feathers, legs and feet with resting circles and bars.

CROCHET PATTERN

Following measurements and colours indicated on diagram, make coat in shell patt as foll:

Make a multiple of 4ch loosely.

1st row. 4tr [dc] into 6th ch from hook, *miss 1ch, ss into next ch, miss 1ch, 5tr [dc] – 1 shell – into next ch, rep from * to last 2ch, ss into last ch. Turn.

2nd row. 3ch, 2tr [dc] in to first ss, ss into centre st of next shell, *1 shell into ss between shells, ss into centre of next shell, rep from * ending with 3tr [dc] into 4th of 5ch. Turn.

3rd row. 1 shell into first ss, *ss into centre st of next shell, 1 shell into next ss, rep from * ending with ss into 3rd of 3ch. Turn.

Rep 2nd and 3rd rows throughout for patt.

Sleeves are also in shell patt in colour B with 4 rows of A at lower edge.

□ **Falcon.** Make falcon separately following diagram and shaping to the proper pattern and join pieces tog.

TO MAKE UP

□ Join side seams of coat. Stitch falcon in position.

□ Join shoulder seams: armhole is a triangular shape.

□ Using A, work 4 rows shell patt round neck edge.

□ Join sleeve seam as far as point M. Sew curved top of sleeve along top two sides of

triangular opening, matching points G and H with corners marked on main piece and M to underarm seam.

□ Embroider eye and beak on falcon.

□ Sew on 3 buttons 16cm (6¼″) apart. Make embroidered button loops.

□ If required, line coat as given for lining rose coat.

Falcon coat pieces and dimensions are given below. Beneath them is a guide to falcon motif, which is appliquéd.

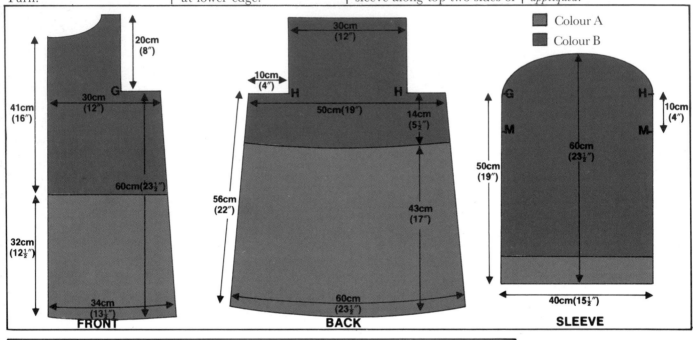

■ Colour A
■ Colour B

20cm (8″)
30cm (12″) G
41cm (16″)
60cm (23½″)
32cm (12½″)
34cm (13½″)
FRONT

30cm (12″)
10cm (4″)
H   H
50cm (19″)
14cm (5½″)
56cm (22″)
43cm (17″)
60cm (23½″)
BACK

G   H
M   M
10cm (4″)
60cm (23½″)
50cm (19″)
40cm (15½″)
SLEEVE

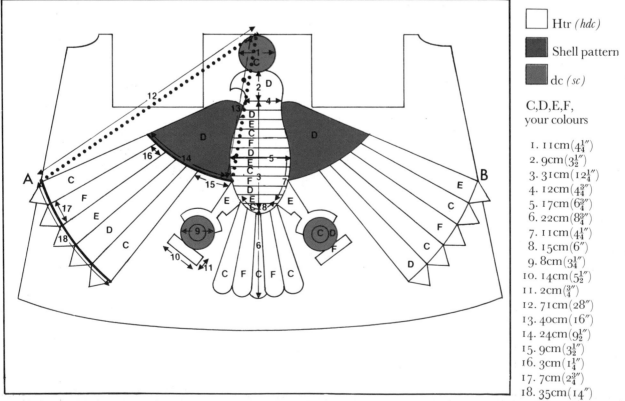

□ Htr (hdc)
■ Shell pattern
■ dc (sc)

C,D,E,F, your colours

1. 11cm (4¼″)
2. 9cm (3½″)
3. 31cm (12¼″)
4. 12cm (4¾″)
5. 17cm (6¾″)
6. 22cm (8¾″)
7. 11cm (4¼″)
8. 15cm (6″)
9. 8cm (3¼″)
10. 14cm (5½″)
11. 2cm (¾″)
12. 71cm (28″)
13. 40cm (16″)
14. 24cm (9½″)
15. 9cm (3½″)
16. 3cm (1¼″)
17. 7cm (2¾″)
18. 35cm (14″)

Baby Waistcoat and Socks

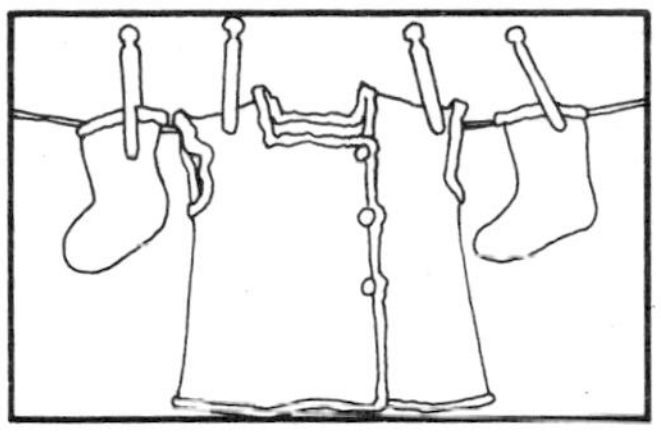

Chest: 41–46cm (16–18")
Waistcoat length: 23[26] cm (9[10½]")

TENSION (GAUGE)
12 sts and 9 rows to 5cm (2") over htr worked on No.3.00 hook.
[*12 sts and 9 rows to 2" over hdc worked on D-3 hook*].

MATERIALS
Yarn: 20[20]gm (¾[¾]oz) of 4 ply yarn in each of 3 colours, A, B and C.
No.3.00 [D-3] hook
3 buttons

BRITISH PATTERN
WAISTCOAT
Using C, make 104[116] ch and work on one piece to armholes.
1st row. 1htr into 3rd ch from hook, 1htr into each ch to end, joining in A on last htr. Do not break off C. Turn. 103[115] sts.
2nd row. Using A, 2ch to count as first htr, 1htr into each htr to end, joining in B on last htr. Do not break off A. Turn.
3rd row. Using B, as 2nd, bringing in C on last htr. Cont in htr, work 1 row each in C, A, B throughout, until work measures 16[18]cm from beg.
Divide for armholes
Next row. 2ch, 32[36]htr, ss over next 4 sts, 46[52]htr, ss over next 4 sts, 16[18]htr. Turn.
Cont on last 16[18] sts for left front. Work without shaping until armhole measures 7[8]cm, ending at armhole edge.
Shape shoulder
1st row. Ss over first 5[6] sts, patt to end. Turn.
2nd row. Patt to last 5[6] sts. Fasten off.
Return to centre 46[52] sts for back. **. Cont without shaping until armholes measure 6[7]cm, ending with a Ws row (2 rows less than left front).
Shape neck
Next row. 2ch, 16[18] htr, turn.
Next row. 2ch, work 2 htr tog, patt to end. Turn. 16[18] sts.
Shape shoulder
Work as given for left front.
Miss centre 12[14] sts for front neck, rejoin yarn, 2ch, patt to end. Turn. 17[19] sts.
Next row. Patt to last 2 sts, work 2 htr tog. Turn. Shape shoulder. Next row: Patt to last 5[6] sts, turn.
Next row. Ss over first 5[6] sts, patt to end. Fasten off.
Return to 33[37] sts for right front. *** Cont without shaping until armhole measures 4[5]cm, ending at armhole edge.
Shape neck
Next row. Patt to last 17[19] sts, turn.
Cont without shaping until armhole measures same as left front, ending with a WS row.
Shape shoulder
Work as given for left back shoulder.

MAKING UP
Join shoulder seams. Using B, join yarn to beg of lower edge, *3ch, 1ss [*sl*] into next st, rep from * along lower edge, then cont in same way all round outer edge and armholes. Sew on buttons using holes in patt for buttonholes.

SOCKS
Using C, make 27[31] ch.
1st row: 1htr into 3rd ch from hook, 1htr into each ch to end, joining in A on last htr. Turn. 26[30] sts.
Cont in htr, working in stripes as on waistcoat, until 10[13] rows have been worked, ending with a row in C.
Next row. Miss first 9[10] sts, join in A to next st, 2ch, 7[9]htr, turn. Cont on these 8[10] sts in A, work 3[4]cm, then dec one st at each end of last row.
Return to where work was left, rejoin A, work 9[10]htr, 8[10]htr along side of foot, 6[8]htr along toe, 8[10]htr along side of foot, then 9[10]htr. 40[48] sts.
Cont in stripes as before, work 2[3] more rows, then work 2[3] more rows, dec one st at each end and 2 sts in centre of every row. Fasten off.

MAKING UP
Join seam at back and under foot. Work edging as given for waistcoat along top.

AMERICAN PATTERN
WAISTCOAT
Using C, make 104[116]ch and work in one piece to armholes.
1st row. 1hdc into 3rd ch from hook, 1hdc into each ch to end, joining in A on last hdc. Do not break off C. Turn. 103[115] sts.
2nd row. Using A, 2ch to count as first hdc, 1hdc into each hdc to end, joining in B on last hdc. Do not break off A. Turn.
3rd row. Using B, as 2nd, joining in C on last hdc. Cont in hdc, work 1 row each in C, A, B throughout, until work measures 6¼[7]" from beg.
Divide for armholes
Next row. 2ch, 32[36]hdc, sl st over next 4 sts, 46[52] hdc, sl st over next 4 sts, 16[18]hdc. Turn.
Cont on last 16[18] sts for left front. Work without shaping until armhole measures 2¼[3¼]", ending at armhole edge.
Shape shoulder
1st row. Sl st over first 5[6] sts, patt to end. Turn.
2nd row. Patt to last 5[6] sts. Fasten off.
Return to center 46[52] sts for back. **. Cont without shaping until armholes measure 2¼[2¾]", ending with a WS row (2 rows less than left front).
Shape neck
Next row. 2ch, 16[18]hdc, turn.
Next row. 2ch, work 2hdc tog, patt to end. Turn 16[18] sts.
Shape shoulder
Work as given for left front.
Miss center 12[14] sts for front neck, rejoin yarn, 2ch, patt to end. Turn. 17[19] sts.
Next row. Patt to last 2 sts, work 2hdc tog. Turn.
Shape shoulder
Next row. Patt to last 5[6] sts, turn.
Next row. Sl st over first 5[6] sts, patt to end. Fasten.
Return to 33[37] sts for right front. ***. Cont without shaping until armhole measures 1½[2]", ending at armhole edge.
Shape neck
Next row. Patt to last 17[19] sts, turn.
Cont without shaping until armhole measures same as left front, ending with a WS row.
Shape shoulder
Work as given for left back shoulder.

MAKING UP
See British pattern.

SOCKS
Using C, make 27[31]ch.
1st row. 1hdc into 3rd ch from hook, 1hdc into each ch to end, joining in A on last hdc. Turn. 26[30] sts.
Cont in hdc, working in stripes as on waistcoat, until 10[13] rows are worked, ending with a row in C.
Next row. Miss first 9[10] sts, join in A to next st, 2ch, 7[9]hdc, turn.
Cont on these 8[10] sts in A, work 1¼[1½]", then dec one st at each end of last row.
Return to where work was left, rejoin A, work 9[10]hdc, 8[10]hdc along side of foot, 6[8]hdc along toe, 8[10]hdc along side of foot, then 9[10]hdc. 40[48] sts.
Cont in stripes as before, work 2[3] more rows, then work 2[3] more rows, dec one st at each end and 2 sts in center of every row.

MAKING UP
See British pattern.

Section Editor:
Margaret Maino

Designers:
Granny squares and babywear are designed by Margaret Maino; coats by Maggi Jo Norton; lace edgings by Jean Litchfield

KNITTING

Knitting is an age-old method of making fabric by creating interlocking loops of yarn, using a pair of needles. A row of stitches is cast on one needle and the stitches are then transferred one at a time to the other needle. As each stitch is transferred, the yarn is wrapped round and this builds the fabric. The methods of transferring each stitch and winding the yarn round the needles creates the textural pattern. But there are only two basic stitches used; one is 'knit' (from which the craft takes its name) and the other is 'purl'. Both are diagrammed in the General Guide on page 241.

TEXTURAL PATTERNS

Garter Stitch is the most basic of textural patterns and consists of horizontal ridges made by knitting row after row. (The woman's sweater shown overleaf is an example.)

Stocking stitch alternates knit and purl rows to produce a smooth fabric with familiar interlocking 'V' shapes. (See tea cosy roof opposite.)

Reverse stocking stitch has the purl, or rough side of the fabric as the finished side and looks rather like garter stitch. (See smocks, page 231).

Ribbing is often used to edge sweaters and is made by alternating one (or two) knit stitches with the same number of purl ones. This creates the ribbed effect.

Moss stitch. This is a variation of ribbing and gives a neat 'seeded' texture. Work the first row as for single rib. On subsequent rows knit each knitted stitch in the previous row and purl each purled stitch.

MATERIALS

Yarn and needles are the main requisites for knitting but you will also need scissors occasionally, and a ruler. The ruler is useful for measuring tension and it is also helpful in reading knitting patterns. By placing the ruler below the first row of instructions and moving it down as you work, you will be less likely to lose your place.

Yarn. Wool is the traditional knitting yarn and it is still a very popular and easily obtainable material, but synthetics of various kinds and textures are increasingly available – as are natural fibres such as cotton, and special wools

such as mohair. As the thickness or 'weight' of yarn directly affects the finished work, always try to obtain the yarn which is recommended, when knitting from a pattern. If you must use another kind, then test the tension before you begin, using the method described below.

The most common 'weight' of yarn is double knitting yarn and this is used for all sorts of knitwear. Heavier, chunky yarns such as double double, Aran – even rug yarn – are also on the market and are gaining in popularity because they knit up relatively quickly and produce fashionably bulky results. As a rule, the thicker the yarn, the larger the needles needed to work it. When buying knitting yarn, always buy enough to complete your project because dye lots vary, even in standard colours, and this could show in the finished work.

Needles. Knitting needles are sold in pairs and are sized according to their diameters. Always work a test sample with the size called for in a pattern since the diameter affects the stitch size and stitches will be looser or tighter depending on whether the needles are smaller or larger than they should be. If, however, your tension turns out differently using a recommended needle, then try a size larger or smaller. (A needle chart in the General Guide at the end of the chapter gives sizes.)

Straight needles in pairs have button-like tips on one end to help keep yarn on, but some needles – for making socks, for instance – are pointed at both ends for knitting in the round. Special circular needles are also available for knitting in the round or for flat knitting where a large number of stitches are involved.

TENSION (Gauge)

The tension is the number of stitches and rows you knit to a given measurement (which is usually a 5cm or 2″ square) with the yarn, needles and stitch pattern you will be using. If your tension square measures less than that stated in the pattern, it means you are working too tightly and your garment will be too small. Change to a size larger needles and test again, continuing until you get it right. If your test square is too big, your work will be too

loose so you should try using a size smaller needle. It is important to get the tension right, because even half a stitch out can add or subtract to or from the final width.

PATTERNS

Knitting patterns are normally given in a very detailed fashion, using abbreviations for each stitch and asterisks to indicate repeat sections. Instructions for reading a pattern and understanding abbreviations are given in the General Guide on page 240.

It is also possible to knit simple garments such as T-shaped sweaters without the use of conventional patterns. Instead, you use your own measurements and then knit in the required stitch until each portion of the garment reaches the desired length. Several designs at the beginning of the chapter involve this free-style method, making a simple introduction to knitting for beginners whilst allowing scope for more experienced knitters to adapt designs to personal tastes.

To measure for free-style knitting, draw the shape and mark in your measurements. Decide how long and wide you want the garment to be. Take bust or chest measurements, add a total of 2cm (¾″) for the seams plus a movement allowance of about 5cm (2″). If the sweater is to fit over the hips allow extra. Divide the total measurement in two for front and back. Work out length, sleeve depth and length in a similar way. Allow about one third of the total width for a neck opening.

FINISHING

It is a good idea to press separate pieces lightly before sewing them together as you can stretch them gently into shape, if necessary. But do this on plain knitting only. Pressing a rib or garter stitch pattern spoils elasticity. Sew the seams together with back stitch, using a blunt-ended needle and matching wool, (choose a matching thinner quality if you have used very thick yarn), but neatly oversew any ribbed parts.

The cottage tea cosy opposite shows the potential of knitting for creating a variety of textural and multi-coloured effects. Detailed instructions are on page 242.

SIMPLE T-SHAPES

Conventional knitting patterns are not necessary for sweaters like the ones shown here. These basic shapes can be knitted by simply taking body measurements, testing the tension of the yarn, needles and stitch you will be using, then knitting the lengths.

The man's sweater is knitted in stocking stitch and the textural pattern made with rows of garter stitch added at regular intervals. The front, back and sleeves are rectangles. A zip is inserted in the neck opening.

The woman's sweater opposite is made in the simplest style imaginable: it is knitted entirely in garter stitch, and in one piece, starting at the right cuff. The rectangular collar, in stocking stitch edged with garter stitch, is attached separately.

The child's hooded sweater illustrates yet another textural possibility. The back and front are in moss stitch, while the sleeves and hood are worked in garter stitch.

Instructions on pages 242 and 243

Sandra Lousada

ARAN

Off the west coast of Ireland lie the rocky promontories of the Aran islands. Their barren, windswept surfaces cannot sustain livelihood and so, for centuries, the men have gone down to the sea in their ships and the women have sat at home, patiently waiting out the storms and keeping busy by knitting heavy woollen sweaters for their men. It is not surprising that the knitting patterns which have become traditional on these islands have names which evoke the hazards of daily life and the religious thoughts of the inhabitants: Trinity, ladder of life, marriage lines and lobster claw cable are a few.

The customary yarn for Aran knitting is a chunky, creamy white called 'bainin', meaning natural; and the traditional textural patterns of cables, crisscrosses and bobbles stand out in it like bas-reliefs carved in marble. But it is also possible to use dyed yarns in colours which evoke the natural environment of the islands – moss and lichen greens, deep browns, heather.

The sweaters shown here are made using three Aran patterns: honeycomb, Trinity and fish net. Honeycomb, (top left in the detail) clearly resembles the cubicles of a hive, while Trinity, opposite it, receives its designation because it is worked 'three in one and one in three'. Fish net evokes the very fabric by which the Aran islanders survive.

There are 42 squares in both the sweaters – 14 of each pattern – but the child's version has smaller squares. All are surrounded by a border of garter stitch. The squares are assembled into a basic T-shape and other sizes than those given here can be made by taking body measurements, as described in the chapter introduction, and dividing front, back and sleeves into squares. *Instructions are on page 244.*

Theo Bergström

229

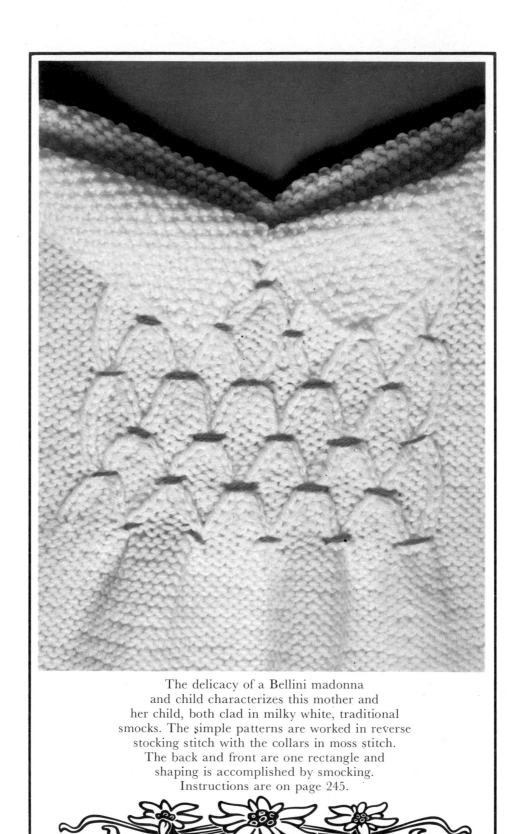

The delicacy of a Bellini madonna
and child characterizes this mother and
her child, both clad in milky white, traditional
smocks. The simple patterns are worked in reverse
stocking stitch with the collars in moss stitch.
The back and front are one rectangle and
shaping is accomplished by smocking.
Instructions are on page 245.

KNITTED
LACE

Although its origins are uncertain, lace for hand knitting was much copied and adapted by the Shetland islanders during the last century. Traditionally, very fine yarns and openwork patterns are combined to form delicate fabrics for edgings, tablecloths and shawls. One of the most famous examples of this gossamer technique is the ring shawl, so fine that it could be pulled through a wedding ring.

To create a lacy fabric, you must increase stitches within a row, bringing the yarn forward or winding it round the needle before you knit the next stitch, thus producing the 'holes'. The increased stitches are accounted for in subsequent stitches. Pattern recipes give detailed instructions on how to work the lace techniques.

Soft mohair yarn adds a feminine touch to the lavender sweater in the picture on the right; it is in a classic lace pattern with deep ribbed welt and stylish tie neck.

The sweater and skirt on the facing page are a clever combination of knitted lace and fabric. The skirt is inset with squares knitted in a matching pattern to the lacy sweater.

Use fine Shetland yarn for this fashionable design, and woollen cloth of a similar weight.

Detailed instructions for these garments on page 246.

Rex Bamber

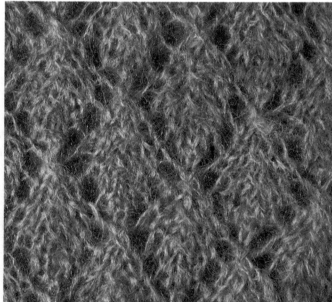

Theo Bergström

FAIR ISLE & JACQUARD

Fair Isle and jacquard are both techniques for creating multi-coloured designs in knitting.
Fair Isle designs combine only two colours in any one row. The method is fairly simple, providing you do not let the separate colours get tangled up. Stocking stitch is used throughout with one colour forming the ground shade and the other forming the pattern. When one colour is being knitted, the other has to be carried across the back of the work until it is needed again.

Jacquards are designs which combine more than two shades in a row. That means that two or more colours have to be 'stranded' or woven across the back of the work until they are needed again. Jacquard is also known to be a single multi-coloured motif on a plain background.
Patterns for Fair Isle and jacquard motifs are given in chart form – each square represents one stitch in a row of knitting. Yarn can be taken over using either the weaving or the 'strand ing' method described on page 238.
Instructions for dresses, page 248.

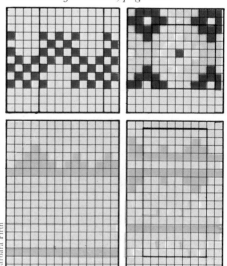

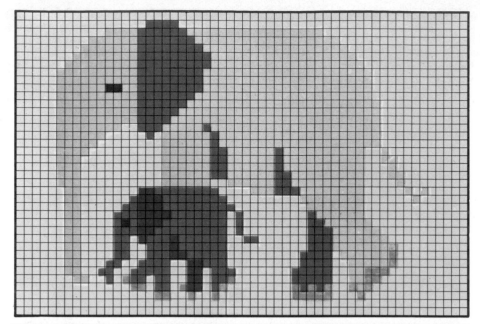

Barbara Firth

234

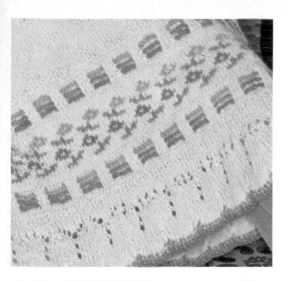

This beautiful coat and skirt in
soft pastel shades are an unusual
combination of Fair Isle and
jacquard techniques.
The skirt has a dainty self-
coloured pattern of contrasting
stitches: the scalloped, lacy hem
is decorated with a knitted-in
border of flower motifs set within
strips of crochet chains threaded
through the fabric. Crochet chains
also make a drawstring fastening at
the waist.
Use rug yarn for the thick, warm
coat in an easy style, patterned
with lozenge shapes, suns and clouds.
Instructions begin on page 249.

John Carter

The two methods of taking yarn over in Fair Isle and jacquard are:

Stranding method. Right side row: knit the given number of stitches in one colour; carry the other colour(s) loosely across *back* of work, making sure the yarn (not in use) is kept loose and not pulled. Then knit required stitches in other colour. Wrong side row: purl the given number of stitches using one colour, carry yarn not in use loosely across *front* of the knitting; purl required number of stitches in the other colour.

Weaving method. This is used when five or more stitches have to be knitted in one colour. Colour(s) not in use should be woven in with every other stitch being knitted in the first colour. To master this, keep colour being knitted in the right-hand and other colours in the left. Right side row: carry yarn at *back* of fabric, knit first stitch (as in pattern) and on the second and every other stitch, insert needle in the normal way – but place the other colour over the top of right-hand needle. Continue knitting with first colour in the usual way. Wrong side row; the stitches have to be purled and yarn woven across *front* of fabric using the same method, changing position of yarn to work in purl. *Cushion instructions, page 251*

Theo Bergström

Jerry tubby

238

KNITTING NEEDLE SIZES

METRIC	9	8½	8	7½	7	6½	6	5½	5	4½	4	3½	3¼	3	2¾	2¼	2
AMERICAN	15	13	12	11	10½	10	9	8	7	6	5	4	3	2	1	0	00
ENGLISH	000	00	0	1	2	3	4	5	6	7	8	9	10	11	12	13	14

KNITTING TIPS

Sizes. Before beginning work look at the measurements stated: check the finished lengths of individual pieces and read the working instructions to see if provision is made for you to make alterations. There may be more than one: instructions for larger sizes are usually given in parentheses. Here, American sizes are given in brackets. Underline the figures relevant to your size throughout the pattern to avoid confusion.

Tension (gauge). For your pattern to be the correct size you must attain the stated tension (gauge). Always work a sample before you begin the pattern.

Materials. If you want to substitute an alternative, see from the tension sample whether the yarn is a comparable weight.

Working instructions. Make the pattern pieces in the order which they appear in the instructions; different pieces may have to be joined before you can continue knitting, or specific instructions may be referred back to at a later stage.

READING A PATTERN

Knitting patterns are given in abbreviated form, a key to these is given opposite.

An asterisk, (*) in a pattern row denotes that you must repeat the sequence of stitches from that point as instructed. A whole section marked with double or triple asterisks at the beginning and end means it is repeated further on.

KNITTING ABBREVIATIONS

alt. = alternate
beg. = begin(ning)
cm = centimetre(s)
cont. = continu(e)(ing)
dec. = decreas(e)(ing)
foll. = following
g. st. = garter stitch
inc. = increas(e)(ing)
K = knit
M1 = make one, by wfd or wrn
mst. = moss stitch
patt. = pattern
psso. = pass slip stitch over
P = purl
rep. = repeat
rem. = remain(ing)
Skpo. = slip one, knit one, pass slip stitch over
sl. = slip
st(s). = stitch(es)
st. st. = stocking stitch
tog. = together
wrn. = wool round needle
yfwd. = yarn forward

COLOUR ABBREVIATIONS

B = beige
Bl = blue
Gr = green
Oc = ochre
Pk = pink
Rs = rust
T = turquoise
Wh = white
Yl = yellow

Special note

Sizes in square brackets refer to American sizes.

HOLDING YARN AND NEEDLES

You must hold the yarn and needles correctly to achieve a firm, neat fabric with consistent tension. If you are right-handed, wind the yarn round the fingers of your right hand (1). Left-handed knitters should work from the reflected version of the diagrams through a mirror. Hold the needle to form the stitch in your right hand and

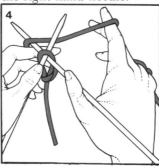

the needle holding the stitches to be worked in your left hand as shown below (2). All stitches are made by transferring loops from left to right-hand needles.

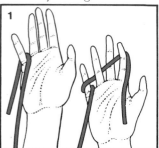

TWO NEEDLE CASTING ON

Make a slip loop about 10cm (4″) from the end of yarn and put the loop onto the left-

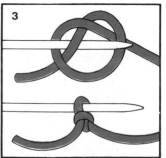

hand needle (3).

Holding the yarn in your right hand, take up the other needle. Insert the right-hand needle into the slip loop from front to back, (4) and with your right hand, wind yarn under and over the point of the right-hand needle.

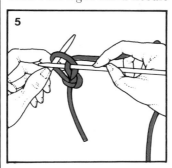

Draw a loop through the slip loop (5), transfer the new loop to the *left-hand* needle. Insert the right-hand needle

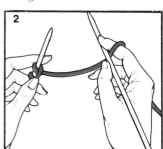

from front to back between the 2 loops on the left-hand needle (6). Wind the yarn under and over the point of the right-hand needle and draw a loop through: transfer the new loop to the left-hand needle as before. Continue working in the same way until you have cast on the required number of stitches.

You are now ready to begin the first row.

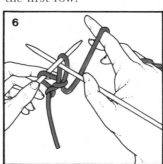

THUMB METHOD CASTING ON

This produces a more elastic and hard-wearing edge than the 2-needle method. Make a slip loop in the yarn some distance from the end; the distance varies according to the number of stitches required, but approximately 1m (1yd) of yarn is enough for 100 stitches. Place the slip loop onto the right-hand needle (1): hold the shorter end of yarn in your left hand by passing it between your index finger and thumb, round the thumb and holding it across the palm of your

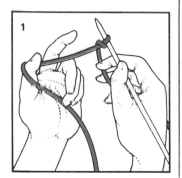

hand with other fingers (1). Insert the needle into the loop on your thumb: wind the yarn from the main ball under and over the point of the needle (2) and draw it through the loop on your thumb so that a new loop is

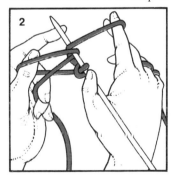

on the needle.
Tighten the last stitch on the needle: wind the yarn round

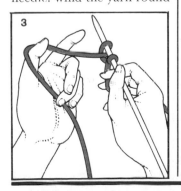

your thumb again (3) ready for the next stitch. Make the number of stitches required in the same way. You are now ready to begin row one.

CASTING OFF

Casting off finished work can be done on a knit, purl or pattern row providing you work each stitch in the correct order before casting it off. With the yarn and needles in the normal working position, work the first 2 stitches to transfer them to the right-hand needle. Use the point of the left-hand needle to lift the *first* stitch knitted over the second one (1) and off the needle, leaving 1 stitch on the right-hand needle.

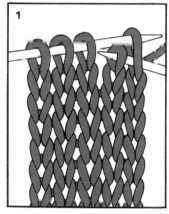

Work the next stitch in the usual way and repeat the process of lifting one stitch over another (2). Continue in this way until you have 1 stitch remaining on the right-hand needle. Secure the last stitch by breaking off the yarn about 10cm (4″) from the knitting; draw the cut end through the stitch on the needle and pull it gently to tighten.

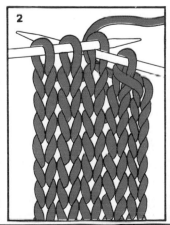

BASIC STITCHES – KNIT

Hold the needle with the cast-on stitches in your left hand and the free needle in your right hand. Insert the right-hand needle from front to back into the first stitch on the left-hand needle (1). Keeping the yarn at the *back* of the work throughout, wind it under and over the top of the right-hand needle. Draw a loop through the

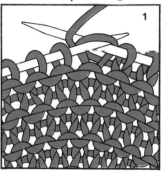

stitch on the left-hand needle (2).
Leave the new stitch on the

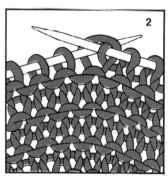

right-hand needle and drop the stitch from the left-hand needle (3). Continue working in this way until you transfer all the stitches to the right-hand needle. To begin the next row change the position of the needles so that the one holding the stitches is in your left hand.
The knit stitch is used to create garter stitch and stocking stitch patterns.

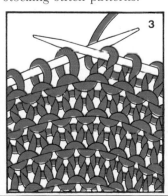

BASIC STITCHES – PURL

Hold the needle with the cast-on stitches in your left hand and the free needle in your right hand. Insert the right-hand needle *from back to front* into the first stitch on the left-hand needle (1). Keeping the yarn at the front of the work throughout, wind it over the top and round right-hand needle. Draw a loop through the

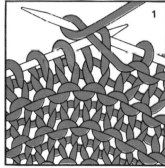

stitch on the left-hand needle (2).
Leave the new stitch on the

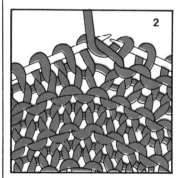

right-hand needle and drop the stitch from the left-hand needle (3). Continue working in this way until you transfer all the stitches to the right-hand needle. To begin the next row change the position of the needles so that the one holding the stitches is in your left hand.
Used in alternate rows with knit stitch, purl makes a stocking stitch pattern.

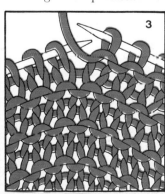

241

Tea Cosy

Height: from base to top of roof, 25cm (10″)
Width: 29cm (11½″) – plus gusset

MATERIALS

Yarn: oddments of wool: about 1 25gm (1oz) ball of 4-ply wool in cream and in white. 1˙25gm (1oz) ball of brown/red fleck (for beams) 1½ 25gm (1oz) balls of blue/green fleck for roof and door. ½ ball of green for base, ½ ball of yellow for base and windows, and ½ ball of rust for windows.
Pair of 4½mm [No.6] and 3¼mm [No.3] knitting needles
Lining, padding
Eyelet hole and bead

TENSION

About 8 sts. to 2.5cm (1″) over sl. st. patt.

PATTERN

GUSSET (2 alike)
Using Gr., and 3¼mm [No.3] needles cast on 26 sts. and work 6 rows in st. st.
7th row. Join in Y1. (1Gr. 1Y1) to end.
8th–10th rows. As 7th row thus alternating colours. (If preferred work more sts. in Gr. or Y.1 to give movement in grass.)
Turn up lower edge and make a hem by taking 1 st. from lower edge and knitting it together with corresponding st. on needle to end.
Next row. P.
** Change to 4½mm [No.6] needles and work in either cream or white to give

exterior 'design effect' and patt. thus:
Next row. *K1, sl. 1. Rep. from * to end.
2nd row. *P1, sl. 1. Rep. from * to end.
Rep. these 2 rows until 18 rows of patt. have been worked.
Change to 3¼mm [No.3] needles and using brown/red fleck yarn work 4 rows in st. st. **
Rep. from ** to ** once more, then using 4½mm [No.6] needles and cream or white, work in sl. st. patt. for 26 rows ***.
Using brown/fleck yarn and 3¼mm [No.3] needles work 4 rows in st. st.
Change to 4½mm [No.6] needles and cream or white and cont. thus:
1st row. (K1, sl. 1) to end.
2nd row. P2 tog., then patt. to last 2 sts., P2 tog. Cont. thus in sl. st. patt. dec. 1 st. each end of every 4th row until 8 sts. rem. Work 2 rows straight then cast off.

FRONT AND BACK
(Both alike)
Using Gr. and 3¼mm [No.3] needles, cast on 64 sts. and work as for gusset to ***.
Cast off 27 sts. at beg. of next 2 rows, then cont. in sl. st. patt. on rem. 10 sts. for 15 rows. Cast off.

DOOR
Using blue/green fleck yarn and 3¼mm [No.3] needles, cast on 14 sts.
1st row. K3, P2, K3, P2, K4.
2nd row. P4, K2, P3, K2, P3.
Rep. these 2 rows 12 times more. Cast off.

ROOF (2 sides alike)
Using blue/green fleck yarn and 3¼mm [No.3] needles, beg. at top of roof and cast on 50 sts.
1st–4th rows. In st. st.
*5th row.** K3 inc. in next st, K. to last 4 sts., inc. in next st., K3.

6th row. P.
7th row. K.
8th row. P3, inc. in next st. P. to last 4 sts., inc. in next st. P3.
9th row. K.
10th row. P*. Rep. from * to * until the 22nd row has been worked. (62 sts.)
23rd row. K3, inc. in next st., K22, cast off 10 sts., K22, inc. in next st., K3. Work on last set of sts.
1st row. P.
2nd row. K.
3rd row. P3, inc. in next st, P. to end.
4th row. K.
5th row. P. to last 4 sts., inc. in next st. P3.
6th row. K. to last 4 sts., inc. in next st., K3.
7th row. P.
8th row. K.
9th row. P3, inc. in next st, P. to end.
10th row. K3, inc. in next st, K. to end.
11th row. P. to end.
12th row. K. to last 4 sts., inc. in next st., K3.
13th–16th rows. In st. st. Cast off.
Go back to other sts., rejoin yarn and work to match other side.

STRIPS FOR VERTICAL BEAMS
Using 3¼mm [No.3] needles and brown/red fleck yarn, cast on 4 sts., and work in st. st. working 8 strips to measure 5cm (2″) and 1 strip to measure 20cm(8″). Cast off.

CHIMNEY
Using 3¼mm [No.3] needles and white, cast on 16 sts. and work 8 rows in st. st., 6 rows in sl. st. patt. 20 rows in st. st., 6 rows in sl. st. patt. and 8 rows in st. st. Cast off.

WINDOWS (9 alike)
Using 3¼mm [No.3] needles and Rs, cast on 12 sts. and work 2 rows in st. st.
3rd row. (1Y1, 3 Rs) to end.
4th row. 1Y1, 1Rs, (3Y1, 1Rs) twice, 2 Y1.

5th row. (1Rs, 3Y1) to end.
6th row. 1Rs (1Y1, 3Rs) twice, 1Y1, 2Rs.
7th row. (1Rs, 3Y1) to end.
8th row. As 4th row.
9th row. As 3rd row.
10th row. As 4th row.
Work 2 rows in Rs in st. st. Cast off.

TO MAKE UP
Press on wrong side lightly. Sew four 5cm (2″) beams to the top panel of each front and back, leaving a larger gap in the centre under the top window (see picture).
Front. At the lower right-hand corner, sew the 20cm (8″) beam, covering the width of the other two panels and following the shape of door. Sew the door inside this, with the larger panel of rib to the right. Now to the left of the door, in the middle white/cream band, and centrally under the vertical beams, sew one window in place. Sew another window to the top flap.
Back. In centre white/cream band, centrally under the vertical beams, sew in 2 windows. Sew another window to the top flap.
Gussets. Sew one window to top band, and another to corresponding band of front and back. Sew gusset in position, matching beams.
Chimney. Fold chimney in half with right sides facing and sl. st. patt. matching. Sew sides. Turn to right side.
Roof. Sew together the front and back of roof sandwiching the chimney. Place wrong side of roof over top edge of front and back. Pin carefully in place, then sew down.
The embroidery. Using oddments of wool, work the herbaceous border.
Attach loose threads of green wool by a couple of oversew sts. at the base, to form the stems of the bunches of flowers. Make the blooms by passing the needle through the end of the green thread

Paul Williams

and knotting. Work 5 bullion sts. (see Embroidery chapter), to form fern leaves at base of bunches of flowers. The creeper is formed by feather st. Make french knots (see Embroidery) in various colours along creeper.

Press work once more.

Sew one eyelet on door, and make long over-sts. through eyelet to represent knocker. Sew a small bead in place for door knob.

Padding. Using knitted tea-cosy as a patt. guide cut out padding and lining for roof and walls in one. Quilt lining by stitching along length at about 5cm (2″) intervals. Sew gussets in place. Pin and tack hem – about 15mm (½″). Machine into place.

Insert padding into tea cosy. Pin base to within 15mm (½″) of base of tea cosy. Hem in place.

Woman's T-Shape Sweater

Bust: 86–91cm (34–36″)
All round: 96cm (38″)
Length: 64cm (25″)
Sleeve seam: 40cm (16″)

MATERIALS
Yarn: 1000gm (35oz) of chunky yarn such as Wendy Naturelle
A pair of 5½mm [No.8] knitting needles. A circular 5½mm [No.8] needle (optional).

TENSION
16 sts and 30 rows measure about 10cm (4″) over g. st.

PATTERN
Beg. at the sleeve edge, fol-

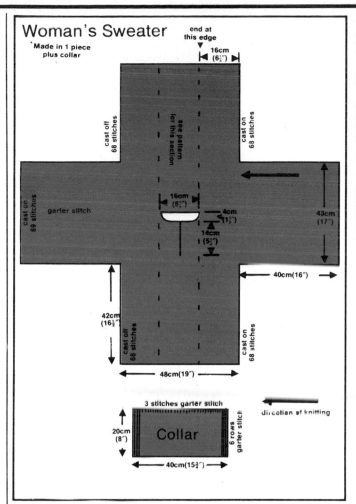

Woman's sweater, diagrammed above, is worked from right to left.

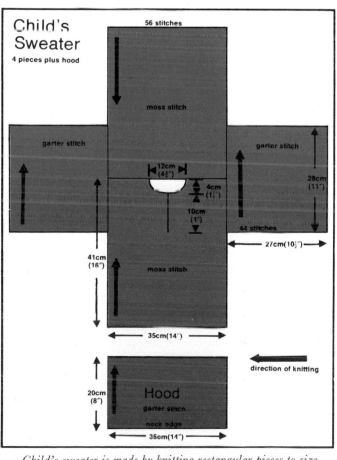

Child's sweater is made by knitting rectangular pieces to size.

low instructions on the diagram (left). Remember that the garment can be made larger or smaller by increasing or decreasing the number of stitches.

Divide for neck
Next row. K102, turn and cont. on these sts. for back neck for 16cm (6¼″) ending with a right side row. Break off yarn and leave sts. on spare needle.

Go back to other 103 sts., then with right side of work facing, rejoin yarn, cast off 3 sts. at beg. of row, 2 sts. at beg. of foll. alt row, then dec. 1 st. at beg of foll. 2 alt. rows. Cont. on these 96 sts. until work measures 8cm (3¼″) from beg. of neck shaping, noting how many rows were worked on the straight and ending with a right side row.
Next row. K73, cast off rem 23 sts. Break off yarn. Cast on 23 sts., then with right side facing K the 73 sts. Cont. straight for same number of rows as on left side shaping, ending with a wrong side row. Now inc. 1 st at beg. of next and foll. alt. row, then cast on 2 sts. at beg. of foll. alt. row and 3 sts on next alt. row.

TO MAKE UP
Join side and sleeve seams. Sew on collar, beg. and ending at top of front opening. Press seams.

Child's T-Shape Sweater

Chest: 66cm (26″)
Width all round: 70cm (27½″)
Length: 41cm (16″)
Sleeve seam: 27cm (10½″)

MATERIALS
Yarn: 500gm (17½oz) of chunky yarn such as Wendy

Naturelle
Oddments of double knitting for edgings
Pair of 5½mm [No.8] knitting needles

TENSION

16 sts. and 20 rows measure about 10cm (4″) over mst; 16 sts. and 30 rows measure about 10cm (4″) over g.st.

PATTERN

Calculate the number of stitches to be cast on for back, front, sleeves and hood. The measurements on the diagram on the previous page fit the measurements stated.

☐ Work following instructions on diagram.

Divide for front opening
Next row. M.st. 28, turn and leave other sts. for the present.

Cont. on first sts. for 10cm (4″) ending at inside edge.

Shape neck
Cast off 6 sts. at beg. of next row, 2 sts. at beg. of foll. alt. row, then dec. 1 st. at beg. of foll. 2 alt. rows. Work 1 row, then cast off.

Go back to other sts., rejoin yarn and work to match first side.

TO MAKE UP

Join shoulders. Measure down from each shoulder, 14cm (5½″) and mark with pins. Sew in sleeves between pins. Join sleeve seams. Sew up side seams leaving 10cm (4″) free at lower edges. Sew hood in position round neck edge. Now using double knitting work blanket st. all round lower edges and slits, around hood, front opening and cuffs. Press seams.

Man's T-Shape Sweater

Chest: 96–102cm (38–40″)
All round: 106cm (42″)

Man's Sweater
4 separate pieces

84 stitches

18 rows garter stitch
6 rows stocking stitch
16 rows garter stitch
6 rows stocking stitch

Continue decreasing garter stitch by 2 rows

10 rows garter stitch
6 rows stocking stitch
10 rows garter stitch
6 rows stocking stitch

Continue

80 stitches

50cm (20″)   17cm (6¾″)

5cm (2″)

35cm (14″)

45cm(18)

69cm (27″)

direction of knitting

53cm(21″)

Diagram of man's sweater shows stitch pattern and construction.

Length: 69cm (27″)
Sleeve seam: 45cm (18″)

MATERIALS

Yarn: approx. 950gm (33½oz) chunky yarn such as Wendy Naturelle.
Pair of 5½mm [No.8] and 6mm [No.9] knitting needles
25cm (10″) zip fastener
Oddments of double knitting yarn in contrast

TENSION

About 16 sts. and 20 rows measure 10cm (4″) on 6mm [No.9] needles, over st. st. About 16 sts. and 30 rows measure 10cm (4″) on 5½mm [No.8] needles over g. st.

PATTERN

Calculate number of stitches to be cast on for back, front and sleeves. Calculations or diagram fit measurements stated.

☐ Work front, back and sleeves using 5mm [No.8] needles for rows of g. st. and 6mm [No.9] needles for rows of st. st.

Divide for opening
Next row. Patt. 42, turn and leave other sts. on spare needle.

Cont. on first sts. and work to match back until 11 rows less than back have been worked thus ending after a right side row.

Shape neck
Cast off 8 sts. at beg. of next row, 2 sts. at beg. of foll. 2 alt, rows then dec. 1 st. at beg. of foll. 2 alt. rows. Work 2 rows, then cast off.

Go back to the sts., rejoin yarn and work to match first side, reversing shapings.

TO MAKE UP

Join shoulders. Measure 25 cm (10″) down from each shoulder and mark with pins. Sew cast off edge of sleeves between pin positions. Join side and sleeve seams. Sew in zip between first g. st. ridge and lower edge of front opening. Using the double knitting wool, work blanket stitch round neck and down either side of front opening to top of zip. Press seams.

Aran Sweaters

Child's Sweater
Chest: 61–66cm (24–26″)
All round: 70cm (27½″)
Sleeve length: 33cm (13″)

Man's Sweater
Chest: 97–102cm (38–40″)
All round: 108cm (42½″)
Sleeve length: 47cm (20″)

MATERIALS

Yarn: approx. 500 (1250) gm. or 18 (45)oz of Aran weight wool.
Pair of 4½mm [No.6] knitting needles
Cable needle

TENSION

Each square measures about 11.5 (18)cm–4½″(7″). Man's sizes are in parentheses.

Note: Special abbreviations C4B = sl. next 2 sts. to cable needle and leave at back of work, K2, then K the 2 sts. from cable needle; C4F = sl. next 2 sts. on cable needle and leave at front of work K2, then K the 2 sts. from cable needle.

PATTERN
FIRST SQUARE
(Make 14)
Cast on 24(34) sts. and K4(6) rows, inc. 1 st. in centre of last row, then cont. in patt. thus:
1st row. K6(7), then (P1, K7) 2(3) times, P1, K2(3).
2nd row. K2(3) P1, K1, (P5, K1, P1, K1) 2(3) times, P3, K2(3).
3rd row. K4(5) then (P1, K3) to last 5(6) sts, P1, K4(5).
4th row. K2(3), P3, (K1, P1, K1, P5) 2(3) times, K1, P1, K2(3).

5th row. K2(3) then (P1, K7) 2(3) times, P1, K6(7)
6th row. As 4th row.
7th row. As 3rd row.
8th row. As 2nd row.
Rep. these 8 rows 2(3) times more, then the first 1(5) rows again. K4(6) rows dec. 1 st. in centre of 1st row. Cast off.

SECOND SQUARE
(Make 14)
Cast on 24(34) sts. and K4(6) rows, inc. 4 sts. evenly across last row, then cont. in patt.
1st row. K. to end.
2nd and alt. rows. K2(3), then P to last 2(3) sts., K2(3).
3rd row. K2(3), * C4B, C4F. Rep. from * to last 2(3) sts., K2(3).
5th row. As 1st row.
7th row. K2(3) *C4F, C4B. Rep. from * to last 2(3) sts., K2(3).
8th row. As 2nd row.
Rep. these 8 rows 2(3) times more, then the first 1(5) rows again.
Next row. K to end, dec. 4 sts. evenly across the row. K3(5) rows. Cast off.

THIRD SQUARE
(Make 14)
Cast on 24(34) sts. and K4(6) rows, then cont. in patt.
1st row. K2(3), P to last 2(3) sts., K2(3).
2nd row. K2(3), * (K1, P1, K1) into next st., P3 tog. Rep. from * to last 2(3) sts., K2(3).
3rd row. As 1st row.
4th row. K2(3), * P3 tog (K1, P1, K1) into next st. Rep. from * to last 2(3) sts., K2(3).
Rep. these 4 rows 4(8) times more, then for 1st size, rep. the first 2 rows again. K5(7) rows. Cast off.

TO MAKE UP
Press work according to ball band instructions. Using a flat seam join squares as shown in diagram, first joining back and front squares tog. Now join the 9 squares of each sleeve, fold and join sleeve seam. Sew in sleeves, then sew up side seams to complete sweater.

Paul Williams

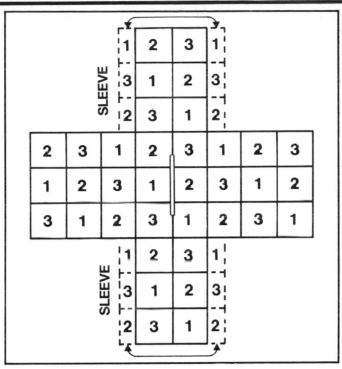

Assembly diagram of Aran squares: (1) honeycomb, (2) fish net, (3) Trinity. Dotted lines indicate fold of sleeves.

Smocks

Woman's Smock

Bust: 86(91:96)cm−34″(36″: 38″)

MATERIALS
Yarn: 16(17:17) 40-gm (2 oz) balls light-weight chunky yarn such as Listers Can-Can. Oddments of contrasting double knitting for smocking.
Pair of 6½mm [No.10] and 5mm [No.7] needles

TENSION
About 3½ sts. and 4½ rows to 2.5cm (1″)

PATTERN
FRONT AND BACK
Using 6½mm [No.10] needles cast on 91(95:99) sts. and work in mst. for 4 (4:5)cm−1½″(1½″:2″).

Change to st.st. and with P side as right side, dec. 1 st. each end of 7th row and every 6th row until 73(77:81) sts. rem. Cont. straight until work measures 43 (44.5:46)cm−17″(17½″:18″)
Begin ribbed panel
Next row. P19(21:23), then (K1, P1) 17 times, K1, P19(21:23).
Next row. K19(21:23) then (P1, K1) 17 times, P1, K19(21:23).
These 2 rows form the smocking patt. Cont. straight until ribbed panel measures 18(19:20)cm−7″ (7½″:8″). End after a K row.
Next row. P19(21:23) and leave these sts. on a spare needle, cast off next 35 sts., P to end.
Work straight on these last 19(21:23) sts. for 5 rows. Cast off. Go back to other sts., rejoin yarn and work 5 rows. Cast off.

SLEEVES
Join shoulders, then measure 18(19:20)cm−7½″ (7¾″: 8″) down from shoulder and mark with pins. Using 6½mm (No10) needles and holding work right side towards you (P. side) pick up and P63(67:71) sts. between pins. Work in reverse st. st.

beg. with a K row, dec. 1 st. at each end of every 3rd row until 49 sts. rem. for each size. Continue straight until work measures 36cm (14″) − or length required, ending after a P row. Change to 5mm [No.7] needles.
Next row. *K2, K2 tog. Rep from * to last st., K1, (37 sts.)
Work in K1, P1 rib for 5cm (2″), then work 5cm (2″) in mst. Cast off in mst.

HALF COLLARS
(2 Alike)
Using 5mm [No. 7] needles cast on 43 sts for each size and work in mst. for 9cm (3½″). Cast off in mst.

TO MAKE UP
Smock ribbed panel, following instructions overleaf and using contrasting yarn and alternating ribs at 5 row intervals − or depth required. Press following instructions on ball band. Sew up sleeve and side seams. Sew on half collars. Press seams.

Child's Smock

Chest: 51(56:61)cm−20″ (22″: 24″).
Yarn: 8(9:10) 20-gm (1oz) balls of machine washable double knitting yarn such as Lister Concorde Easy Wash
Contrasting yarn for smocking
Pair of 4½mm [No.6] and 3mm [No.2] knitting needles

TENSION
20 sts. measure 10cm (4″).

PATTERN
FRONT AND BACK
Begin at Front. Using 4½mm [No.6] needles cast on 81(87:95) sts. and work in mst for 5(6:7) rows.
Change to reverse st. st. with P side as right side and work until front measures 20(26.5:29)cm−8″. (10½″: 11½″) ending after a K row.
Next row. P20(23:27) then (K1, P3) 10 times, K1, P20(23:27).
Next row. K20(23:27) then (P1, K3) 10 times, P1,

K20(23:27).

These 2 rows form the smocking patt. Cont. straight until ribbed panel measures 11.5(13:14)cm– 4½″(5″:5½″) ending after a K row.

Divide for neck

Next row. P20(23:27) and leave on spare needle, cast off next 41 sts., P20(23:27). Cont in reverse st. st. on the 20(23:27) sts. for 13(15:15) rows, thus ending at neck edge. Leave for the present. Rejoin yarn to neck edge of other sts. and work in reverse st. st. for 14(16:16) rows, cast on 41 sts. and P across other sts. Now work across all sts., working the 41 sts. in ribbed patt. as for front until back ribbed panel measures as front, then cont. straight in reverse st. st. for 18.5 (24: 26.5)cm – 7¼″(9½″:10½″). Change to mst. and work for 5(6:7) rows. Cast off in mst.

SLEEVES

Fold work in half, and mark shoulder line, then measure 10(11.5:13)cm – 4″(4½″:5″) down from shoulder line and mark with pins. Using 4½mm [No.6] needles and holding work right side facing (P side) pick up and P60(70:80) sts. between pins. Work in reverse st. st. dec. 1 st. at beg. of every row until 44(54:64) sts. rem. Cont. straight until sleeve measures 11.5(15:19)cm– 4½″(6″:7½″) or length required, ending after a P row. Change to 3mm [No.2] needles.

Next row. K8(3:3) then K2 tog. to last 8(3:3) sts., K8(3:3)–30(30:35) sts. Now work in K1, P1 rib for 3.5cm (1½″). Change to mst. and work for 2(2.5:2.5)cm ¾″(1″:1″). Cast off in mst.

HALF COLLARS
(2 alike)

Using 3mm [No.2] needles cast on 45(49:49) sts. and work in mst. for 5.5(6:6)cm– 2¼″(2½″:2½″). Cast off in mst.

TO MAKE UP

Smock ribbed panel, (figs. 1a and b) using contrasting yarn and alternating ribs at 5 row intervals – or depth required. Press lightly. Sew up sleeve and side seams. Sew on half collars. Press seams.

How to Smock

The smocking is worked in honeycomb stitch, in double rows about 2.5cm (1″) apart on the large smock and 2cm (¾″) apart on the child's version.

☐ Starting at the top left-hand corner of the panel to be smocked, bring the needle through to the right side of the knitting, outside the first rib.

☐ Keeping the wool above the needle, insert the needle across the next rib in the same row from right to left, and then over the first rib again, fig. 1a; pull ribs together.

☐ Insert needle again from right to left over the second rib and pass it on the wrong side of the knitting to second rib of second row.

☐ With the needle above the thread, stitch the second and third ribs in the second row together as before, fig 1b. Pass needle on the wrong side to come out beyond the first row.

☐ Continue stitching two ribs together on each stitch on alternating rows. This produces the honeycomb.

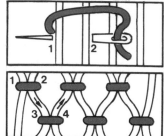

1a and b. Honeycomb smock.

Mohair Sweater

Bust: 91–96cm (36″–38″)
Length from shoulder: 70cm (27½″)
Sleeve seam: 44cm (17½″)

MATERIALS

Yarn: 14 balls of mohair.
Pairs of 3¾mm [No.4], 5mm [No.7] and 6mm [No.9] knitting needles

TENSION

About 15 sts. and 18 rows to 10cm (4″) over patt. on 6mm [No.9] needles.

PATTERN

1st row. Sl. 1, K2 tog., K2 *wrn, K1, wrn, K2, sl. 1, K2 tog, psso, K2. Rep from * ending last rep., wrn, K1, wrn, K2, sl. 1, K1, psso, K1.
2nd and alt. rows. P.

3rd row. Sl. 1, K2 tog., K1. *wrn, K3, wrn, K1, sl.1, K2 tog., psso, K1. Rep. from * ending last rep. wrn, K3, wrn, K1, sl. 1, K1, psso, K1.
5th row. Sl. 1, K2 tog., * wrn, K5, wrn, sl. 1, K2 tog., psso. Rep, from * ending last rep. wrn, K5, wrn, sl. 1 K1, psso, K1.
7th row. Sl. 1, K1, * wrn, K2, sl. 1, K2 tog., psso, K2, wrn, K1. Rep. from * to last st., K1.
9th row. Sl. 1, K2, * wrn, K1, sl. 1, K2 tog., psso, K1 wrn, K3. Rep. from * to end.
11th row. Sl. 1, K3, * wrn sl. 1, K2 tog., psso, wrn, K5. Rep. from * ending last rep. K4 instead of K5.
12th row. P.
These 12 rows form the patt.

BACK

Using 3¾mm [No.4] needles, cast on 74 sts. and work 15cm (6″) in K1, P1 rib, inc. 1 st. at end of last row. Change to 5mm [No.7] needles and work in the 12 row patt. for 1 row, then change to 6mm [No.9] needles and cont. straight until. work measures 49.5cm (19½″).
Shape armholes. Keeping continuity of patt. work thus: cast off 3 sts. at beg of next 2 rows, then cast off 2 sts. at beg. of next 6 rows. 57 sts. rem. Continue straight until work measures 68cm (26¾″) ending after a wrong side row.

Shape neck and shoulder

1st row. Patt. 26 sts., turn. Leave rem. sts. on spare needle.
2nd–4th rows. Cast off 4 sts. at beg. of rows.
5th row. Cast off 5 sts., work to end.
6th row. Cast off 4 sts., work to end.
Cast off rem. 5 sts.
Go back to other sts., rejoin yarn to centre, cast off 5 sts., work to end. Work to match other side, reversing shapings.

FRONT

Work as for back until armhole shaping is completed and 57 sts. rem., then cont. straight until work measures 65.5cm (25¾″) ending after a wrong side row

Shape neck and shoulder

1st row. Patt. 27 sts., turn. Leave rem. sts. on spare needle.
2nd row. Cast off 3 sts., work to end.
3rd row. In patt.
Rep. last 2 rows twice more.
8th row. Cast off 2 sts., work to end.
9th row. Cast off 4 sts., work to end.
10th row. As 8th row.
11th row. Cast off 5 sts., work to end.
12th row. In patt.
Cast off rem. 5 sts.
Go back to other sts., rejoin yarn, cast off centre 3 sts., patt. to end. Now work to match other side, reversing shapings.

SLEEVES

Using 3¾mm [No.4] needles, cast on 42 sts. Work 10cm (4″) in K1, P1 rib.
Next row. Rib 4 (inc. in next st., rib 1) to last 4 sts., rib. 4 59 sts.
Change to 5mm [No.7] needles and work first row of patt., then change to 6mm [No.9] needles and cont. in patt. until work measures 44cm (17½″).

Shape Top. Cast off 3 sts. at beg. of next 2 rows, 2 sts. on next 6 rows, 1 st. at beg. of next 14 rows. Now cast off 2 sts. at beg. of next 2 rows and 5 sts. at beg. of next 2 rows. Cast off rem. 13 sts.

NECKBAND

Using 3¾mm [No.4] needles, cast on 176 sts. and work 10 rows in K1, P1 rib.
Next row. Cast off 48 sts., rib 90 sts. – including st. already on needle from casting off, cast off 38 sts. Now cast off centre 90 sts.

TO MAKE UP

Do not press. Sew side, shoulder and sleeve seams. Sew in sleeves. With right side facing sew cast off 90 sts. of neckband to neck leaving 6.5cm (2¾") in front free. Knot ties.

Lace Sweater and Skirt

Bust: 86(91:97)cm–34" (36":38")

MATERIALS

Yarn: 6 50-gm (2oz) balls 4-ply wool such as Jaeger Celtic Spun for sweater and 4 50-gm (2oz) balls for skirt.
Skirt fabric: 170cm×90cm (67"×36") fabric which matches a knitted square in weight.
20cm (8") zip
1m (1yd) petersham
Hooks and eyes, thread
Pair of 3¼mm [No.3] and 3¾mm [No.4] knitting needles.

TENSION

About 12½ sts. and 18 rows measure 5cm (2") over patt using 3¾mm[No.4] needles.

SWEATER PATTERN
BACK
Using 3¼mm [No.3] needles cast on 77(81:85) sts. and work in K1, P1 rib until work measures 7cm (3"). Change to 3¾mm [No.4] needles.
Next row. K1, * K1, inc. in next st. Rep. from * to end. 115(121:127) sts.
Next row. P to end.
Now work in patt. thus:
1st row. K1, *yfwd, sl. 1, K1, psso, K1, K2 tog., yfwd, K1. Rep. from * to end.
2nd and every alt. row: P.
3rd row. K1, * yfwd, K1, sl. 1, K2 tog., psso, K1, yfwd, K1. Rep. from * to end.
5th row. K1, * K2 tog., yfwd, K1, yfwd, sl. 1, K1, psso, K1. Rep. from * to end
7th row. K2 tog., * (K1, yfwd) twice, K1, sl. 1, K2 tog., psso. Rep. from * but ending last rep. sl. 1, K1, psso instead of sl. 1, K2 tog. psso.
8th row. As 2nd row. These 8 rows form the patt. Cont. straight until work measures 48(51:53)cm – 19"(20":21") ending after a wrong side row.
Shape neck and shoulders
Keeping continuity of patt., work thus.
Next row. Patt. 40(42:44) sts., turn and leave rem. sts. on spare needle.
Next row (neck edge). Cast off 2 sts., patt. to end.
Next row. Cast off 7(7:8) sts., patt. to end.
Rep. last 2 rows twice more. Patt. next row. Cast off rem. sts.
Go back to other sts., sl. centre 35(37:39) sts. on to a holder for centre back neck, rejoin yarn to rem sts. and patt. to end.
Next row. Cast off 7(7:8) sts., patt. to end.
Next row. Cast off 2 sts., patt. to end.
Rep. these last 2 rows twice more. Cast off rem. sts.

FRONT
Work as for back until front measures 43(46:48)cm–17" (18":19") ending after a wrong side row.
Shape neck
Next row. Patt. 46(48:50)

sts., turn and leave rem. sts. on spare needle.
Cast off at beg. of next and every alt. row, 3 sts. once and 2 sts. twice then dec. 1 st. at neck edge on every alt. row until 34(36:38) sts. rem. Cont. straight until work measures as back to shoulder ending at side edge.
Shape shoulder
Cast off at beg. of next and every alt. row 7(7:8) sts. 3 times and then work 1 row straight. Cast off rem. sts. Go back to other sts., sl. centre 23(25:27) sts. on spare needle for centre front neck, rejoin yarn to rem. sts. and patt. to end. Patt. one row, then work to match first side, reversing shapings.

SLEEVES
Using 3¼mm [No.3] needles cast on 37 sts. and work 14 rows in K1, P1 rib. Change to 3¾mm [No.4] needles.
Next row. K10, (inc. in next st.) 18 times, K9. 55 sts.
Next row. P1, * inc. in next st. Rep. from * to end. 109 sts.
Now work in the 8 row patt. until sleeve measures 47 (49:52)cm–18½"(19½":20½" ending after a 7th patt. row. Cast off.

NECKBAND
Join left shoulder. Now using 3¼mm [No.3] needles, and with right side of work facing, pick up and K12 sts. down right back neck, K across back neck sts., pick up and K12 sts. up left back neck and 30 sts. down left front neck K across front neck sts., then pick up and K 30 sts. up right front neck – 142(146:150) sts.
Work in K1, P1 rib until neckband measures 7.5cm (3"). Cast off in rib.

TO MAKE UP
Join right shoulder. Press work, following instructions on ball band and avoiding the ribbing. Sew in sleeves, first measuring down 20cm (8") from shoulder seam, and placing sleeve top between this measurement.
Sew up side and sleeve

seams. Turn neckband in half to wrong side and sl. st. loosely. Press seams.

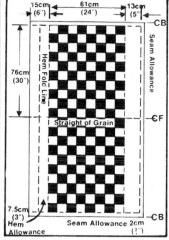

The skirt inset pattern.

THE SKIRT
The square. (80 needed)
Using 3¾mm [No.4] needles cast on 19 sts. and work in the 8 row patt. as for sweater for 23 rows. Cast off on wrong side. Pin out squares to 7.5cm (3") and press.

TO MAKE UP
Prepare fabric. Make sure the edges are on the straight of the grain. Cut a length 91cm×156cm (36"×61½"). Finish the edges. Using tailor's chalk and tacking thread, mark on the fabric a grid as shown in the diagram. Mark the alt. squares as shown in the diagram. Zigzag 1cm (⅜") inside these squares, so that it will have a finished edge when the inside square is cut away, but do not cut the fabric until the knitted squares have been sewn on.
Using the knitting yarn, blanket st. the squares over the marked squares, making sure that the knitted squares cover the zigzagging. Sew on all the squares. Now snip away the surplus fabric behind the knitted squares. Remove the tacking thread. Make up the skirt as follows. Gather along the waist seam line.
Sew centre back seam leaving 22cm (8¾") open at top. Sew in the 20cm (8") zip along free edge.
Cut a waistband to size, allowing extra for an overlap

Trevor Lawrence

to fasten the waistband. Stiffen band with the petersham.

Now place the gathers evenly onto the waistband, excluding the overlap. Seam and fold the waistband. Finish the waistband with hook and eye.

Turn up a 7.5cm (3″) hem. Press all seams.

Children's Dresses

Elephant Motif

Chest: 56cm (22″)

MATERIALS
Yarn: 25gm (1oz) balls of washable double knitting yarn such as Sirdar Superwash in the following amounts: 6 balls in light green (main) 2 balls each of light pink (1st contrast) and dark pink (3rd contrast), 1 ball of medium pink (2nd contrast). Oddments.
Pair of 3¼mm [No.3] and pair of 4mm [No.5] knitting needles
4 small buttons

TENSION
11 sts. and 14 rows measure about 5cm (2″) on 4mm [No.5] needles.

PATTERN
BACK
Using 3¼mm [No.3] needles and with main colour cast on 100 sts and work 9 rows in st. st.
Next row (wrong side). K to form hemline.
Change to 4mm [No.5] needles and beg. with a K row cont. in st. st. for 6 rows. Cont. thus:
** **Next row.** (3rd contrast) K.
Next row. (main) P.
Next row. (main) K.
Next row. (1st contrast) P.
Next 5 rows. (main). In st. st. beg. with a K row. ** Join in 3rd contrast and follow patt. from Fair Isle graph on page 234 working 1st row thus: K 1st and 2nd sts., then rep. from 3rd–10th sts. 12 times, then 11th and 12th st. When Fair Isle chart is completed, cont. in main only and dec. 1 st. each end of next row and every 8th row until 84 sts. rem. Work straight until back measures 33cm (13″) ending after a P. row.
Decrease for yoke
Next row. K 11, *K2 tog., K1. Rep. from * to last 13 sts, K2 tog., K11. (63 sts.)
Next row. P to end.
Shape armholes
1st row. Using main, K9, then work from jacquard graph (page 234) foll. sts. across row to last 9 sts., K9 main.
2nd row. Cast off 9 sts. in patt. to last 9 sts., cast off 9 main.
Cont. in patt. on rem. 45 sts. until work measures 14cm (5½″) from armhole, ending after a P row. Cast off 10 sts. and place wool marker in 10th st. to indicate shoulder, cast off next 25 sts., place a marker in last st., cast off rem. sts.

FRONT
Work as for back until the 7th row after 1st graph has been worked (thus ending after a K. row (98 sts.) Work elephant motif from graph.
Next row. P36 Gr., 2 Oc., 2 Gr., 1 Oc., 2 Gr., 1 Oc., 1 Gr., 2 Oc., 6 Gr., 5 Oc., 3Gr., 1 Oc., 36 Gr.
Now remembering to dec. each end of every 8th row (as for back) cont. to follow graph until completed, then cont. in main only, matching back, dec. for yoke and shaping armholes, then cont. straight until yoke measures 11cm (4¼″) from beg. of armhole ending after a P row.
Shape neck
Next row. K14, and leave on spare needle, cast off 17 sts., K to end.
Working on last sts., dec. 1 st. at neck edge on next 4 rows.
Cont. straight until work measures as back to shoulder. Cast off.
Go back to other sts., rejoin yarn and work to correspond with other side.

SLEEVES
Using main colour and 3¼mm [No.3] needles cast on 38 sts. and work 6cm (2½″) in K2, P2 rib.
Change to 4mm [No.5] needles.
Next row. K6, K twice in to every st. to last 6 sts. K6. 64 sts.
Now work in st. st. for 5 rows, then work in st. st. working stripe patt. as for back from ** to **.
Foll. Fair Isle graph, rep. 3rd–10th sts. 8 times. When Fair Isle is completed, work in main in st. st. until work measures 27cm (10½″) from beg. ending after a P row.
Work the first 4 rows of stripe patt., then 2 rows in main and 1 row in 3rd contrast.
Work 13 rows in st. st. in main. Cast off.

THE BACK NECKBAND
Using main and 3¼mm [No.3] needles and with right side of work facing, pick up and K24 sts. from back neck (between wool markers).
Work 4cm (1½″) in K2, P2 rib. Cast off loosely in rib. Fold neckband in half to wrong side, slip stitch down.

FRONT NECKBAND
Using main and 3¼mm [No.3] needles and with right side of work facing, pick up and K10 sts. from left side neck, 16 sts. from front neck, 10 sts. up right side neck. 36 sts. Work 4cm (1½″) in K2, P2 rib. Cast off loosely in rib. Fold neckband in half to wrong side and slip stitch down.

SHOULDER EDGINGS
With right side facing and 3¼mm [No.3] needles and main, beg. at armhole edge, pick up and K10 sts. from shoulder and 6 sts. from top of neckband edge. (16 sts.)
Next row. (K2. P2) rib to end.
Next row. Rib 5, wrn, K2 tog., rib 5, wrn, K2 tog., rib 2.
Rib 3 more rows and cast off in rib.
Work other side to match, but beg. from neck edge to armhole edge and reversing buttonhole position. Work back shoulder edges to match front, but omitting buttonholes.

TO MAKE UP
Press work following instructions on ball band. Lap front shoulders over back shoulders and sew at armhole edge to secure. Sew in sleeves sewing the last 13 rows in main st. st. to cast off armhole sts. Join side and sleeve seams. Turn up hems at lower edges and sl. st. down neatly.
Sew 2 buttons on each back shoulder to correspond with buttonholes.

Giraffe Motif

Chest: 56cm (22″)

MATERIALS
Yarn: 25gm (1oz) balls of double knitting wool such as Sirdar Superwash, in the following amounts: 7 balls in main colour (blue), 1 ball each of green, yellow, fawn and brown.
Pairs 3¼mm [No.3] and 4mm [No.5] needles
4 small buttons

TENSION
As for elephant motif dress.

PATTERN
Follow instructions for elephant motif dress, but use the other graphs on page 234 for borders and yoke.
Beginning on the row after border pattern has been worked, knit 45 sts. in main colour. Join in brown and follow pattern in graph. Dec. one st. at each end of every 8th row until 84 sts. remain.

Coat and Skirt

Skirt

Sizing: Back and front over main part measures 58cm (23") wide and 74cm (29") long. The length is adjustable and the width, pulled in to required waist measurement.

MATERIALS

Yarn: 8 balls of 50gm (2oz) double knitting wool in white.

1 50gm (2oz) ball of double knitting in each of pink, blue and green.

Pair of 6mm [No.9] and 5mm [No.7] knitting needles

4mm [5–F] crochet hook

TENSION

21 sts. and 27 rows measure 10cm (4") over main patt.

PATTERN
BACK AND FRONT
Using pk and 6mm [No.9]

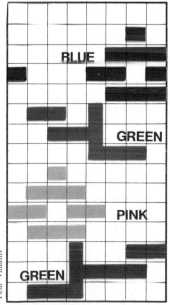

Fair Isle repeat pattern.

needles, cast on 120 sts. loosely, and work 3 rows in mst working 1 row bl, 1 row gr and 1 row wh. Cont in wh.

4th–9th rows. Beg. with a K row, work 6 rows in st. st.

10th row. *K7, catch a loop through the cast on row with the right-hand needle, pull tight, and transfer the st. thus formed to left-hand needle, K tog. the new st. with next st. on needle. Rep. from * to end.

11th row. P.

12th row. *K3, M1, K3, K2 tog. Rep. from * to end.

13th and 14th rows. In st. st. beg. with a P. row.

15th row. *P2 tog., P3, M1, P3. Rep. from * to end.

16th and 17th rows. In st. st. beg. with a K. row.

18th row. *K3, M1, K3, K2 tog. Rep. from * to end.

19th row. P2 tog.,* P2, M1, P1, M1, P2, P3 tog. Rep. from * to last 6 sts., P2, M1, P1, M1, P1, P2 tog.

20th row. K2 tog., M1, K3, M1, K1, K3 tog., *K1, Rep. from * to last 6 sts., M1, K3, M1, K1, K2 tog.

21st row. P2 tog., *M1, P5, M1, P3 tog. Rep. from * to last 6 sts, M1, P6.

Change to 5mm [No.7] needles.

22nd and 23rd rows. In st. st. beg. with a K. row.

24th row. K3, *P1, K7. Rep. from * to last 5 sts., P1, K4.

25th row. P3, *K1, P1, K1, P5. Rep. from * to last 5 sts., K1, P1, K1, P2.

26th row. K1, *(P1, K1) twice, P1, K3 Rep. from * to last 7 sts., (P1, K1) twice, P1, K2.

27th row. (P1, K1) to end.

28th row. (K1, P1) to end.

29th–31st rows. P3 rows.

32nd row. K1, *M1, K2 tog. K1, K2 tog., M1, K3. Rep. from * to last 7 sts., M1, K2 tog., K1 K2 tog., M1, K2.

33rd row. P.

34–37th rows. Rep. 32nd and 33rd rows twice more (3 rows of holes formed).

38th–40th rows. K.

41st row. P.

42nd–55th rows. Work the 14 rows of Fair Isle, rep. 1st–8th sts. across row 15

times.

56th row. K.

57th row. P.

58th–60th rows. K.

61st row. P2, M1, P2 tog., P1, P2 tog., M1, * P3, M1, P2 tog., P1, P2 tog., M1). Rep. from * to last st., P1.

62nd row. K.

63rd–66th rows. Rep. 61st and 62nd rows twice more.

67th–69th rows. P3 rows.

70th row. (K1, P1) to end.

71st row. (P1, K1) to end.

72nd row. K1,* (P1, K1) twice, P1, K3). Rep. from * to last 7 sts., (P1, K1) twice P1, K2.

73rd row. As 25th row.

74th row. As 24th row.

75th row. P.

76th–81st row. In st. st. beg. with a K row.

82nd row. (K7, P1) to end.

83rd row. P1, K1, * P5, K1, P1, K1). Rep. from * to last 6 sts., P5, K1

84th row. (K7, P1) to end.

85th row. P.

86th–91st row. In st. st. beg. with a K row.

92nd row. K3, *P1, K7. Rep. from * to last 5 sts., P1, K4.

93rd row. P3, *K1, P1, K1, P5. Rep. from * to last 5 sts., K1, P1, K1, P2.

94th row. As 92nd row. These last 20 rows – rows 75–94 form the main patt. Rep. them until work measures 68cm (20½") from beg., ending with a P row.

Now work 58th–69th rows for holes for drawstrings, with g. st. ridge below and above. Work 6 rows of mst. and cast off.

DRAWSTRINGS

Using the 4mm [5–F] crochet hook work crochet chains in each of the contrast yarns, working each one 2m (2yd) long. For the lower edges, work crochet chains, twice in each contrasting yarn, long enough to thread through holes. (See Crochet chapter for making chains.)

TO MAKE UP

Press work on wrong side with warm iron over damp cloth. Back stitch side seams. Thread drawstrings through lower holes, in rotation of Pk,

Gr., then Bl. Thread drawstring through waist, beg. at front, and draw up to fit waist. Tie in bow.

Coat

Please bear in mind the following when knitting this pattern:

The lozenge pattern (rows 50–69). Always carry both ends of yarn to end of section. It it very important *not* to pull at the strands of yarn which are not being knitted – those carried across back of work between groups. If pulled, the work will become narrower, and the tension incorrect.

The cloud and sun pattern (rows 100–114). Different balls of different colours are used here and are *not* carried across. Use separate balls twisting the new colour over yarn just knitted to avoid a hole.

When casting off fronts and collar, cast off loosely, as a tight tension will cause coat to hang incorrectly.

Bust: 86–91cm (34–36") bust, worn loosely.

Length: about 118cm (46½") – adaptable.

MATERIALS

Yarn: in rug wool, 1000gm (35oz) in turquoise, 600gm (21oz) in beige, 500gm (18oz) in pink and 500gm (18oz) in white.

Pair of 10mm [No.15] knitting needles

TENSION

About 21 rows and 20 sts. measure 20cm (8").

PATTERN
BACK

Using B cast on 80 sts. ** K5 rows, working, 1 row B, 2 rows Pk. 2 rows Wh.** Then using T, work 4 rows in st. st. Now K6 rows working 2 rows Wh, 2 rows Pk and 2 rows B. Work sl. st. patt. thus:

16th row. Wh. *K3, sl. 1 Rep. from * to end.

17th row. Wh. Yarn to P side, sl. 1, yarn back to K. side, K3. Rep. from * to end.

18th row. Pk. K1, *sl. 1, K3.

Knitted Coat

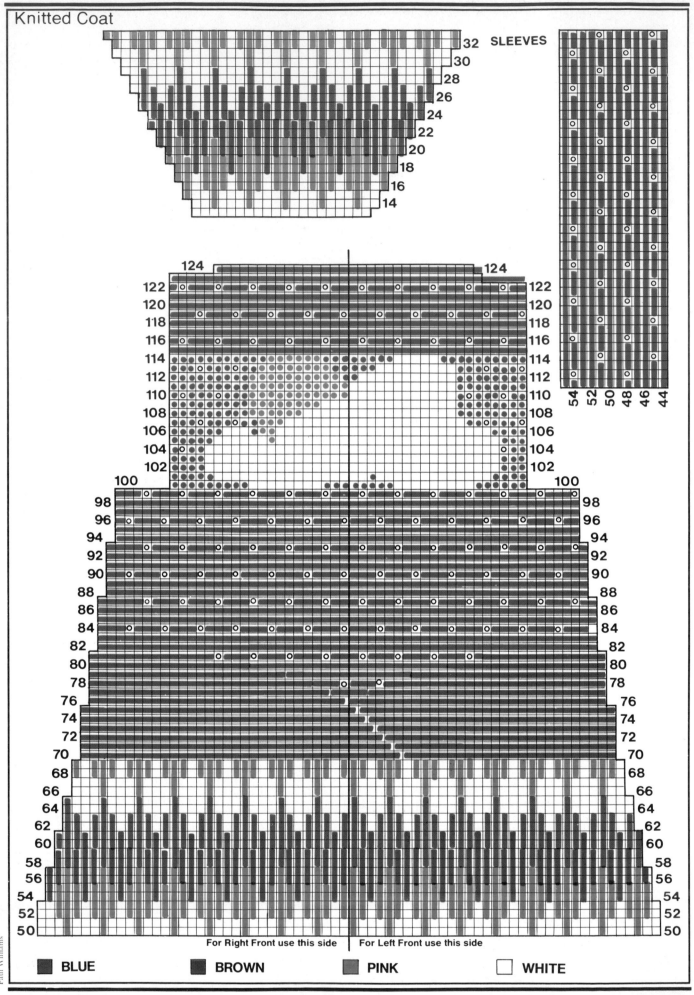

SLEEVES

32
30
28
26
24
22
20
18
16
14

54 52 50 48 46 44

124   124
122   122
120   120
118   118
116   116
114   114
112   112
110   110
108   108
106   106
104   104
102   102
100   100
98   98
96   96
94   94
92   92
90   90
88   88
86   86
84   84
82   82
80   80
78   78
76   76
74   74
72   72
70   70
68   68
66   66
64   64
62   62
60   60
58   58
56   56
54   54
52   52
50   50

For Right Front use this side | For Left Front use this side

■ BLUE   ■ BROWN   ■ PINK   □ WHITE

250

Paul Williams

Rep. from * to last 3 sts., sl. 1, K2.

19th row. Pk. K2, * yarn to P. side, sl. 1, yarn back to K. side, K3. Rep. from * to last 2 sts., yarn to P. side, sl. 1, yarn back to K side, K1.

20th and 21st rows. As 16th and 17th rows.

22nd and 23rd rows. As 18th and 19th rows.

24–39th rows. Rep. last 8 rows twice more.

Now dec. 1 st. at beg. of next 10 rows, knitting 2 rows Wh, 2 rows st. st. in T, K2 rows Pk, 2 rows in st. st. in T, K2 rows B. 70 sts. rem.

50th–69th rows. Following graph as given dec. 1 st. each end of every 4th row 4 times, then on next 5th row. 62 sts. Using B work in st. st. for 6 rows, dec. 1 st. each end of next and every 6th row following thus 76th row will read K2 tog., K28, join on T, K2 T, join on another ball of B, K28, K2 tog. B. Continue to follow chart, still dec. as before until 99th row has been worked. 52 sts.

Shape Armholes
Cast off 6 sts. at beg. of next row, patt. to last 6 sts. cast off 6 sts. Rejoin yarn and continue straight at armhole edge, and follow chart keeping continuity of 'snow flakes' either side of Wh. cloud, using separate balls of yarn where necessary until the 122nd row has been worked.

Shape Shoulders
Cast off 5 sts. at beg. of next 2 rows. Cast off rem. 30 sts.

LEFT FRONT
Using B, cast on 40 sts, and work to match back, working from right side of graph until the 116th row has been worked.

Shape Neck
Cast off 6 sts. at next neck edge row, then dec. 1 st. on next 4 rows at neck edge. Work 1 row, then cast off rem. 10 sts.

RIGHT FRONT
Work to match left front, reversing all shapings and work chart from left side.

SLEEVES

Using B. cast on 20 sts. and work from ** to ** of back, then work 2 rows in st. st. in T, K2 rows Wh, 2 rows Pk and 2 rows B. Now work from chart, inc. 1 st. at beg. of next 20 rows. (40 sts.) 33rd row completed. Now K2 rows B, 2 rows st. st. in T, K2 rows Wh, 2 rows st. st. in T, K2 rows Pk.
Work in 'snowflake' patt. for 11 rows. Cast off.

FRONT BAND
With right side of work facing, pick up and K78 sts. along each front edge about 2 sts. for every 3 rows. Work in g. st. working 1 row T, 2 rows Wh, 2 rows Pk, 1 row B. Cast off in B.

COLLAR
Join shoulders. With right side facing, pick up and K3 sts. from top of border, 7 up front to shoulder 8 sts. from back neck, 7 sts. down front, and 3 sts. along top of border. Now work in st. st. for 4 rows beg. with a K row. K2 rows Wh, 2 rows Pk, 2 rows B, 1 row T and cast off in T.

POCKETS (Both Alike)
With right side of work facing, pick up and K10 sts. between B rows of 70–81. Then beg. with a P row, work 12 rows in st. st., dec. 1 st. each end of 3rd row. Cast off.

TO MAKE UP
Press work, with warm iron over damp cloth. Back stitch top of sleeves along straight part of armholes, then side of sleeve down to the beg. of the 'snowflake' patt. to cast off armhole sts.
Sew up side and sleeve seams, matching patt., and leaving an opening for pocket.
Sew in pockets. Turn coll. at band to right side – in half, and slip stitch down neatly.
For the ties, (4 required), work a twisted cord from 51cm (20") of T yarn. Sew 2 to neck edge, and 2 more about 20cm (8") from previous ties.

Cushions

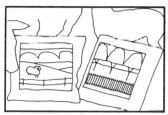

The panels are worked in a 4-ply weight yarn. An interesting and representational landscape can be pro-duced by using textured and tweedy yarns i.e. bouclé for trees, brushed mohair for grass. A random effect is made by working two different coloured finer yarns together as one, always remembering that a 4-ply weight should be maintained overall.

Size: the finished cushion is 35.5cm (14") square.
Panel: 23cm (9") square.

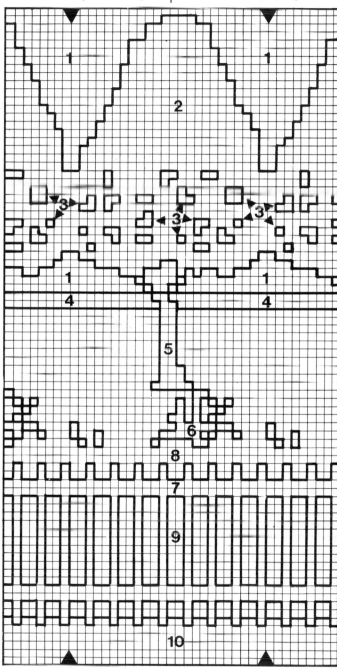

Graph repeat pattern of cherry tree cushion. The following colours are indicated by the numbered sections.

1. Grey
2. Light brown bouclé
3. Pink for blossoms

1. Light green
5. Light brown
6. Turquoise/pink for flowers
7. Dark brown
8. Green and yellow mixed
9. Mixture: green/pink bouclé
10. Green mohair

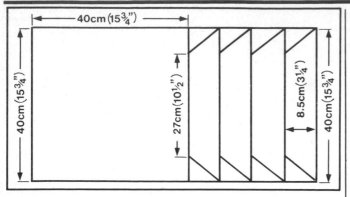

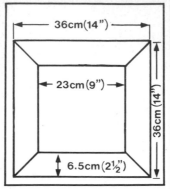

1. Cutting layout of cushions.

2. Assembly of cushion fabric.

MATERIALS

Yarn: oddments of 4 ply wool in 11 colours
Pair of 3¼mm [No.3] knitting needles
40cm (½yd) of 140cm (54″) wide fine tweed fabric
25cm (10″) zip

TENSION

7 sts. and 9 rows measure about 2.5cm (1″).

PATTERN

The panels are worked in stocking stitch. Using 3¼mm [No.3] needles, cast on 58 stitches. Following the design diagram from right to left, knit the 1st row using the first selected colour. Purl the 2nd row, following diagram from left to right. Continue thus changing colours as required. When the 81 rows have been completed, cast off.

TO MAKE UP

Pin out panels to measure 23cm (9″) square, then press with a warm iron over a damp cloth. Textured yarns, such as brushed mohair, can be 'raised' by gentle brushing to give more depth and life to the landscape. Any loose ends must be sewn in securely.

Cut fabric as in fig. 1. Sew borders together with 2cm (¾″) seams to make a frame fig 2, and press seams.

Position knitted square in centre and oversew seams together on WS. Sew backing square to front with 2cm (¾″) seams leaving open 25cm (10″) on one side for zip. Insert zip.

Consultant:
Frances Rogers

Designers:
T-shape sweaters by Margaret Maino; tea-cosy by Annette Critton; aran sweaters by Jean Litchfield; children's dresses by Sarah Dunkley; mohair sweater by Angela Cash; lace sweater and skirt by Judith Hodgson; coat and skirt by Jo Compton; knitted cushions by Ginny Hubble.

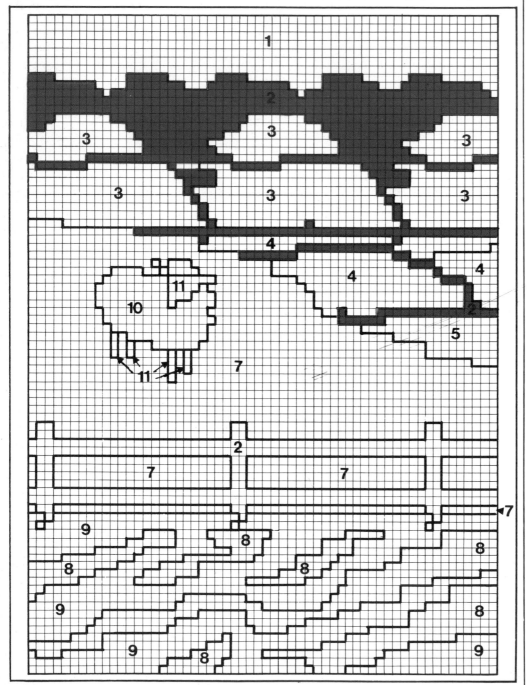

The graph pattern above is a guide to working the multi-coloured sheep cushion. The numbers indicate colours used.

1. Grey
2. Dark brown
3. Lovat green
4. Light green
5. Bottle green
6. Mixed wool, medium green
7. Mid green
8. Green mohair stripes
9. Mixture: light green
10. White bouclé
11. Black

Paul Williams

252

TRANSFERRING DESIGNS

Direct Transfer

To make a tracing, grease-proof paper is needed or the special tracing paper obtainable from most art supply shops.

Place tracing paper over the design to be copied and draw along outline, using a fairly sharp, soft pencil. (Anchor tracing paper to prevent shifting.)

TRANSFERRING TO PAPER

If using greaseproof paper, shade the reverse side of the traced design with a pencil, making sure the whole outline is covered thoroughly and fairly heavily.

Place the tracing paper, design side uppermost on the plain paper.

Anchor with masking tape and re-trace whole outline so that the shading is transferred.

TRANSFERRING TO WOOD

Typewriter carbon (or dressmaker's carbon) can be used for this, but take care not to smudge the surface.

Place carbon paper between the tracing and the wood. Anchor with masking tape. Re-trace outline of design with a pencil, then carefully remove tracing and carbon.

TRANSFERRING TO FABRIC

A wax transfer pencil provides a simple way of making a design on fabric; however, it does not show up on dark colours well. It is wise to test whether the pencil marks can be removed by experimenting with a piece of your fabric first.

Use the transfer pencil to trace the initial design on tracing paper, then place the tracing face down on the fabric and iron it so that the design is transferred.

Dressmaker's carbon is an alternative to the transfer pencil. It is available in both light and dark shades so that it will register on any colour. It is not suitable for heavy, thick materials.

BASTING

This is the best method when fabric is too heavy to register a transfer. It is also excellent for embroidery.

Pin traced design to fabric, having darkened outline first with a felt tip.

Using a thread which contrasts with the colour of the material, baste along the outline with running stitch. Remove tracing paper gently, leaving the stitches intact.

Enlarging

If you wish to enlarge or reduce the size of the design you have chosen, the simplest and most widely used method is to use a grid as your guideline.

Improvised grid. For a simple, very distinct outline, you can easily draw your own grid; all you need is a sharp pencil, a ruler and plain or tracing paper.

Make a rectangle round the original design which you wish to enlarge or reduce (if you do not wish to mark the original, take a tracing of it and draw the rectangle on that instead). Divide the rectangle you have drawn into equal, numbered squares (fig. 1).

On another piece of paper, draw a second rectangle, proportionately larger or

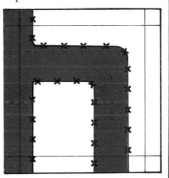

1. Original motif on a grid.

smaller than the first e.g. double or half its dimensions. Divide this into the *same number* of squares as before.

Number the squares on the second rectangle and you are ready to begin copying. By carefully observing the outline of the original in relation to the grid lines through which it passes, it is possible to copy the figure or pattern accurately, but to different dimensions from the original.

Note where the lines cross the side or corner of a square in the first design, and make a dot at the equivalent position on the second grid. By making a series of marks, in this manner (fig. 2), even a convoluted line can be copied with ease.

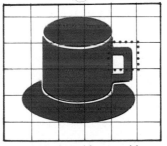

2. Motif copied on larger grid.

Graphs. Many of the designs and motifs given in this book are already placed on a graph, for your convenience. In copying one of these, another piece of graph paper can be used to enlarge or reduce the figure.

Simply draw a rectangle to the size you require. The number of squares to the centimetre (inch) is given beside each design, so it is merely a matter of altering the ratio of squares to the centimetre (inch).

If working without graph paper, use tracing paper to enable you to draw the rectangle accurately.

Place the tracing paper over the design in the book and trace the two adjacent sides of design's frame (A C, CD), fig.3. Extend the diagonal

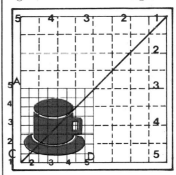

3. Tracing a ready-made graph.

from C. Continue these lines as far as you require, according to whether the design is being enlarged or reduced. Draw in the other two sides of the rectangular frame, and divide larger frame into same number of squares as in the original. Number the squares on your copy and copy outline as described previously.

ENLARGING BY PROJECTOR

If the design is obtainable in the form of a slide or is small enough to fit into a slide holder, a projector provides a very satisfactory means of enlarging.

If the design is not on a slide, transfer it to tracing paper and darken the outline with a felt tip or black ink. Put the tracing or slide into the projector in the usual way. Focus the design on another piece of paper pinned to the wall, or to a board. (Make sure that this paper is exactly upright or the design will look warped at the top or bottom.) If the design is to be transferred to yet another surface, it should be projected on tracing paper pinned to a white background. Vary the distance between the projector and the paper until the required size is obtained. Draw along the projected lines.

INDEX

MAIL ORDER SUPPLIES

The following sell handicraft supplies by mail order:

UNITED KINGDOM

WHI Tapestry Shop,
85 Pimlico Road, London SW1 — Needlepoint materials

Candlemaker's Supplies,
28 Blythe Road, London W14 — All materials required for candlemaking

Eaton Shell Shop,
16 Manette Street, London W1 — Shells

Ells & Farrier, Limited,
5 Princes Street, London W1 — Bead merchants

R. D. Franks,
Kent House,
Market Place, London W1 — Sewing accessories

The Needlewoman,
146 Regent Street,
London W1 — Supplies for all forms of needlecraft, plus macramé and rug making

Hobby Horse,
15 Langton Street, London W1 — Macramé, beads, printing supplies

Reeves & Sons Limited,
178 Kensington High Street,
London W8 — Macramé and printing supplies

S. Tyzack,
341 Old Street, London EC1 — Wood carving tools

Royal School of Needlework,
25 Prince's Gate, London SW7 — Embroidery & needlepoint

U.S.A.

Erica Wilson Needleworks,
717 Madison Avenue,
New York 10021 — Needlepoint and embroidery supplies

Sax Art & Crafts,
207 N. Milwaukee Street,
Milwaukee,
Wisconsin 53202 — Supplies for printing, beadwork, candlemaking, rug making

American Crewel & Canvas Studio,
PO Box 298,
Boonton, New Jersey 07005 — Needlepoint and embroidery supplies

Eye Squared,
361 Delaware Avenue,
Buffalo, New York 14202 — Needlepoint and rug making supplies

Berry's of Maine,
20/22 Main Street,
Yarmouth,
Maine 04096 — Rug making supplies and tapestry wool

The Hidden Village,
215, Yale Avenue,
Claremont,
California 91711 — Supplies for needlepoint, embroidery, macramé and rug making

Jewelart,
7753, Densmore Avenue,
Van Nuys,
California 91406. — Bead merchants

AUSTRALIA

Craft World,
PO Box 139,
Burwood 2134,
N.S.W. — Macramé, rug making and bead supplies

256

City Gems'n'Crafts,
127 York Street,
Sydney 2000 — Supplies for needlepoint, embroidery, candlemaking, rug making, beadwork, printing and macramé

CANADA

Lewiscraft,
40 Commander Boulevard,
Agincourt,
Ontario MIS 3S2 — Supplies for needlepoint, embroidery, printing, candlemaking, macramé, beadwork, knitting, crochet, woodwork and rug making

Leonida's Embroidery Studio Limited,
99, Osborne Street,
Winnipeg,
Manitoba R3L 2R4 — Needlepoint and embroidery supplies

Helio Dyes and Crafts Div.
2140 West 4th Avenue,
Vancouver 9 — Macramé and candlemaking supplies

NEW ZEALAND

Golding Handcraft Centre,
158, Cuba Street,
Wellington. — Supplies for needlepoint, embroidery, printing, candlemaking, beadwork, macramé, crochet and rug making

Shorts (Hobby & Artcrafts) Limited,
Maidstone Mall,
Upper Hutt, — Supplies for needlepoint, embroidery, printing, candlemaking, beadwork, rug making, knitting and crochet

Handcraft House,
37, Oranga Avenue,
Onehunga,
Auckland — Supplies for needlepoint, macramé, embroidery, candlemaking, beadwork, knitting, crochet and rug making

SOUTH AFRICA

Art, Leather & Handcraft Specialists,
493/495 West Street,
Durban — Supplies for needlepoint, embroidery, printing, beadwork, macramé, crochet, rug making and candlemaking

ACKNOWLEDGEMENTS

p. 9 – yarn, J & P Coats; p. 49 – jacket, Leon Jaeggi & Sons, London; p. 50 & 61 – T-shirts, Dickens & Jones, London
p. 69 – all articles, Browns, London; p. 70 – poultry, Anthony Redmile, London; p. 74 – shirt & belt, Nick Nacks, London
p. 84 – colours by Dylon; p. 85 – basket & glasses, The Neal St. Shop, London; clothes & cutlery, Dickens & Jones; p. 86 – sweater, Dickens & Jones; p. 87 – skirt & petticoat, Fenwicks; dresses, Laura Ashley; p. 89 – blouse & petticoat, Fenwicks, London; basket, The Neal St. Shop; clogs, Du Du, London; p. 96 – desk accessories, Wright Allison
p. 103 – skirt & scarf, Laura Ashley; petticoat, Fenwicks; p. 109 – beret & braces, Dickens & Jones; blouse, tie, petticoat, Fenwicks; p. 110 – accessories, Fenwicks; p. 113 – clogs, Hanky Panky
p. 130 – bottle garden, Selwyn Davidson; p. 132 – blouse & bangles, Fenwicks; pill box, Dickens & Jones
p. 146/7 – tools , Burgess & Galer, London; clothes, Nick Nacks; p. 148 – toys etc. Galt Toys, London; p. 150 – doll's furniture, Galts; dolls, Heal & Sons, London; clothes, Dickens & Jones

p. 157 – peasant dress, Bianca Buscaglia, London; mola work, courtesy of Herta Puls; p. 158/61 – clothing & accessories, Dickens & Jones; p. 162 – wallpaper, Laura Ashley; bed linen, Casa Pupo; tea set & vase Heal & Sons; p. 167 – courtesy of Reading Schools' Library; p. 171 – bottles & vase, Browns; beads and powder puff, Dickens & Jones; p. 174 – machine by Elna; p. 187 – wool & hooks, The Needlewoman, London; p. 190 – rug, Browns Living; p. 191 – chairs, Omnia Designs, London
p. 195 – wool, The Needlewoman; basket, The New Neal St. Shop; p. 197 – adult's clothing & accessories, Fenwicks; child's clothing, Dickens & Jones; p. 202 – skirt, Fenwicks; boots, Gamba; black slip, Fenwicks; p. 207/8 – clothes & accessories, Dickens & Jones; p. 226 – polo neck, Fenwicks; p. 227 – clothes & accessories, Fenwicks; child's trousers, Dickens & Jones; p. 229 – check shirt and trousers, Nick Nacks; gumboots & fishing gear, Moss Bros; p. 233 – bangles, Fenwicks; p. 236 – shoes, Joe & Ada Bloggs, London; other articles, Fenwicks
Location: Rosetti's, London
Page 1 – detail of felt appliqué by Linda Brill.
Title page – Embroidered picture designed and worked by Julia Sorrell.